Law and healing

Manchester University Press

CONTEMPORARY ISSUES IN BIOETHICS, LAW AND MEDICAL HUMANITIES

Contemporary Issues in Bioethics, Law and Medical Humanities, edited by Rebecca Bennett and Simona Giordano, of the University of Manchester, was established to publish internationally respected book-length works – primarily monographs and edited collections, but also specialist textbooks – in contemporary issues in bioethics, law and the medical humanities and as such welcomes proposals from this range of academic approaches to pertinent issues in this area. The series focuses on the strong foundations and reputation of the University of Manchester's world-leading scholars in bioethics and law, and its internationally respected Centre for Social Ethics and Policy. Works from across the humanities, brought to bear on contemporary, historical, and indeed future bioethical questions of the highest social and moral concern and interest, will find a perfect home within this series.

Law and healing

A history of a stormy marriage

Margaret Brazier

MANCHESTER UNIVERSITY PRESS

Published by Manchester University Press
Oxford Road, Manchester M13 9PL

www.manchesteruniversitypress.co.uk

British Library Cataloguing-in-Publication Data
A catalogue record for this book is available from the British
Library

ISBN 978 1 5261 2918 5 hardback
ISBN 978 1 5261 9587 6 paperback

First published 2023
Paperback published 2026

The publisher has no responsibility for the persistence or
accuracy of URLs for any external or third-party internet
websites referred to in this book, and does not guarantee
that any content on such websites is, or will remain, accurate
or appropriate.

EU authorised representative for GPSR:
Easy Access System Europe – Mustamäe tee 50,
10621 Tallinn, Estonia
gpsr.requests@easproject.com

Typeset by Newgen Publishing UK

For Rodney and Vicky

Contents

Table of cases

Table of statutes

Legislation

Table of statutes

Secondary legislation

Preface

The law's relationship with health care is rarely out of the news. The courts and the legislature are kept busy with a plethora of matters concerning law and health care, and the media regularly highlights medico-legal problems. Medical law is offered as an optional course unit to virtually all law students in the United Kingdom. Academic and popular literature abound. In this book, I look back to 'yesterday', to explore aspects of the history of law's engagement with medicine and health care in England, questioning assumptions that only in recent times has the law engaged with medical practice and the delivery of health care, or the moral dilemmas which arise from what we now term biomedical science. To the contrary, a study of history demonstrates that the relationship between medicine and the law is long-standing and often fraught with difficulty – a stormy marriage. Legal battles and problems relating to health care and the practice of medicine prove to be far from new. The explosion of interest in medical law from the 1980s marked a rebirth not a birth.

I seek to demonstrate how reflection on that history can contribute to the development of law today. I do not aspire to provide answers, agreeing that: 'History does not provide answers to the problems today: it merely helps to frame the question.'[1]

When well over a decade ago I fell in love with the history of law and medicine, there was little research on that history undertaken by legal academics in England. In 2009, Imogen Goold and Catherine Kelly described the story of the inter-relationship of medical professionals to the development of laws and legislation as greatly under-researched – highlighting that 'historical considerations of medico-legal issues that are available are

---

1 J G Wofford 'The Blinding Light: The Uses of History in Constitutional Interpretation' (1964) 31 *University of Chicago Law Review* 502, 533, cited in B Abbott Goldberg 'Horseshoers, Doctors and Judges and the Law on Medical Competence' (1978) 9 *Pacific Law Journal* 107, 144.

generally case-studies of a single area, most often focused on contraception or abortion'.[2] That 'research gap' is gradually being met. I hope to encourage more research and attention to medico-legal history.

Law and Healing: A History of a Stormy Marriage, not *History of Medical Law*, or *Medico-Legal History*. Its purpose is to explore historical perspectives on the relationship of the law and healing including, but not restricted to, the emergence of a medical profession, the status and regulation of health-care practitioners and the doctor/patient relationship. In particular, I also examine how developments in biomedical 'science' influenced laws. I do not attempt to offer a comprehensive account of the history of medical law. When I started my research, I worried that there would not be enough material for a book. To the contrary,[3] my problem has been an over-abundance of material including legal cases, Acts of Parliament, Royal Charters, canon law, the writings of jurists from the thirteenth century and more relatively recent works authored by medical and legal professionals from the eighteenth to the nineteenth centuries.[4] Most importantly, I do not pretend to be a historian. I offer a lawyer's perspective on and analysis of aspects of medico-legal history which may shed new and brighter light on the role of the law.

The book is about English law. While focusing principally on the sixteenth to nineteenth centuries, at times I delve back to the thirteenth century, a journey in time necessary to understand the difficult and complex relationship of law and healing. I end my journey in the late nineteenth to the early twentieth centuries, the period of time in which the legal system, and the medical and legal professions underwent radical change. And the relationship of medicine and law acquired a much closer resemblance to their relationship in the twenty-first century. In focusing on 'older' history, I seek to show that the apparent differences conceal fundamental themes as relevant today as in the thirteenth to nineteenth centuries. As I say in Chapter 1, *'Medical law' is not new: it just looked different*. The rebirth of

2 I Goold and C Kelly (eds) *Lawyers' Medicine: The Legislature the Courts and Medical Practice* (Hart Publishing, 2000) 2–3.

3 I am aware important areas of health law, including forensic medicine, mental and public health law are not addressed. Space limited how much could be packed into one book. And happily, history of those three areas has attracted considerably more research than other areas of medico-legal history; see Goold and Kelly (n 2) 4.

4 See R M Kerrison *An Inquiry into the Present State of the Medical Profession in England containing an Abstract of all the Acts and Charters granted to Physicians, Surgeons and Apothecaries and A Comparative View of the Profession in Scotland, Ireland and on the Continent* (Longman, Rees, Hurst, Orme and Brown, 1814); J Willcock *Laws relating to the Medical Profession with an Account of the Rise and Progress of the Various Orders* (J & W T Clarke, 1830).

interest in the relationship between law and medicine sparked fervent argument about how the 'new' field of practice and enquiry should be named.[5] I eschew this debate and, for the sake of simplicity and clarity, I refer to the burgeoning area of practice and scholarship engendered by the rebirth as 'modern medical law'.[6]

After examining in Chapter 1 why medico-legal history merits attention, Chapters 2–5 consider how law regulated healing and the obligations of healers. Any account of encounters between law and medicine must embrace more than the letter of the law and confront both the battle for dominance between different groups of health practitioners, and the quest by many of those practitioners for a social status akin to the lawyer or the clergy. Chapters 6–10 address what might today be designated bioethical questions, such as the value of human life, what you could do with your living body, matters of reproduction, fetal status and the treatment of the dead. It will be seen that the 'marriage' of law and healing is not just about legal 'rules' governing practice. A two-way process can be perceived with developments in medical knowledge influencing laws for good or ill.

I aim to interest a broad audience including, of course, readers from law and medicine; it addresses 'our' professional history. But it is a history which belongs to everyone touching as it does on the most intimate and troubled matters of human life and death. I have often been told that 'surely law is boring'. Perhaps the story told in this book may change their minds.

5 See J Montgomery 'What's in a Name? Labelling Effects on the Analysis of the Role of Law in Medicine' (2019) 7 *Journal of Medical Ethics and Law* 111.
6 M Brazier and J Montgomery 'Whence and Whither "Modern Medical Law"?' (2019) 70 *Northern Ireland Quarterly* 5, 6.

Acknowledgements

I am indebted to my colleagues, my students, my family and friends for their patience and support in listening to me as I wrote this story of law and healing. I cannot name everyone without devoting most of the book to a list of names. I wrote much of the final draft under the shadow of the COVID pandemic. Continuing contact with colleagues kept me sane. Never an IT fan, I give thanks for Zoom.

I acknowledge the financial assistance of the Leverhulme Trust by way of the award of a Leverhulme Trust Emeritus Fellowship (EM-2018-067/8). I would also like to thank the staff at the Trust and especially Anna Grundy for their support over the last three years. The Fellowship enabled me to engage a post-doctorate Fellow to assist me with this work and other research within the Fellowship. I was immensely fortunate to be able to appoint a real historian, Dr Sarah Fox. Sarah was a brilliant colleague, not only a highly skilled researcher but also a fount of enthusiasm and encouragement.

I owe particular thanks to Emma Cave, Sarah Devaney, Sara Fovargue, Sarah Fox, Alex Mullock and Chloe Romanis who read and commented on draft chapters. Their comments were invaluable. Their help at a time when university staff faced such exceptional challenges was over and beyond any 'call of duty'. In the decade or so that I have been fascinated by medico-legal history, well before this book was even conceived, other colleagues helped me develop my work. Presentations at seminars and informal conversations over coffee clarified my thinking and encouraged me to carry on. Maureen Mulholland was as ever generous with her time and her knowledge. A number of doctoral students helped me with research. I thank especially Jenny Bell, Sarah Brown, Anna Nelson, Sacha Waxman and Hannah Wishart. I am grateful to Lucy Burns and Manchester University Press for their encouragement and patience.

I must also acknowledge two people who inspired my love of history long ago, Dorothy Butcher and Mr Watson. Gloriously eccentric, Miss Butcher's lessons were the highlight of each week. Returning home from boarding school to join the sixth form at Queen Mary School for Girls, I feared that no teacher would come close to matching Miss Butcher. Happily, I was wrong. The terrifying Mr Watson (we never knew his first name) proved to be another giant among teachers. My first love of history, however, was born in early childhood sparked by my mother. She transmitted her passion for history to me. She read voraciously, books propped up on the window-sill while she cooked or washed up. Conversations over family meals moved seamlessly from planning my birthday party to discussing whether the execution of Charles I was justifiable.

Last, but far from least, I thank my husband, Emeritus Professor Rodney Brazier. Always supportive of my work, this book would not have been completed without his practical help. He proofread every chapter and made valuable suggestions for improvements, in particular regarding accessibility for a general audience.

1

Medico-legal history: why bother?

Snapshots from history

I begin with some brief snapshots depicting encounters between law and healing across five centuries.

In 1215, Canon 18 of the Fourth Lateran Council prohibited priests and monks in the higher orders from practising surgery.

In 1368, the first Guild of Master Surgeons (also referred to as the Fellowship of Surgeons) was founded. The Guild formed part of the medieval system of craft Guilds that sought to regulate and maintain the standards of their trades. The Guild set out a Code of Ethics which was comparatively sophisticated for its time and focused principally on the injunction to 'do no harm'.

In 1421, in the reign of Henry V, a Draught (*sic*) Bill was presented to Parliament, which, had it entered into force, would have established a secular system for the regulation of healing enforced across the realm by the Sheriffs. The Bill recited that the King was well aware many untrained and unlicensed people sought to practise medicine 'to great harm and slaughter of many men'. The Bill proposed that only a man holding a degree of Bachelor or Doctor of Medicine within 'some University' be permitted to 'practise in Physic'. The Bill further directed that '[N]o woman use the practise of Physic'.

In 1522, in the reign of Henry VIII, an Act of Parliament entitled 'The Privileges and Authority of Physicians in London' declared that it was expedient and necessary that no person should 'be suffered to practise physic, but only those persons that be profound, sad and discreet, groundly learned and deeply studied in physick'. The statute granted the College of Physicians extensive powers to license those lawfully permitted to practise 'physic' in London, or within a seven-mile circuit around London, and authority to investigate, judge and punish unlicensed practice or malpractice regardless of whether the offender was a member of the College or not.

In 1614, in *Everard v Hopkins* a claim was brought against a 'common chyrurgeon' (surgeon) engaged by the plaintiff to treat his servant who had been injured by a cart wheel. The plaintiff agreed to pay the surgeon five marks for his services. The plaintiff alleged that the defendant surgeon was not 'onely careless of the cure ... but he had also applied unwholsome medicines'. The servant could not work for a year. It was held that the servant 'cannot have an action upon this agreement, but he may have an action on the case for his supplying of unwholesome medicines to him'. The surgeon's undertaking to treat the injury to the servant created a duty of care to the patient independent of the contract.

In 1732, Eleanor Beare stood trial for performing abortions. She was accused that (1) she provided a poison to Nich. Wilson to give to his wife to destroy the child in her womb; (2) she inserted an 'iron instrument' into the body of Grace Belfort causing her to miscarry; (3) she similarly used an instrument and/or gave an abortifacient to a woman 'unknown to the jury'. Eleanor was found guilty on the first two indictments. She was sentenced to stand in the pillory and to three years' imprisonment. Had she been convicted sixty-nine years later she might have faced the death penalty.

In 1832, the first Anatomy Act provoked riots and arson. In 1858, Parliament, after decades of wrangling, passed the Medical Act 1858 which began the process of unifying the three orthodox medical professions (physicians, surgeons and apothecaries) and instituted a degree of state control of medical practice.

Why bother?

These brief snapshots shine light on the myriad ways in which law and healing interacted in the past. They cannot answer the question: why bother examining medico-legal history? The question assumes that the relationship of law and medicine has a substantive history. In the latter three decades of the twentieth century, the assumption tended to be to the contrary. Medical law was said to be 'new', with little history, certainly very little relevant history. In 2000, Ian Kennedy and Andrew Grubb stated:

> Medical law is still a comparatively young subject. It emerged in English law over the past two decades or so as a distinct subject, both as an area of importance in legal practice and as an academic discipline.[1]

---

1 A Grubb (ed) *Kennedy and Grubb: Medical Law* (3rd edn) (Butterworths, 2000) 3. And see I Kennedy 'The Patient on the Clapham Omnibus' in I Kennedy *Treat Me Right* (Oxford University Press, 1988) 175; originally (1984) 47 *Modern Law Review* 454.

They argued that the courts and the legislature only rarely engaged with medicine. Moreover, when the courts had engaged with medicine, the judges displayed 'historic deference from one learned profession (the law) to another (medicine)'.[2] Judges endorsed medical paternalism.[3] Any relationship between law and medicine was tenuous, far from any sort of 'marriage'. If a marriage could be discerned, then given the amenability of English law towards its medical spouse, that marriage was not stormy. I shall seek to show that there *is* an extensive history of a close and complex relationship between law and medicine in England, a history which is increasingly being paid more attention by legal academics.[4] Medical and social historians have long explored the 'marriage'.[5]

Kennedy's Reith Lectures, published in 1981 as *The Unmasking of Medicine*,[6] are often cited as marking the birth of medical law and ethics in the United Kingdom (UK).[7] Kennedy challenged the dominance of the medical profession in decision-making about health care and a culture of deference to doctors. In the 1980s, the number of cases relating to medical practice reaching the courts increased. Patients became less willing to accept that 'Doctor Knew Best', and judges retreated from the deference which had characterised judicial attitudes to medicine for much of the twentieth century. Academic interest burgeoned. Books, articles and conferences proliferated. Undergraduate and postgraduate courses were established. Doctoral students chose medical law for their PhD theses. Research centres in medical law and ethics were set up in many universities in the UK.[8] 'For a legal scholar coming to medical law in that era, it felt new.'[9]

Rebirth not birth

Feelings can mislead. The 1980s marked a *rebirth* of medical law, not its birth. A rich history of law and medicine in England from medieval times to

---

2 M Brazier and J Montgomery 'Whence and Whither "Modern Medical Law"?' (2019) 70 *Northern Ireland Quarterly* 5, 6.

3 H Teff *Reasonable Care: Legal Perspectives in the Doctor/Patient Relationship* (Clarendon Press, 1994) 69–93.

4 I Goold and C Kelly (eds) *Lawyers' Medicine: The Legislature the Courts & Medical Practice* (Hart Publishing, 2000) 2–3.

5 C Crawford 'Medicine and the Law' in W F Bynum and R Porter *Companion Encyclopaedia of the History of Medicine* (Routledge, 1993) 1619, 1619.

6 I Kennedy *The Unmasking of Medicine* (Allen and Unwin, 1981).

7 D Wilson *The Making of British Bioethics* (Manchester University Press, 2014) 105–139.

8 Ibid 187–219.

9 Brazier and Montgomery (n 2) 7.

the late nineteenth century was temporarily rendered invisible. The neglect of a 'history' of medical law is not surprising, if consideration of any history is limited to the late nineteenth and the first seven or so decades of the twentieth century. English case law and legislation relating to medicine during that period was sparse. When questions of medical law were addressed, they were not labelled 'medical law'.

There was equally little evidence of medical law as an academic sub-discipline. Scholarly papers examining aspects of law and medicine were published before 1981, notably by Peter Skegg, Gerald Dworkin and Kennedy himself. Glanville Williams's provocative book *The Sanctity of Life and the Criminal Law*, first published in 1957,[10] covered a huge range of matters including the law relating to abortion, contraception and euthanasia. Williams's book, like the journal articles published about law and medicine in the 1950s to 1970s, was not perceived as contributing to a core sub-discipline focused on medicine's relationship with law, but rather as analyses of other legal disciplines in the context of medicine (in Williams's case criminal law). Kennedy and Grubb's designation of medical law as comparatively young at the turn of the millennium is unsurprising. Their 'young subject' grew up fast. This phenomenon of rapid growth was not confined to medical law. The numbers of reported cases on all aspects of law soared. In the legal academy the nature of academic writing and legal scholarship began to change.[11] English legal academics focused less on writing principally for students and legal practitioners, and more on critical inquiry. They wrote much more. They expanded legal research from traditional emphases on fundamental principles of common law, equity and theoretical jurisprudence, to examination of how law affected human life in contexts such as the family and the environment. The absence or invisibility of a sub-discipline of 'medical law' in 1981 was 'in common with many of the categories we use to organise legal scholarship today'.[12]

If there is no doubt that from the 1980s medical law flourished, why cavil at the suggestion that the decade marked the birth of medical law and insist on describing the developments post-1981 as rebirth? I do so because birth suggests something brand new, yet delving further back in history reveals abundant evidence that the courts, Parliament, the Sovereign and the Church were heavily involved in the relationship of law and healing.

---

10 G Williams *The Sanctity of Life and the Criminal Law* (Alfred A Knopf, 1957).
11 W Twining 'Professionalism in Legal Education' (2011) 18 *International Legal Education* 165; W Twining *Blackstone's Tower: The English Law School* (Stevens and Sons, 1984).
12 Brazier and Montgomery (n 2) 15.

From the fourteenth century and before, English law engaged with health and healing, in what proved to be a stormy 'marriage'.

Exploring some of the history of that union from late medieval times to the close of the nineteenth century reveals fascinating stories, embracing comedy and tragedy and telling us a great deal about the lives of the men and women who preceded us. Writing about early case law on medical competence and care, and the difficulties in dealing with medieval law reports, US judge B Abbott Goldberg commented that 'in these dusty, fusty antiques are the first glimmers of modern law of the quality of medical care'.[13] Glimmers of modern medical law can be found in nearly all the areas where law and healing engaged. Attention to medico-legal history casts light on persistent questions which still trouble law-makers, health workers and society in the twenty-first century. Examination of case law, legislation and jurisprudence from the past uncovers myths which have distorted the development of medical law. In surveying law and healing it becomes apparent that while law regulated healing and its practitioners, developments in 'biomedical science', for example, theories about human reproduction, also shaped the development of law, sometimes in areas of law not generally considered to be anything to do with modern medical law.

Metaphors and 'marriage'

The interaction of Law and Medicine has attracted several metaphors. Why, even if partly in jest, choose 'marriage'? Lawyers are often depicted as predators by doctors,[14] not a good basis for wedlock. Warmer feelings between the two are invoked in the portrayal of medical and legal practitioners as siblings, learned brethren. David Faigman notes the use of a courtship metaphor to explain the relationship between Law and Science.[15] Each depiction tells us something about that relationship. Predators, siblings, sweethearts, all can choose to end their relationships. 'Marriage', or as satirist A P Herbert described it, *Holy Deadlock*,[16] is, or was, for life. Law and Medicine are yoked together. Their courtship was not smooth. 'Medical men' struggled to be recognised as equal in social status to the barrister

---

13 B Abbott Goldberg 'Horseshoers, Doctors and Judges and the Law on Medical Competence' (1978) 9 *Pacific Law Journal* 107, 115.

14 G J Annas 'The Art of Medicine: Doctors and Lawyers and Wolves' (2008) 371 *The Lancet* 1832.

15 D L Faigman *Legal Alchemy: The Use and Misuse of Science in the Law* (W H Freeman and Company, 2000) 9. He proposes his own 'more dramatic metaphor', based on the Greek myth of Heracles slaying the three-headed Hydra.

16 A P Herbert *Holy Deadlock* (Penguin, 1934).

or clergyman. From the sixteenth to the nineteenth century, if regarded as brethren at all, the doctor may often be deemed an inferior sibling. Medicine looked to Law, to the law courts and Parliament to enhance their standing as professionals, to endow the medical 'bride' with some of Law's prestige. Within the 'marriage' the 'spouses' battled for dominance.

Interaction between Law and Medicine was not exclusively concerned with the relationship of their practitioners, doctors and lawyers. The relationship of the two disciplines, of Law and biomedical Science merits equal attention. Faigman says of the two disciplines 'Science explores what is; the law dictates what ought to be'.[17] The shifting balance of power within the marriage witnessed Medicine claiming an ever-stronger voice in determining what ought to be in relation to moral dilemmas in medicine, and the regulation of emergent biomedical science. And gradually Medicine sought to be the arbiter of responsible opinion in all matters relating to their practice, be it at the bedside or the laboratory bench.

Health care: what health care?

Before considering how the law related to healing, the question arises about how far health care itself has a relevant history prior to the late nineteenth century, a question which becomes more pressing the further back in time we travel. Did anyone save for our richest ancestors have access to health care of any sort, for if there was little health care, there would be little for law to address? Waddington suggested that in the eighteenth century 'the demand for qualified medical care was relatively highly concentrated amongst the wealthier sections of the community'.[18] Yet in 1814, Kerrison, a surgeon-apothecary campaigning for medical reform, designated health as 'the most valued possession of every individual'.[19] Tracing the history of medicine from classical times, he wrote that:

> It cannot be doubted, indeed, that a science so useful in preserving life and so desirable in rendering its tenure tolerable under the pressure of multiplied and protracted infirmities must soon have been held in high estimation, and its aid sought after with avidity.[20]

17 Faigman (n 15) 6.
18 I Waddington *The Medical Profession in the Industrial Revolution* (Gill and Macmillan, 1984) 181.
19 R M Kerrison *An Inquiry into the Present State of the Medical Profession in England containing an Abstract of all the Acts and Charters granted to Physicians, Surgeons and Apothecaries and A Comparative View of the Profession in Scotland, Ireland and on the Continent* (Longman, Rees, Hurst, Orme and Brown, 1814) vii.
20 Ibid 2.

Modern medical historians, notably Margaret Pelling,[21] reject assumptions that 'most of the population before the nineteenth century had no access to medical services worthy of the name' and that 'medical care was necessarily confined to the rich'.[22] Nor was access to health care limited to residents of London.[23] In common with their descendants, 'early modern people were obsessed with health, with its fragility and with the means of preserving it'.[24] The crucial importance of health to people well before the nineteenth century created a space for law and lawyers. And, as today, there is evidence that laypeople, the consumers of health care, sought 'rights over their own lives and bodies'.[25]

Who were the 'doctors'?

Who provided the care that people sought? The Medical Act 1858 began a slow process whereby a distinct medical profession could be identified. Before 1858, medical practitioners in England were far from unified. Following, if imperfectly, the tripartite division of medicine prevalent in Continental Europe, there were three 'orders of medicine': physicians, surgeons and apothecaries. University-educated physicians sought to dominate medical practice. Summoned to the bedside, a physician would diagnose your ill, perhaps by sniffing your urine or consulting astrological charts. He might then 'prescribe' treatment.

Should bloodletting or any form of operation be required, the actual procedure would be carried out by a surgeon. Medicines prescribed by the physician would be made up by an apothecary. Sometimes seen as the forebears of the modern pharmacists, apothecaries were more than just mixers and purveyors of potions. In most towns and villages in England the apothecary resembled the modern general practitioner.

The orthodox aspired to be recognised as professional gentlemen equal to the lawyer or the clergyman. Within the extensive literature published by medical historians, physicians, surgeons and apothecaries are variously referred to collectively as regulars, or the regular orders, or orthodox practitioners, or simply as the medical professions. I shall generally use the term orthodox to describe those practitioners who belonged to the College of

---

21 M Pelling *The Common Lot: Sickness, Medical Occupations and the Urban Poor in Early Modern England* (Routledge, 1998).
22 Ibid 5.
23 R S Roberts 'The Personnel and Practice of Medicine in Tudor and Stuart England Part I: The Provinces' (1962) 6 *Medical History* 363.
24 Pelling (n 21) 5.
25 Ibid 8.

Physicians, the Royal College of Surgeons and the Society of Apothecaries, or their predecessors in title. Those august institutions I refer to collectively as the medical corporations. Internecine conflicts between the orthodox were regularly played out in the law courts and Parliament.

The orthodox were not the only healers. 'Any balanced view of medicine in the early modern period … must take account of all practitioners dispensing medical care.'[26] Two other groups, female midwives and retail chemists, partially co-existed with the orthodox. Until the early years of the eighteenth century, female midwives licensed by the Church provided most obstetric care, delivering babies and caring for women and their infants in childbirth. By the end of that century, a relatively new group of 'healers', 'retail chemists and druggists',[27] emerged to challenge the apothecaries, undercutting apothecaries by selling medicines more cheaply. Reformers sought to regulate and control both groups, but, for the most part, reserved their vitriolic campaign against quackery to attack the myriad ranks of traditional healers.

That host of other healers offered a range of services. They included herbalists, bone setters, phlebotomists and 'cunning women'. Many such men and women were traditional healers learning their skills from family members already working as a healer. Purveyors of 'miracle medicines' peddled their wares. A common hatred of these 'healers' united the physicians, surgeons and apothecaries. As with the conflict *between* the orthodox, the temporarily united trio resorted to the courts and Parliament in attempts to drive out of business all those 'other' healers, variously denominated by their powerful rivals, the orthodox, as 'irregulars', 'empirics', or 'quacks'. Margaret Pelling and Charles Webster make a strong case for avoiding such derogatory labels, deciding 'not to take at face value judgments made by contemporaries designating individuals and indeed major groups as "quacks"' or "empirics"'.[28] They acknowledge that unscrupulous opportunists did infiltrate medicine but refuse to give way to what they refer to as 'the special pleading of contemporary pressure groups'.[29]

The battles between the medical corporations, and the constant efforts of the orthodox to exclude other healers from practice, resulted in a plethora

---

26 M Pelling and C Webster 'Medical Practitioners' in C Webster (ed) *Health, Medicine and Mortality in the Sixteenth Century* (Cambridge University Press, 1979) 166.

27 H Marland 'The "Doctor's Shop": The Rise of the Chemist and Druggist in Nineteenth-century Manufacturing Districts' in L H Curth (ed) *From Physick to Pharmacology: Five Hundred Years of British Drug Retailing* (Ashgate, 2006) 79–104.

28 Pelling and Webster (n 26) 166.

29 Ibid.

of litigation. Resort to the courts and the legislature to establish the status and authority of one form of healing over others met with a mixed reception until late in the nineteenth century when the orthodox gradually achieved some success and, for a short period of time, law was for the most part a deferential and supportive 'spouse' to medicine.

Church and State: a third party in the marriage

'Law has deeply religious roots.'[30] The relationship between secular law and healing was not exclusive. As the next chapter elaborates, another actor, the Church, played a significant role in providing and regulating healing and in the development of laws addressing moral controversy in medicine. Canon law as well as secular law must thus be addressed. The ban on clergy of the higher orders practising surgery imposed by Canon 18 of the Fourth Lateran Council in 1215, re-enforced the divide between physic and surgery. The withdrawal of the Church from front-line health care by no means spelled an end to ecclesiastical engagement in healing. First the Roman Catholic Church, and after the Reformation, the newly established Church of England, were entrusted by the Crown and the legislature with the licensing and regulation of surgeons across the realm and physicians outside the capital. To this day, controversially, the Church of England retains a voice on matters of medicine and morals via the presence of Anglican Bishops in the legislature. Moreover, in the conjoined twins case, the Roman Catholic Archbishop of Westminster was permitted to give evidence to the court.[31]

Christian doctrine undoubtedly influenced the common law as it addressed matters of life and death, sexual morals, the unborn child and the status of women – questions central to medical law. Often labelled sanctity of life, the pervasive influence of religious doctrine relating to such questions has been attacked as incompatible with the values of a society where few people now practise that faith. I suggest in Chapter 6 that the extent to which religious dogma dominated the common law relating to medicine has been exaggerated.

Does medico-legal history matter in practice?

Even if the relationship of law and healing enjoys a long and diverse history, does it matter? Former Secretary of State for Education, Charles Clarke,

---

30 Faigman (n 15) 9.
31 *Re A (children) (Conjoined Twins: Surgical Separation)* [2000] Fam 147.

said of any study of medieval history, 'I don't mind there being some medi-
evalists about for ornamental purposes, but there is no reason for the tax-
payer to pay for it'.[32] Clarke would no doubt say of medico-legal history
that studying old law may be a suitable hobby for a retired academic. No
public money should be wasted funding others to develop research into the
far past unless some concrete practical benefit derives from the enterprise.
I agree with Margaret Pelling when she said:

> Finally, there is the vexed issue of how useful history should be. The 'safe'
> position is that history is valuable for its own sake. While more than ready to
> defend this position, I do not see why history should not inform the present
> especially since the subjects we choose, and the ways in which we write about
> them, undoubtedly reflect current concerns.[33]

Scholarship offering knowledge of, and insight into, the past has intrinsic
value. I reject Clarke's argument that it is *only* if such study has immediate
and obvious usefulness that it should be pursued. Where and when knowledge is also useful to guide us towards better understanding of 'current
concerns', it should of course be put to such use. But unless we unearth
such knowledge in the first place, we cannot identify uses to which it might
be put.

Considering any practical importance of medico-legal history confronts
an obvious obstacle. Medicine today is, thankfully, wholly different from
1215 when the Lateran Council prohibited priests from undertaking surgery, or 1518 when the College of Physicians received its first Royal Charter.
In 1215 or 1518 should a wounded leg become infected, the best a surgeon
could do was amputate the leg and apply leeches to cleanse the wound.
Summon a physician in the 1500s and he would be unlikely to examine you,
and never do so were you a woman.[34] Even though, occasionally, ancient
remedies are found to have beneficial effect, for example, leeches to clean
wounds, little can be learned about how to treat and cure illness from such
history. David Wootton has commented:

> [I]f we define medicine as the ability to cure disease then there was very little
> medicine before 1865. The long tradition that descended from Hippocrates,
> symbolized by reliance on bloodletting, purges and emetics, was almost totally
> ineffectual, indeed positively deleterious, except in so far as it mobilized the
> placebo effect.[35]

32 www.theguardian.com/uk/2003/may/09/highereducation.politics.
33 Pelling (n 21) 8.
34 D Wootton *Bad Medicine: Doctors Doing Harm Since Hippocrates* (Oxford
    University Press, 2007) 64–66.
35 Ibid 283.

Demonstrating that treatments offered to patients by any healer, empiric or Fellow of the College of Physicians were rudimentary and crude does not, however, undermine the case for identifying benefits from greater knowledge and understanding of the relationship of law and healing. Useful insights do not derive from examining the 'cures' which healers provided, but from a better understanding of the role played by legislation and case law in determining how healing was organised and practised, the rights and obligations within healer/patient relationships, and how law has responded to bioethical controversies over time. Common themes persist across the ages and remain relevant in response to current concerns.[36] Context and environment differ. The fundamental questions change little. Ignoring how those questions have been addressed in past times risks constantly 'reinventing the wheel'. Vague knowledge, little more than folk memory, results in myths which distort the law.

Persistent themes

Persistent themes underlying law's engagement with healing include (1) the social organisation of, and access to, healing; (2) regulating healers, and the legal framework governing the relationship of healer and patient; (3) the value attached to human bodies, in particular female bodies, and who has sovereignty over those bodies; (4) conflict between popular opinion and the elite. A theme may disappear from view but persist 'underground' and surface unexpectedly. More than one theme can often be instructive when looking back to examine how today's concerns were addressed yesterday.[37] And debates that are thought to be modern frequently prove to have ancient roots.

By way of illustration, consider access to health care. The fundamental principle of the National Health Service (NHS) of care 'free at the point of use' is regarded as the gift of the Beveridge Report published in 1942.[38] Any 'medical marketplace' where different sorts of healers compete for custom was long gone. Towards the end of the twentieth century, 'markets' re-emerged on the political agenda. Free market economists challenged the principle 'free at the point of use'. So far, no government has proposed to dismantle the NHS, opting rather to smuggle elements of competition

---

36 Brazier and Montgomery (n 2) 10–12.

37 See Brazier and Montgomery (n 2). I have tweaked the five themes we described as *enduring* themes: (1) the social organisation of healing; (2) the sphere of regulation; (3) the significance of human bodies; (4) fear of science; and (5) the impact of scandal.

38 *Beveridge Report on Social Insurance and Allied Services* Cmd 6404 (1942).

into the NHS. In debates about the future of the NHS it may be useful to note that the 'Beveridge' concept of a duty to treat those less fortunate and unable to fund their own care long precedes Beveridge. In the Middle Ages, the monasteries provided care free of charge, as a canonical obligation, not simply charity. In the sixteenth to eighteenth centuries, midwives swore an oath that they would 'helpe every Woman labouring with Childe, as well the poore as the rich: and in time of nessitie [sic]'.[39] Healers of all varieties claimed to treat the poor pro bono, even if their claim might sometimes be more theory than reality.[40]

The importance of regulation to protect patients from incompetence, charlatans and exploitation stretches back across the ages. Re-visit the snapshots. Questions asking who should be the regulator, and how far self-regulation should be countenanced, were mooted from the fifteenth century, when, in 1421, a Bill proposed a national system for regulating health-care workers. The monarch's responsibility to their subjects for the quality of healing was embodied in the 1518 Charter granted to the College of Physicians and confirmed by an Act of Parliament in 1522. Case law on medical negligence, akin to clinical negligence claims today, can be found from the fourteenth century and is discussed in Chapter 5.

Healing our bodies prompted, and still prompts, questions about con-trol of those bodies at each stage of life – in the womb, from birth to death, and after death. How far your body was (or was not) 'yours', vesting choices about what could be done to the body in you and you alone, per-vades the development of laws relating to medical practice and biomedical science. The status of the fetus has 'troubled' jurists and judges from time immemorial. Key questions in the context of bodies and healing address the extent to which the medical professions influenced law-making in, for example, nineteenth-century legislation on abortion, and the regulation of anatomy. Women's bodies have attracted particular attention. Medical opinion may be seen to frame laws imposing significant legal incapacities on married women.

In Chapter 10, I address the controversy generated at the turn of the millennium by revelations that pathologists had retained hearts, brains and other organs after post-mortem examinations without appropriate consent. The 'scandal' highlighted multiple themes. It emphasised the importance attached to physical bodies. It questioned the adequacy of regulation.

39 'A Seventeenth Century Midwife's Oath' Book of Oaths 1649 (anon) in D Evenden *The Midwives of Seventeenth-Century London* (Cambridge University Press, 2006) Appendix B 206–207.
40 *William Rose (Plaintiff in Error) v College of Physicians (London)* (1703) 2 English Reports 857.

Public outrage revealed a huge chasm in attitudes to the bodies of the dead between, on the one hand, medical professionals, lawyers and many bioethicists, and, on the other, families affected by organ retention and many of the public. Distinguished medical practitioners were at a loss to understand why there should be such opposition to practices designed to facilitate medical research, bemoaning the effect of the scandal on the supply of organs and tissue for transplant as well as research.[41] Bitter debates echoed earlier conflicts relating to the use of body parts from the dead. The risks of mutual distrust and antipathy between sections of the public and the 'elite' were thus exposed once again.[42]

Debunking myths

The invisibility of history may have deprived modern medical law of insights into how problems similar to those engaging law-makers in the twentieth century were addressed in the past. A little knowledge can be even more dangerous, perpetuating harmful myths.

Consider two examples – midwives and leprosy. Examined further in Chapter 8, a well-known myth, popularised by Charles Dickens, was the depiction of nineteenth-century midwives as drunken sluts. Lurid allegations about female midwives which had little, if any, basis in fact dominated and distorted parliamentary debates about the regulation of midwifery in the nineteenth century. The leprosy myth (addressed in the next chapter) influenced laws to control leprosy in the British Empire in the nineteenth century. Many public health doctors and colonial administrators wrongly believed that draconian laws imposing isolation of lepers brought about the decline in leprosy in medieval England. They based their policy to combat leprosy in the Empire, focusing on enforced segregation, on what they believed to be medieval precedent. Public health legislation relating to communicable diseases generally in Victorian Britain was, in turn, heavily influenced by similar mistaken beliefs about law relating to lepers in medieval England.

The most pervasive myth, however, is the myth of judicial deference, suggesting that when the courts engaged with medical practice a tradition of judicial deference to medical men had from 'time immemorial' dominated those encounters. Harvey Teff, writing in 1994, suggested that 'nondisclosure and deference have been among the hallmarks of the paternalistic

---

41 R Tallis *Hippocratic Oaths: Medicine and its Discontents* (Atlantic Books, 2004) 186–192.
42 See the 'Afterword' in R Richardson *Death, Dissection and the Destitute* (2nd edn) (Chicago Press, 2000) 409–428.

tradition which has dominated orthodox medical practice over a period of some 2,500 years'.[43] Twentieth-century judges were wary of any criticism of medical practitioners. For example, in 1954, in *Hatcher v Black*, Lord Denning directed a jury that they should not find 'a medical man' (*sic*) negligent unless his conduct was 'deserving of censure'.[44] Three years later, in *Bolam v Friern Hospital Management Committee*, McNair J's ruling that a doctor was not liable in negligence as long as he acted in accordance with 'a practice accepted as proper by a responsible body of medical men skilled in [the] particular art' began a series of cases which, in effect, handed control over standards of practice to the medical profession.[45] Subsequent judgments extended *Bolam* well beyond negligence to almost all decision-making in health care. The courts ceded to the medical profession authority to make decisions that were at best little to do with clinical judgement. Michael Davies described the judicial approach as '[w]hen in doubt *Bolamise*'.[46] José Miola charted the gradual transfer of power to decide questions of medical ethics and patients' rights to the medical profession.[47] Law took a subservient role in the marriage.

The rebirth of modern medical law saw a growing cohort of academics in battle against an entrenched tradition of deference to medicine. We were fighting a straw man. Before the Medical Act 1858, a formidable difficulty affected any notion of judicial deference to practitioners. How were judges to identify the 'responsible medical man' given that several different sorts of healer claimed to represent responsible opinion, scorning the claims of other competing groups of healers?

Had deference been ingrained in law's relationship with healing, it might be expected that before 1858 judges would have preferred, and deferred to, orthodox practitioners licensed by the medical corporations. In particular, one might expect to find deference to the physicians who claimed to be the educated elite of medicine and thus the repository of 'responsible practice'. Yet, the language and attitudes of judges before 1858 often reveals a distinct lack of deference to any sort of doctor, be he licensed or not. Faced with an argument that if an unlicensed man (traditional healer) treated a patient

---

43 H Teff *Reasonable Care: Legal Perspectives on the Doctor-Patient Relationship* (Clarendon Press, 1994) 69.
44 *Hatcher v Black*, *The Times* 2 July 1954.
45 [1957] 2 All ER 118.
46 M Davies 'The "New Bolam": Another False Dawn for Medical Negligence' (1996) 12 *Professional Negligence* 10.
47 J Miola *Medical Ethics and Medical Law: A Symbiotic Relationship* (Hart Publishing, 2007).

who died within three days there was a presumption of homicide, Park J (undeferentially) commented that the test of gross negligence was the same for any kind of healer as it mattered not 'whether the individual consulted be the president of the College of Physicians, the president of the College of surgeons or the humblest bone-setter in the village'.[48]

Little evidence of deference is not evidence of the contrary, of consistent judicial scepticism questioning medical 'expert' opinion. The majority of negligence actions where judges accorded little weight to medical opinion concerned surgeons and apothecaries, seen as artisans, and not the gentlemen of the College of Physicians who regarded themselves as brethren to the lawyer and the clergyman. True, in *Bonham's Case* in 1609,[49] Sir Edward Coke was dismissive of claims by the College that it alone could judge malpractice. Coke declared that any judge with a university education could find whether a medical treatment had been handled correctly or not.[50] Holt CJ later poured scorn on Coke, ruling that it was not for judges to decide if prescribed medicines were wholesome or not.[51]

Evaluating judicial attitudes towards medical practitioners must take account of the broader social context. Judicial disdain reflected the fact that lawyers did not regard medical men as brethren, gentlemen of similar social standing. The medical man was simply another sort of craft or tradesman akin to the farrier or vintner. Pelling suggests that the overall status of medical practitioners before the mid-nineteenth century 'was probably much lower than has been assumed'.[52]

George Eliot's famous novel *Middlemarch*,[53] set in the 1830s, illustrates how social attitudes to doctors were far from deferential. Despite aristocratic family connections, Mr Lydgate, the surgeon-apothecary who had studied in Paris, was still not regarded as a gentleman. His wife regrets his choice of occupation as 'not a nice profession'.[54] His uncle, the baronet, refusing him financial help, declares he could have gone into the army or

---

48 *R v St John Long No 1* (1830) 172 English Reports 759.
49 *Dr Bonham's Case* (1609) 77 English Reports 638.
50 H J Cook 'Against Common Right and Reason: The College of Physicians versus Dr Thomas Bonham' (1985) 29 *American Journal of Legal History* 301.
51 *Case 50 Dr Groenvelt v Dr Burwell and others, Censors of the College of Phyisicians* (1698) 92 English Reports 865.
52 Pelling (n 21) 11.
53 G Eliot *Middlemarch* (Penguin Classic, 1994); discussed in M Pelling 'Scenes from Professional Life: Medicine, Moral Conduct and Interconnectedness' in P Ghosh and L Goldman (eds) *Politics and Culture in Victorian Britain* (Clarendon Press, 2006) Chapter 13.
54 Eliot (n 53) 458.

the Church,[55] medicine being no job for a gentleman. Lady Chettam prefers her medical man 'more on a footing with the servants'.[56] Lydgate is a surgeon, not a physician. Physicians fare little better with Eliot: she damns the venerable colleges 'which used great efforts to secure purity of medicine by making it scarce'.[57]

'Medical law' is not new: it just looked different

The engagement of law with healing and healers is as aged as medicine itself.[58] By the fifteenth century, the law courts, the Church, the Crown and the legislature were engaged in addressing questions now considered to be part of the corpus of 'modern medical law'. The contents of a book on 'Medical law' in 1600 or 1700 would not differ significantly from a modern textbook. Developments as yet undreamt of, such as assisted conception, organ transplants, and artificial life support, would necessarily be missing from the Table of Contents. Nevertheless, 'old' law is still called on to cast light on 'new' medicine.[59] In the absence of legislation designed to address developments in biomedical science and new technologies, judges look to history, to fundamental principles of the common law to play a part in regulating such innovations.[60] 'Old' attitudes persist. Reflect on the common law's antipathy to single motherhood which surfaced in debates about Section 13(5) of the Human Fertilisation and Embryology Act 1990.[61]

Identifying analogies between law's engagement with healing centuries ago and modern medical law is complicated by the fact that the same issues may look different. Clinical negligence is a simple example. As Chapter 5 explores, malpractice litigation and doctors' fears of a malpractice crisis have a long history, but the form taken by litigation in the sixteenth to nineteenth centuries may look different. Rather than the aggrieved patient bringing a claim for negligence, litigation was often initiated by the doctor, suing in contract for unpaid fees. The action presented as a claim for debt. The defendant patient would contend that the plaintiff doctor was negligent, and

---

55 Ibid 664.
56 Ibid 91.
57 Ibid 145.
58 See the Code of Hammurabi: R Porter *The Greatest Benefit to Mankind: A Medical History of Humanity from Antiquity to the Present* (Fontana Press, 1997) 45.
59 S MacLean *Old Law, New Medicine: Medical Ethics and Human Rights* (Pandora, 1999).
60 See, for example, *Re A (children) (Conjoined Twins)* (n 31).
61 E Jackson 'Conception and the Irrelevance of the Welfare Principle' (2002) 65 *Modern Law Review* 176. And see Chapter 8 below.

not entitled to payment. Archaic language and the common law's attachment to complex procedural rules further complicate and obscure the similarities between the case law from before the nineteenth century and now.

Another difficulty is that some of the most pressing questions in medical law have tangled roots. Principles now used to frame law governing medicine and medical science often evolved in markedly different contexts. The law relating to consent to treatment has its source in laws to prevent violence in breach of the King's Peace. Chapter 9 examines how fetal status was addressed in litigation about succession to property of a child in utero at the date of their father's death. Chapter 6 shows how the roots of the ubiquitous appeals to sanctity of life are found in cases relating to homicide far removed from the context of end-of-life decisions in the twenty-first century. Moral and social dilemmas relating to assisted dying are on the surface dramatically different to the crew of a lifeboat adrift at sea eating the cabin boy.[62] Yet, the questions whether and when killing can be justified apply to both the wretched seamen and physicians treating a dying patient.

What about 'science'?

John Harrington, examining the interaction of medicine and the common law, explains how in the mid-to-late 1800s legislation gradually unifying the orthodox professions combined with the emergence of biomedical science based on laboratory investigation, rigorous testing and assessment of results granted medicine 'a position of unprecedented prestige and influence'.[63] 'Science' offered 'new certainties' to replace folklore and to challenge religion. Porter traced the development of fact-based experimental medicine across Europe and in the USA.[64] Raymond Tallis hailed the miracle of scientific medicine emerging in the nineteenth century.[65]

Recalling Wootton's condemnation of much of medicine before 1865 as 'ineffectual indeed positively deleterious',[66] we have to ask again whether, prior to the advent of Tallis's miracle, any useful understanding can be teased out of 'older' history to illuminate legal and ethical quandaries generated by modern scientific discoveries and science more generally. Put brutally, even if greater knowledge of the law relating to the relationship of practitioners

---

62 *R v Dudley and Stephens* (1884) 14 QBD 273.
63 J A Harrington ' "Red in Tooth and Claw": The Idea of Progress in Medicine and the Common Law' (2002) *Social and Legal Studies* 211, 213.
64 Porter (n 58) 304–347.
65 Tallis (n 41) 14–27.
66 Wootton (n 34) 283.

of healing and their patients offers insights into such matters as the doctor/patient relationship, is it a waste of time to explore the relationship between English law and biomedical science before late in the nineteenth century? 'Science' has always been a presence in the marriage, 'sometimes as an honored guest, sometimes as an unwanted interloper, and sometimes both at the same time'.[67] Science was not a term limited to activities of gathering knowledge empirically but embraced 'any body of knowledge that resulted from systematic and rigorous study'.[68] Theology and philosophy were deemed sciences. Religion and natural philosophy provided accounts of the human condition long before any lab technician donned a white coat, or reached for a petrie dish. Boundaries between different sorts of science were blurred. The same scholar might undertake study of several disciplines which we now classify as medicine, physics, biology, moral philosophy and theology.

Looking back to evaluate how law engaged with theories of science in its older, broader meaning informs us about how law both 'regulated' science and how science 'made law'. By way of example, Chapter 9 considers how the concept of 'quickening' framed abortion law for centuries. Medical 'knowledge' combined with religious dogma to create a fiction; a fiction endorsed by the law. It does not matter that the concept was later proven wrong, what is instructive is how law related to, and adjudicated between, competing bodies of knowledge accessible at the relevant time. Chapter 8 explores how learned men and philosophers from Aristotle onwards contended that the woman contributed nothing or very little to the child she bore. She only nourished the seed. One theory held that the whole of the child was present in the father's sperm. A wife was de facto a genetic carrier. The influence of this claim to paternal exclusivity in creating his child explains laws on succession to property and the status of women.

Reaching back to explore law's relationship with science also illustrates that what the public understood or misunderstood about scientific 'evidence' was as crucial as the reality. The horror felt by a pauper who believed in the Resurrection and whose wife's body was taken for dissection, was no less acute for lack of empirical evidence. Again and again scornful dismissal of popular beliefs and cultural preferences as superstition and ignorance by the educated elite has fuelled discord.

Were the shades of the common law jurists from the Middle Ages to Victorian England to be summoned to debate the status of the fetus, their discourse would not be much different to debates today. Of course, medical technology has opened up possibilities undreamt of by our grandparents,

---

67 Faigman (n 15) xi.
68 Ibid 7.

never mind remoter ancestors. As with litigation and regulation of medical practice, what matters, what can be learned from the past, is not dependent on the scientific detail but, rather, identifies insights into persistent features of human life. A childless woman in 1600 seeking a remedy for her 'barren' womb, might be instructed on the best conditions for conception, prescribed some nostrum, and advised to resort to prayer and pilgrimage. Such 'fertility treatment' bears scant resemblance to the assisted reproductive technologies (ARTS) developed following the success of in vitro fertilisation. But forget science for a moment and look at the social context. Medieval fertility aids were profitable businesses, as is the fertility industry today. Fundamental questions about regulation, access and the ethics of profit are much the same. Determining when a fetus gestating in an artificial womb acquires legal personality appears to be wholly unrelated to any 'knowledge' before the end of the twentieth century. If we strip away the technology of ectogenesis, a pesky persistent question comes out of the shadows: once a fetus is not dependent on a woman's body, is it thus born alive with the same right to life as its naturally gestated sibling?

Questions raised by the law, healing and the human body in sickness and in health are diverse; only a handful are dealt with in this book. One thread linking the very different scenarios is whose voice has been dominant in framing the law. If a gangrenous leg needed amputation, the surgeon in 1518 or today was and is best placed to explain what can be done and carry out the operation. Proposals to legislate to regulate the acquisition of corpses required evidence of practice and need from the anatomists. Judges and legislators need expert opinion about what can be done and how it could be done. What should or should not be done was, and is, a quite separate question. The weight accorded by law to medical 'expertise' has swung to and fro over the centuries creating acrimony between the parties.

And finally, Lord Atkin's ghosts

Uncovering some of the stories of law's relationship with healing in the next nine chapters will (I hope) prompt useful reflections on the relationship of law and healing today. The stories to be told may provoke mixed emotions in twenty-first century readers. The longevity of a principle of access to care, and the more patient-focused approach of Edward Coke, may be applauded. Evidence of midwifery as a thriving female occupation with a 'code of ethics' embodied in the Midwives Oath, addressing such matters as candour and 'whistle-blowing' prescient of professional ethics today, may be welcomed. Other insights are uncomfortable. Parts of the Midwives Oath may be forward-looking, but the duty to 'grass' on women who sought to conceal a birth and the midwife's role in enforcing the Infanticide Act are less palatable. The notion that you could not use your own body as you wished is unnerving. The relationship of law and science cementing imagery of women which reduced further women's rights over their bodies, jars with liberal thinking. The evidence can be depressing that in debating some persistent questions, exemplified by disputes about fetal status, the same arguments are repeated ad nauseam over nine centuries.

Speaking of the convoluted and sometimes incomprehensible rules of procedure developed by the common law, a highly regarded judge, Lord Atkin, said:

> When these ghosts of the past stand in the path of justice clanking their medieval chains the proper course for the judge is to pass through them undeterred.[69]

Should we follow Atkin's precept and not bother with medico-legal history? I hope not. Meeting a ghost of medico-legal history, we should rather pause and interrogate the spectre. It may be that she offers us little enlightenment and should be passed through 'undeterred'. She may, though, cast light on the present, counselling us as much about what not to do as to how we might do better. And even if she offers no positive prescriptions from her time, she will have a story to engage us.

---

69 *United Australia Ltd v Barclays Bank* [1941] AC 1, 29.

2

Medical brethren

The Church and healing

The ubiquitous presence of a third party, religion, in the marriage of law and healing is central to the story of law's relationship with healing. The pervasive influence of first the Roman Catholic Church, and after the Reformation the Church of England, has survived for many centuries. Anglican Bishops still sit in the Upper Chamber of the legislature.[1] The extent of clerical influence in relation to law-making in response to moral controversies arising from healing and human bodies is weaker and more contested in a society where religious faith and practice is waning, or perhaps it is more accurate to say Christian, and in particular Anglican practice, is declining.

The picture of the tripartite marriage was dramatically different in medieval England. The Roman Church was the dominant partner. In medieval Europe, Roy Porter said simply 'Medicine and religion intersected at many points'.[2] The key role or roles of the medieval Church were downgraded by many Protestant commentators in the nineteenth century. Rawcliffe commented:

> The symbiotic relationship between religion and medicine and the overwhelming influence of the Catholic Church in matters to do with sickness and health has at times been treated dismissively and Victorian doctors and theologians regarded the relationship as one that smacked of popish superstition to Anglicans living in an age of untrammelled scientific progress. Yet it is the bedrock upon which any serious study of pre-modern medicine must be founded and is crucial to an understanding of medieval attitudes to extreme human suffering.[3]

1 E Wicks 'Religion, Law and Medicine: Legislating on Birth and Death in a Christian State' (2009) 17 *Medical Law Review* 410.
2 R Porter *The Greatest Benefit to Mankind: A Medical History of Humanity from Antiquity to the Present* (Fontana Press, 1997) 110.
3 C Rawcliffe *Leprosy in Medieval England* (Boydell Press, 2006) 6.

The relationship between medicine and religion has not always been comfortable. Nor has the interaction of lawyers and judges with their medical and clerical brethren always been harmonious. The days of ecclesiastical dominance are long gone. Christian doctrine may have limited impact in public debate but in seeking to understand the history of the relationship of law and healing in England and its impact on modern health care, the enduring influence of the Christian churches cannot be ignored.

Language still used in relation to health-care workers echoes the language of the Church. The very word 'profession' resonates with the notion of the monk and nun's solemn vows.[4] Health-care professionals, especially doctors and nurses, are often said to be pursuing a 'vocation' as does a priest. Even in a secular society, the belief continues that health care is somehow a different calling demanding higher standards of personal behaviour than other trades or professions. Codes of ethics for doctors and nurses require that they respond to emergencies even outside their workplace or working hours; albeit rarely, health professionals must act pro bono. Doctors and nurses can be charged with unfitness to practise concerning alleged misconduct unrelated to their conduct at work. In debates on controversial questions, for example abortion and assisted dying, argument rages as to whether the law should permit a health professional to refuse to treat a patient on the grounds of conscientious objection, objection often deriving from the professional's religious faith.

Prior to the Reformation, the Church in Rome effectively legislated on many matters that we would now consider medical law. Canon law addressed both general principles relating to medical treatment, for example the nature of disease and the uses of the human body (living and dead), and also particular questions, for example the treatment of lepers. Canon law applied across Western Europe[5] wherever the Roman Catholic Church held sway.[6] For so long as England retained allegiance to the papacy, canon law relating to illness and healing was incorporated into English law.[7] Post the Reformation the reformed churches, including the Church of England, continued to play a key role in shaping laws relating to healing. Unlike the pre-Reformation Church in Rome, while the Church of England could and did seek to influence both the legislature and the courts, it could not

---

4 M Pelling *The Common Lot: Sickness, Medical Occupations and the Urban Poor in Early Modern England* (Routledge, 1998) 251–253.

5 Rawcliffe (2006) (n 3) 9.

6 Canon law as promulgated by the Church in Rome did not of course apply in the countries that adhered to the Eastern Orthodox traditions.

7 J R Guy 'The Episcopal Licensing of Physicians, Surgeons and Midwives' (1982) 56 *Bulletin of the History of Medicine* 528, 529.

'make law' as had the Roman Church. The establishment of the Church of England as the state church, however, gave, and still gives, the Anglican Church a privileged role in law-making.[8] The break-up of the Roman Catholic dominance in Europe and its replacement in parts of Europe by diverse reformed religions and churches inevitably meant that across the continent divergence emerged in religious pronouncements on 'medieval/early modern' bioethical debates.

In exploring the impact of the Church on the relationship of law and healing, religion engaged with law and healing in at least four different ways.[9]

(1) Canon law. The Roman Catholic Church 'made law' in certain cases, for example, the decrees of the Lateran Council in 1179 relating to the treatment of lepers, and later the response to the plagues.

(2) Providing healing. For much of the Middle Ages medical practitioners and lawyers were literally brethren. Lawyers and doctors were often monks educated and practising in or from monasteries throughout England. The Church was directly responsible for a considerable proportion of the delivery of health care. Its role was not limited to matters of medicine and morals. The majority of physicians were priests and the monasteries provided much of the care of the sick. Within the monasteries, monks acted as healers. Outside the monasteries, an array of other healers, including 'wise women, empirics and herbalists actually constituted the great majority of practitioners at work among the sick': healers trained only by experience and sometimes informal apprenticeships.[10]

(3) Regulating healers. Towards the end of the medieval era and the start of the early modern era, the Church came to play a role regulating secular health care by way of episcopal licensing. Across Europe, secular laws required physicians, surgeons and midwives to obtain a licence from the local bishop before they could lawfully practise independently. In England after the Reformation episcopal licensing continued with Church of England bishops 'inheriting' the powers and duties of their Roman Catholic predecessors. As will be seen in the next chapter, however, episcopal licensing of physicians and surgeons was gradually supplanted by other forms of regulation. The role of the Church in midwives and regulating midwifery continued well into the eighteenth century.

(4) Theology shaping secular laws. Theological debates within the Church influenced secular law-making. For example, consider the influence on

---

8 Wicks (n 1).

9 Note the jurisdiction of the ecclesiastical courts in matters of morals e.g. adultery; J Baker *An Introduction to English Legal History* (5th edn) (Oxford University Press, 2019) 135–138.

10 C Rawcliffe *Medicine and Society in Later Medieval England* (Sandpiper Books, 1995) xv.

laws regulating abortion of the teaching of St Thomas Aquinas relating to 'quickening', as the stage in gestation when the soul entered the body of the fetus.

By the late fifteenth century, the role of the monks and the monasteries in directly delivering health care declined as a growing number of laymen began to practise as physicians, often men who had studied at one of the great medical schools in Continental Europe. Lay people were well established as surgeons. The Church's ban on priests in the higher orders carrying out surgery created a space in which the 'doctor' practising surgery was free of clerical competition. Gradually the predominance of the priest-physician declined and a cohort of lay medical practitioners began to emerge. The dual role of priest and doctor did not disappear altogether. A number of Anglican clergymen controversially continued to combine care of the souls of their parishioners with some level of medical practice.[11]

This chapter focuses on the first three roles, canon law, providing healing, and regulating healers. I begin by assessing the doctrine of the pre-Reformation Roman Church on the interface between law and healing and the nature of illness. I then address an example of canon law exposing the risk that a little knowledge is a dangerous thing. The chapter goes on to examine the Church as a provider of healing focusing on the rise and fall of the monasteries in providing health care, charting the move from clerical to secular health care and exploring the changing role of the Church from provider to regulator. The particular facets of clerical regulation of female midwives are briefly noted at the end of this chapter and are more fully developed in Chapter 8. The broader and controversial questions of the persistent influence of Christianity on English law in the context of debates about medicine and morals, debates which today might be classified as bio-ethical controversy, are considered in Chapters 6 to 10.

Body and soul: illness and sin

The medieval Church, and much of medieval society, would have regarded suggestions that you could distinguish in any major way between body and soul as misguided. Illness of the body might indicate sickness of the soul. Illness was often regarded as the result of sin. Healing the body required more than the physical care that lay physicians or surgeons could offer. Healing could include supernatural intervention. Such interventions might

---

11 I Mortimer 'Rural Medical Marketplace in Southern England c 1570–1720' in M Jenner and P Wallis (eds) *Medicine and the Market in England and its Colonies c 1450–c 1850* (Palgrave Macmillan, 2007).

be classified as benign and offered by the Church itself, as in the example of healing shrines across Europe.[12] Supernatural interventions might also be malign, the result of witchcraft and/or demonic possession. Witches, it was believed, meddled in healing to disguise their evil purpose. The witch might harbour an ' "ancient and secret" knowledge of herbs, healing and hurtful'.[13] In its cure of souls, the Church unsurprisingly perceived ecclesiastical control and monitoring of healing as 'essential'.[14] The body should not be neglected for it 'belonged to God and had to be properly looked after'.[15] The soul took priority. In a canon in the thirteenth century Pope Innocent III mandated that no physician for the body:

> [s]hall prescribe to a sick person anything that may prove perilous to the soul. But when it happens that he is called to a sick person, he shall first of all effectually persuade him to send for the physicians of the soul; that after the sick person hath taken care of his spiritual medicament, he may with better effect proceed to the cure of his body.[16]

In the Middle Ages the physician for the body and the physician of the soul were often the same individual – a priest-physician. The stance taken by the Church and articulated by Popes over time demonstrated mixed feelings within the Church to the dual role of cleric as physician of the soul and physician for the body. The Church recognised the contribution made by the physician for the body and gradually accepted 'a role, but a subordinate one for secular medicine'.[17]

The growth of secular medicine did not diminish the importance of care of the soul and spiritual healing. As Kusukawa says 'it is best to interpret these "spiritual therapies" as an extension of healing'.[18] The emphasis on the soul in the canon law of the Roman Catholic Church should not be underestimated. In Chapter 8, it will be seen that the Roman Church's interest in licensing midwives originally derived in part from the role of midwives in 'emergency' baptisms of a child who might not live. An unbaptised infant was condemned to limbo. The reformed churches largely rejected the dogma of limbo, resulting in changes to the Midwife's Oath and her

---

12 Porter (n 2) 111.
13 Guy (n 7) 530.
14 Ibid.
15 Porter (n 2) 87.
16 Guy (n 7) 531.
17 Porter (n 2) 87.
18 S Kusukawa 'Medicine in Western Europe in 1500' in P Elmer (ed) *The Healing Arts: Health Disease and Society in Europe: 1500–1800* (Manchester University Press, 2004) 1–19.

professional obligations post the Reformation. Changes in religious teaching influenced regulation of professional practice.

The notion of the priority of the care of the soul over the cure of the body will be alien to most modern readers, many of whom do not believe in the soul. The underlying principle in medieval healing, that the health and care of the physical body is not the whole story of the person, nor the sole objective of health care, resonates with the emphasis today on holistic medicine. A less palatable outcome of the priority of the soul flowed from teachings that illness might ensue from sorcery, or be punishment for sin. Mental illnesses in particular were often thought to be caused either by demonic possession or derived from sinful behaviour on the part of the sick patient, or both.[19] In modern England, the notion of sorcery as a cause of illness would be dismissed as fantasy in mainstream medicine, yet fears of demonic possession hover on the fringes of health care, as illustrated by the tenacity of stories of Satanic sexual abuse.[20] More widespread is the recurring argument that certain kinds of illness result from morally blameworthy activity on the part of the stricken patient. Blame has the effect of transforming the sick into burdens on society, even threats to society. To the medieval Church, sexual sin dominated debates. Twenty-first century physicians and public health officials are more likely to focus on the patient's smoking or drinking habits. Responses to the advent of the HIV pandemic demonstrated that modern people remain susceptible to moral panic and debates about criminalisation of transmission of HIV echo some of the language and imagery of medieval responses to leprosy and the plague.[21]

Lessons from leprosy: an early myth

[C]ancer and AIDS have become the iconic diseases of the late twentieth century, so leprosy has also been presented as representative of 'the Dark Ages'.[22]

Now named Hansen's disease in an attempt to reduce the stigma attached to leprosy, most people have read something about the fate of the leper in the Middle Ages. The Church and common law are often presented as imposing the cruellest treatment on unfortunate lepers, perceived as deformed and cast out of society. The story recounts that in accordance with biblical

19 The sick person's sin might have made him more vulnerable to demonic possession.
20 'Satanic Panic on Greater Manchester Council Estate' *Manchester Evening News* 15 March 2021.
21 C Stanton and H Quirk *Criminalising Contagion: Legal and Ethical Challenges of Disease Transmission and the Criminal Law* (Cambridge University Press, 2016).
22 Rawcliffe (2006) (n 3) 17.

injunctions, the leper was to be segregated from the community; a ghastly ritual (to be found in the Sarum Missal) was performed forbidding the leper from all normal human contact. Canon 23 of the Lateran Council 1179 was supposed to have ordered that lepers be excluded from the community. The 'leper mass' pronounced the leper 'dead among the living'.[23] If they were lucky a leper might find a place in a lazar house, often described as akin to the worst Victorian workhouse.

However harsh that response to leprosy appeared, many (though not all)[24] colonial administrators and doctors dealing with leprosy in the British Empire in the nineteenth century believed that it was such a stringent regime of imposing isolation on lepers which brought about the decline in leprosy in medieval England. They based their response to leprosy in the Empire on segregation, on what they believed to be medieval precedent. Moreover, public health legislation relating to communicable diseases in Britain itself was, and is, influenced by similar beliefs about law relating to lepers in medieval England. For those who argue that we should learn from history and are inclined to cheer the use of history in law-making relating to medicine, the trouble is much of what is believed about the laws relating to the treatment of lepers in medieval England is wrong. In *Leprosy in Medieval England*, Carole Rawcliffe marshals a powerful argument that much of the popular understanding of the treatment of medieval lepers is myth not reality.[25] She warns of the:

> [F]antasies and misapprehensions about 'the medieval leper' propagated during a period when microbiologists, colonial administrators and evangelicals turned to the past for evidence to support their own campaign for mandatory segregation.[26]

I can only highlight some key points in Rawcliffe's compelling book.

The growth of the myth of segregation as the 'cure' for leprosy is in part explained by theological debates on disease and sin. Many medieval theologians regarded leprosy as caused by depravity, probably sexual depravity. Some argued that intercourse during menstruation (a sin according to canon law) resulted in children with leprosy. Many believed leprosy to be a sexually transmitted disease. The widespread belief that the leper brought their fate upon themselves by self-indulgence is incontrovertible. In her earlier

---

23 Porter (n 2) 121–122.
24 C Creighton *A History of Epidemics in Britain, From AD 664 to the Great Plague* (London 1894 reprinted 1965).
25 Rawcliffe (2006) (n 3).
26 Ibid 5.

work published in 1995, *Medicine and Society in Later Medieval England*, Rawcliffe quoted a contemporary homily:[27]

> For just as leprosy makes the body ugly, loathsome and monstrous, so the filth of lechery makes the soul very loathsome spiritually and the swelling of secret pride is leprosy that no man may hide.[28]

The language of prejudice is patent. That prejudice, however, did not translate into the grim picture of exile to a living death described above. The reality is more complicated. Canon 23 of the Lateran Council 1179 said nothing about forced isolation and quarantining of lepers: it focused on the duty of priests to make provision for lepers to hear Mass and be given Christian burial. The obligation to live apart, an obligation derived from Mosaic law, was taken as read. Canon 23 addressed the reciprocal obligation of the community. In *Leprosy in Medieval England* Rawcliffe describes Canon 23 as 'unambiguously designed to provide support for such [leper] communities'.[29] The care of lepers at risk to one's own health was regarded by the Church as a high form of sacrifice and virtue. Rawcliffe demonstrated that the dreaded lazar houses were for the most part not much different in comfort and care from the monastic hospitals which catered for those sick from other illnesses.[30] An afflicted person's principal problem was finding a bed in the lazar house of their choice.[31]

The 'leper mass' and the ritual in the Sarum Missal driving lepers out of society and condemning them to living death are found by Rawcliffe to be myths, not appearing in any Missal or liturgy until at least 1520 when leprosy had more or less disappeared from England.[32] The persistence of the myth is remarkable; even Roy Porter takes it for truth.[33] Nor were all lepers driven out of society. Afflicted persons who accepted their fate and kept apart from others taking such precautions as were then thought to be effective to prevent passing on the disease often continued to live 'socially distanced', but still within in the community. Baldwin IV, King of Jerusalem in the twelfth century, was a leper. Making provision to live apart was much easier for what were described as noble lepers.[34] The precedent of mandatory segregation relied on to support nineteenth-century legislation

27 Rawcliffe (1995) (n 10) 14.
28 J Small (ed) *English Metrical Homilies* (Edinburgh, 1862) 129–130.
29 Rawcliffe (2006) (n 3) 257.
30 Ibid 302–344.
31 Ibid 291.
32 Rawcliffe (2006) (n 3) 19–21.
33 Porter (n 2) 121–122.
34 Rawcliffe (2006) (n 3) 54–55.

was deeply flawed by its misunderstanding of canon and common law. And its 'scientific' claim that segregation resulted in a decline in leprosy was also probably wrong. Improved nutrition, better housing and increased immunity are more likely causes.[35]

What then of the law relating to lepers in medieval England? There appears to be no secular legislation, akin to the modern Public Health (Control of Diseases) Act 1984 and its predecessors, providing for the isolation of lepers or punishment of those who refused to live apart and who thus might be seen to threaten the public. Reference is made by some authors[36] to a 'statute' of Edward III in 1346. The so-called statute is not an Act of Parliament with national force, but rather an Edict of the King ordering the removal of all lepers from within the walls of London.[37] Rawcliffe explains that for the most part action against lepers was a matter for local law and custom, informed in part by canon law. Legal proceedings were usually instigated by local authorities by way of presentment of the supposed leper as a risk to the public by creating a great nuisance.[38] Supporters of the myth that a rigorous policy of segregation was applied nationally argue that a royal writ *de leproso amovendo* constituted the legal basis for enforcement of such a policy are confounded by Rawcliffe's finding that such a writ was used only twice and that there are perhaps six occasions when other royal writs formed the basis of action to exclude lepers from the community.[39] Presentment by the local authorities was often influenced by panic over epidemics and the character and class of the defendant. The 'offence' might primarily be seen as anti-social behaviour.

Rawcliffe also demonstrates that claims that the common law consistently condemned all lepers to a living legal death are misplaced. Leprosy did not at canon or common law dissolve a marriage, nor did the leper forfeit his existing property nor lose his rights to invoke the law by pleading in the Royal Courts. He might be barred from entry to the physical space of the courtroom but he could appoint an attorney to act for him.[40] Entry into a monastic *leprosarium* did entail the usual legal consequences of entry into

35 Ibid 344–345.
36 John Stow *Survey of London* (1598) cited in Rawcliffe (2006) (n 3) 23.
37 Rawcliffe (2006) (n 3) 22–23.
38 In 1995, the antique offence of causing a public nuisance was resurrected to prosecute a doctor who knowing that he had tested positive for Hepatitis B concealed his condition and continued to operate. See *R v Gaud* (1995) (unreported) discussed in M Mulholland 'Public Nuisance a New Use for an Old Tool' (1995) 11 *Professional Negligence* 70.
39 Rawcliffe (2006) (n 3) 22.
40 Ibid 273.

a religious house, and so like monks and nuns who freely chose religious life the leper became subject to vows of poverty and chastity. He could not thereafter own property or enter into contracts.

A brief examination of the medieval response to leprosy offers a helpful insight into the relationship of canon and secular law. Can any more be claimed? In the light of Rawcliffe's debunking of myths about the medieval responses to leprosy and the role of that myth in informing later legislation, does the history remain instructive? I think it does, subject to a health warning that great care is needed to ensure as far as possible the accuracy of the historical precedent. The picture of the law's response to leprosy in the Middle Ages illustrates fundamental dilemmas in making laws which seek to balance the liberties of the individual against threats to the health of the community. In that context, HIV and leprosy highlight a very particular problem. Contrary to popular opinion neither leprosy then, nor HIV now, are particularly effective infectious agents. 'We still do not know precisely why so many people who are regularly exposed to it [leprosy] enjoy immunity, while a small minority do not. For, contrary to popular myth, the risks of succumbing to infection are generally slight.'[41] Unlike many communicable diseases the person with HIV and the person with leprosy will survive for many years, rather than as for example the cholera victim either dying swiftly or recovering and no longer being infectious.[42]

A 'Monastic Health Service'?

Until well into the fourteenth century, much of the health care provided in England was delivered by monks some of whom, though not all, were physicians, or before 1215 surgeons. The ubiquity of clerics as trusted healers is explained by Willcock: '[N]one but the learned could be deemed fully accomplished in this science and none but the clergy paid the slightest attention to learning.'[43]

Monastic hospitals cared for the sick. Access to monastic care was in theory free of charge. The hospitals took in the poor man at the gate as well as the rich man from his castle. Until the later years of the medieval era, monks did not only treat the 'sick poor'. They also cared for wealthier and more aristocratic members of society. The king and the court had their own physicians and surgeons.[44] The local gentry might share a roof, if not

---

41 Ibid 2.
42 M Brazier and J Harris 'Public and Private Lives' (1996) 4 *Medical Law Review* 171.
43 J W Willcock *Laws relating to the Medical Profession with an Account of the Rise and Progress of the Various Orders* (J & W T Clarke, 1830) 6–9.
44 Usually trained abroad: Rawcliffe (1995) (n 10) 112.

a room[45] with the sick peasant. The number of monasteries and hospitals in all save the remotest parts of England suggests that a form of 'monastic health service' (MHS) existed in England over 600 years before the inception of the National Health Service (NHS) in 1948.

The NHS arguably created a right of access to health care. Were the monasteries simply providing cold charity on the lines of later foundations of secular charitable hospitals such as St Bartholomew's or the provision for outdoor and indoor medical relief in the Poor Laws? Consider the Rule of St Benedict: 'The care of the sick is to be placed above and before any other duty, as if indeed Christ himself were being directly served by waiting on them.'[46] Benedictine monks were obliged to offer care to any in need who came to their doors. They were forbidden to act for gain. Providing care without charge is charity in a legal sense but note the emphasis on duty. The monasteries were in theory not free to pick and choose. The monks must serve their patients as they would serve Christ, not treat their guests as common sorts of persons to be condescended to and patronised.

The difference between the monastic hospitals and the great charitable hospitals founded in London and the larger cities, such as St Bartholomew's, is stark. Only the worthy sick poor could enter the hospital doors and must then abide by rules. Children and the terminally ill were unlikely to be admitted at all.[47] The wealthy citizens who contributed to hospital funds and became hospital governors saw munificence as helping the unfortunate as praiseworthy but not a duty.

A second objection to an analogy between NHS and 'MHS' could be that monastic health care was not health care. In the twelfth to fourteenth centuries, treatments were limited and often bizarre. In speculating that the monasteries offered a 'Monastic Health Service' a key question is, did they provide access to such healing and care as was known at the time? Fifty years from now, our great grandchildren may laugh at the unsophisticated way breast cancer is treated today. It does not follow that there is no health service now. It does seem to be the case that care (in the sense of active interventions) in monastic hospitals was more limited than the treatment which lay medical practitioners might offer outside the monasteries. In treating their patients, monks focused more on cleanliness, warmth, simple herbal remedies and nutrition and avoided the regular administration of clysters and enemas that patients who were tended by lay physicians in the

45 Porter (n 2) 113.
46 As cited in Porter (n 2) 111.
47 T Crane *The Statutes of the General Infirmary at Chester* (printed by Elizabeth Adams, 1763) LIV.

Royal Courts might face. Gentler, less invasive, care may have benefited the patients.[48]

A further objection to the concept of an 'MHS' even vaguely resembling the NHS is the argument that the monasteries cared more for the soul – prioritised a good death. Grell argues that monastic hospitals were:

> [v]ery different from the modern equivalent. They were primarily religious institutions, dedicated to saving souls – both those of the patients and the individuals who cared for the sick or who financed such care.[49]

Grell further claims that monastic hospitals spent most of the money donated to them on altar screens and other accoutrements for the church; on religion and not the sick.[50] Such charges against the monasteries were common at the time of the Reformation and included related claims that monasteries also misused money donated for the relief of poverty. Rushton has shown that the latter charge is not supported by the evidence.[51] Evidence that medieval monastic hospitals paid attention to spiritual welfare as well as the health of the body does not demonstrate that the hospitals should be dismissed as extensions of the Church where prayers were supplemented by a little crude medicine and which were in no sense analogous to modern hospitals. Sick patients in the Middle Ages cared deeply for the fate of their soul. Any healer, lay or religious, treating a patient would have regard to spiritual and bodily welfare, to the whole person (the *particular patient*).[52] Monastic care may indeed be seen as holistic.

The most difficult question to address in examining the nature of monastic health care and canon law is the ambivalence of the Church towards clerics in holy orders practising as physicians. Although at least one Pope, John XXI, was himself a practising physician,[53] papal attitudes to priests combining the roles of physician of the soul and physician for the body varied over time. Amundsen presents a cogent case that an absolute prohibition of the practice of physic, as opposed to surgery, by any man in holy orders was never canon law.[54] At times the leaders of the Church expressed concern

---

48 Rawcliffe (1995) (n 10) 58–81.

49 O P Grell 'Medicine and Religion in Sixteenth-Century Europe' in Elmer (ed) (n 18) 84, 85.

50 Ibid.

51 N S Rushton 'Monastic Charitable Provision in Tudor England: Quantifying and Qualifying Poor Relief in the Early Sixteenth Century' (2001) 16 *Continuity and Change* 9.

52 See *Montgomery v Lanarkshire Health Board* [2015] UKSC 11.

53 D W Amundsen 'Medieval Canon Law on Medical and Surgical Practice by the Clergy' (1978) 52 *Bulletin of the History of Medicine* 22, 38.

54 Ibid.

about a dual role fearing that the priest/physician might neglect his religious function. That concern was part of a broader anxiety about monks leaving their monasteries to pursue secular studies and practice, including secular law.[55] There are many examples of priests and monks undertaking the study of law to become advisers to the monarchs of Europe. The Church deplored their 'desertion' of the cloister. Amundsen makes it clear the pursuit of 'temporal gain' was classed as 'evil and detestable'.[56] 'Commercial' practice as a physician outwith the Church was deplored.

Surgery was a different matter. Canon 18 of the Fourth Lateran Council 1215 headed 'Clerics to dissociate from the shedding of blood' is generally regarded as imposing an absolute prohibition on the higher orders of clergy engaging in surgery.[57] Canon 18 forbade all clerics from participating in punishments involving the shedding of blood or participating in such punishment. Nor might a cleric be involved with 'mercenaries, crossbowmen or other men of blood' or play a role in trials by 'ordeal of boiling or cold water or of the red-hot iron'. Canon 18 imposed a prohibition of clerical involvement with cruel treatment and torture and combat. The canon additionally stated that '*nor may a subdeacon, deacon or priest practise the art of surgery, which involves cauterising or making incisions* (my emphasis)'. The inclusion of surgery within a canon barring the clergy from participation in the nastier aspects of the medieval judicial process and of warfare seems unlikely to be explicable on the ground that the Church regarded surgery as on a par with torture. Only the higher orders were banned from surgery. In France and other countries on the continent some priests obtained exemptions allowing them to practise surgery.[58] Amundsen suggests that the ban resulted from doctrine that for a cleric to be responsible for any death incurred a 'canonical irregulatory' (*sic*). Surgery was much more likely to be linked to a death than physic.[59] Whatever the rationale for Canon 18 the principal effect was to hand surgery over to lay practitioners seen as pursuing a manual craft.[60] Writing in 1830, Willcock states that 'the abandoned profession of surgery fell into the hands of the barbers and the smiths'.[61] It opened up a gap between the intellectual and technical aspects of medicine and contributed to the bitter divisions between physicians and surgeons as the Middle Ages gave way to the early modern era.

55 Ibid 33.
56 Ibid 28.
57 Ibid 41.
58 Rawcliffe (1995) (n 10) 112.
59 Amundsen (n 53) 39.
60 Rawcliffe (1995) (n 10) 112.
61 Willcock (n 43) 13.

The effect of the ban on surgery was not necessarily all bad for the medieval patients in monastic hospitals. The monks could call on lay assistance when surgery was needed. Canon 18 extended to a favourite remedy of practitioners outside the monasteries – bloodletting. The monastery patient spared regular blood loss may have been better off.

Rigorously comparing systems of health care over 600 years apart is an impossible endeavour, especially for someone who is a lawyer, not a historian. Features of the monastic system resonate with debates about the NHS today. Unlike any later initiative to provide health care for all citizens, until the foundation of the NHS in 1948, the Church recognised a duty to treat regardless of ability to pay. Later generations treated in the charitable hospitals or within the schemes for poor relief were just that, objects of charity. Patients in monastic hospitals enjoyed, whether they knew it or not, an entitlement to care. In the canons of the Church and literature on medieval medicine, the case that healing and the care of the sick should not be dependent on temporal gain resonates with work on rights to health care and Richard Titmuss's advocacy of altruism.[62] Healing should not be traded in the marketplace. The concept of some sort of obligation requiring health workers to treat the poor endured the translation of healing from the monasteries to the warring professions and the secular domain. How far it was rhetoric rather than reality is a more difficult question.

The dissolution of the monasteries in 1536 sounded the death knell of monastic care, but the dominance of the Church in delivering health care was already in decline. The prohibition of clerics in the higher orders from conducting any kind of surgery enabled surgeons to thrive outside the clerical domain.[63] Wealthier families began to avoid the open doors of the monasteries preferring personal physicians, often educated abroad. No longer benefiting from the system the rich were less willing to make charitable gifts to maintain the hospitals. Education became accessible outside the Church so that bright boys could attend schools without committing to the priesthood. And after lagging behind Europe for many decades the 'poorly developed' medical schools of England's only two universities, Oxford and Cambridge, began to develop medical education outside the Church.[64]

The road to a medical degree was long and arduous.[65] The two universities also enjoyed the power to 'license all classes of practitioner, giving authority

62 R M Titmuss *The Gift Relationship* (Allen & Unwin, 1971).
63 Rawcliffe (1995) (n 10) 113.
64 M Pelling and C Webster 'Medical Practitioners' in C Webster (ed) *Health, Medicine and Mortality in the Sixteenth Century* (Cambridge University Press, 1979) 165, 189–206.
65 Ibid 189.

to practise medicine or surgery throughout the nation'.[66] The newly licensed physician fresh from several years of study at Oxford or Cambridge might have studied relatively little physic or any surgery. He would be well versed in Latin, Greek, philosophy and theology. By the sixteenth century the curriculum began to focus more on matters medical. The universities sought to educate 'a humanistically inclined scholar, familiar alike with classical tongues and the medical sciences'.[67] It was not illegal to practise healing of any kind without a university licence. Many practised physic without the dubious benefit of an English university education. Brighter students often opted to study abroad. The universities guarded their privileges as medical educators fiercely, a stance which was to lead to conflict with the College of Physicians founded in 1518.

From clerical to secular medicine

As the monastic hospitals closed and the Church's role in providing care atrophied, the role of the Church transmuted from provider to regulator. In 1511, Parliament passed 'An Act for the Appointment of Physicians and Surgeons'. The Act marked the beginning of a long series of statutes relating to the regulation of healing. At least two prior attempts had been made to define the legal status of medical practitioners and give legal force to licensing powers. The earliest attempt in England which I can identify from the prolific work of the medical historians as an embryonic move to self-regulation by a group of healers was the foundation in 1368 of the first Guild of Master Surgeons (also referred to as the Fellowship of Surgeons).[68] The Guild formed part of the medieval system of craft Guilds that regulated and maintained the standards of their trade. The Guild of Surgeons, following the pattern of all craft guilds, provided for the apprenticeships and examination of trainee surgeons. The Master Surgeons used the Guild framework to formalise the power of the trade/profession to license practitioners. The location of the surgeon within a system designed to regulate and protect the interests of the manual crafts and commercial trades contributed to the perception encouraged by the physicians that surgeons were not gentlemen and that surgery played 'second fiddle to physic'.[69] Further 'evidence' of the inferiority of surgeons derived from the role of the lowly barbers who, in addition to their usual work, took on tooth-drawing and bloodletting and

66 Ibid 190.
67 Ibid.
68 Porter (n 2) 186.
69 Ibid.

other surgical procedures. Some barbers worked 'almost exclusively' as surgeons styling themselves barber-surgeons. The barbers were in conflict with the better-educated elite of the Guild who never throve in terms of numbers, yet these elite surgeons created a formal system of regulation and training 150 years before the College of Physicians obtained their Charter in 1518. The Guild set out a Code of Ethics which was comparatively sophisticated for its time and focused principally on the injunction to 'do no harm'. The reason for the surgeons staking out their own model of self-regulation so long before the physicians is a further consequence of the Lateran Council's ban on priests undertaking surgery. As long as most physicians were in holy orders, they were subject to the authority of the Church. Surgeons outside the clerical domain were free to establish their own organisation.

In 1421, as greater numbers of lay physicians began to practise, especially in London, the physicians 'sought some form of state control and a more exact definition of their responsibilities'.[70] The physicians eschewed the Guilds and sought the authority of the Crown for their model of regulation and the power to control entry to the profession. Led by the two university 'scoles of Physik'[71] (the Faculties of Medicine at Oxford and Cambridge) the physicians petitioned Parliament for an Act of Parliament controlling entry to the profession and providing for regulation of practice. Raach sets out the petition in full,[72] and Willcock includes a copy of the Draught (*sic*) Bill presented to Parliament.[73] I note some key points. First the physicians clearly aligned themselves with what they perceived as the other learned 'Sciences', Divinity and Law, and noted that practice in these 'cunnings' (fields of learning) was largely limited to the 'most cunning men (learned) in the same Sciences'. But, as the King was well aware, many untrained unlicensed people sought to practise Physic 'to great harm and slaughter of many men'. The petition begged that only a man holding a degree of Bachelor or Doctor of Medicine within 'some University' be permitted to 'practise in Physic'. Violation of such a rule would result in hefty fines and imprisonment. Furthermore, the Bill declared that '[N]o woman use the practise of Physic' subject to the same penalties. As no university would admit women to study physic or anything else, the petition effectively barred any woman from becoming a physician. Enforcement of the law would rest with the Sheriffs of the counties who were to be empowered

70 J H Raach 'English Medical Licensing in the Early Seventeenth Century' (1944) 16 *Yale Journal of Biology and Medicine* 267, 268.
71 Rawcliffe (1995) (n 10) 120.
72 Raach (n 70) 268.
73 Willcock (n 43) 11.

to investigate allegations of unlicensed practice and could impose a fine of up to £40, and imprisonment.

It seems that Parliament approved the petition, adding a provision that only persons who had been examined and licensed by the Master Surgeons could lawfully practise surgery. In the event, there is some doubt that Royal Assent was ever granted and the system envisaged proved unworkable and was quietly abandoned. The universities could not supply sufficient graduates to meet demand for services, especially in the provinces. The country lacked the infrastructure to enforce the system across the realm especially in the chaos following the death of Henry V.[74] Two years later, more modest proposals were put to the authorities of the City of London. A joint college of physicians and surgeons should be established to control and license all forms of medical practice in London. The mayor and corporation acceded to this request but then proceeded to allow the barbers in London to continue to practise surgery, rather defeating the objective of the exercise to vest power and responsibility in the college for the practice of medicine in the capital. Rawcliffe outlines the collapse of the college which only ever had one president.[75]

Raach commended the physicians' proposals as an early instance of concern for patient welfare, 'groping in the direction of social legislation'.[76] He is perhaps a little starry-eyed, and in an incisive critique of the first successful statute relating to the regulation of medicine, the Act of 1511, Guy expressed scepticism about physicians' concerns for the well-being of the King's people.[77] The failed attempts at legal regulation of healing are, however, of considerable legal interest highlighting tensions between different objectives in regulation. The 1421 petition combined, as did the Medical Act 1858 over 400 years later, the grant of a monopoly to benefit licensed practitioners, coupled with a stated aim of protecting the patient from unqualified, incompetent practitioners. The tension in medical regulation between the protection of the professionals and the protection of their patients by the regulatory body of the profession endured until 2002 when Section 1 of the Medical Act 1983 was amended to provide in Section 1A that the main objective of the General Medical Council is to 'protect promote and maintain the safety of the public'.[78] Of particular interest in the Draught Bill of 1421 is the role proposed for the State. Sheriffs would enforce the Act. Unlawful practice would become a crime. The profession would designate

74 Raach (n 70) 270.
75 Rawcliffe (1995) (n 10) 120–121.
76 Raach (n 70) 268.
77 Guy (n 7) 529–530.
78 The Medical Act (Amendment) Order 2002, SI /3135 (2002).

how a man qualified to practise. The responsibility and power to regulate would have lain principally with the State. In contrast to later legislation the element of self-regulation was small.

In 1511, the 'Act for the appointing of Physicians and Surgeons' received Royal Assent from Henry VIII. As had the petition in 1421, the Act envisaged a system of regulation of medical practice applying across the realm. In opting for episcopal licensing of physicians and surgeons, the 1511 Act signalled the changing role of the Church from delivery to regulation of healing. In 1511, England and its King still owed allegiance to the Church in Rome. The Act provided:

> [T]hat no person within the City of London, nor within seven miles of the same, take upon him to exercise or occupy as a physician or surgeon except he be first examined, approved and admitted by the bishop of London or by the Dean of St Paul's.

The examination should be conducted by the bishop or dean convening a panel of four 'doctors of physic' or in the case of a surgeon four 'expert persons in the Faculty's leading Master Surgeons'. Hefty fines would be imposed on any person who sought to practise without an episcopal licence. Outside the capital and the surrounding seven-mile cordon, no person could lawfully practise physic or surgery without first being examined and approved by the bishop or his vicar-general of the diocese in which he sought to practise. The bishop, or his vicar-general, in determining whether to license the applicant, should call for expert advice; the experts should provide the bishop with 'letters testimonial'. Finally, but crucially, the Act provided that nothing in the Act should 'be prejudicial to the universities of Oxford or Cambridge … or to any privileges granted to them'.

On its face the 1511 Act imposed a national system of external licensing and regulation of physic and surgery. Bishops, not the professions themselves, determined who might be granted a licence, but in placing the examination of the applicant in the hands of 'medical experts' summoned by the bishop the licensing process accorded a substantial role to the professions.[79]

Raach applauded the 1511 Act as an attempt to protect the public from inadequate, unsafe medical care. He suggested that the choice of the bishops to police the system was because the Church had 'a national organization permeating every part of the country with an elaborate administrative and judicial hierarchy'.[80] He portrays the Church as acting for the secular state in a regulatory role designed to deter bad practice, a model not immensely

---

79 Raach (n 70) 271–272.
80 J H Raach *A Directory of English Country Physicians 1603–1643* (Dawsons, 1962) 10.

different from modern models of regulation.[81] Guy disagrees, arguing that
the 1511 Act was more concerned with theology than patient safety.[82] The
bishops in 1511 still owed fealty to the papacy. In Guy's judgement, the
Preamble to the statute gives away its roots in canon rather than secular law.
As had the 1421 petition, the Preamble to the 1511 Act begins by asserting
that physic and surgery require great learning and yet are 'daily within this
realm exercised by a great multitude of ignorant persons' with no learning
and some of whom were illiterate. These ignorant people include 'common
artificers, as smiths, weavers and women'. In taking in 'great cures' such
unlearned people:

> [p]artly use sorcery and witchcraft, and apply such medicines unto the disease
> as be very noxious, and nothing meet therefore to the high displeasure of God,
> great infamy to the faculty, and the grievous hurt, damage and destruction of
> many of the king's liege people, most especially of them that cannot discern the
> uncunning from the cunning.

Guy contends that by placing the evil of sorcery and witchcraft first in the
order of the mischiefs which the Act sought to address, and placing God's
displeasure before harm to the King's people, the statute's primary concern
is the teaching of the Church. It was, Guy claims, 'in the main a highly conservative piece of legislation, rooted ultimately in medieval canon law, and
reflecting the priorities and preoccupations of the age'.[83]

The 1511 Act lies on the cusp of the gradual move of responsibility for
the regulation of medical practice from the clerical to the secular domain.
Is it irrational to suggest that Raach and Guy may both be right? The Act
does seek to protect patients; even in its reference to witchcraft it is not only
addressing theology. Lay people including the highest in the land believed
in witchcraft as a cause of disease. Protection against disease caused by a
'doctor' engaged in witchcraft would have been as important to sixteenth-
century patients as protection from a ham-fisted surgeon. Unspoken in
the Act is the conferral of a monopoly benefiting those practitioners who
obtained their licence in physic or surgery. Nothing in the 1511 Act expressly
dictated that only recognised physicians with a university education or only
surgeons belonging to the Guild of Surgeons could be licensed. No express
ban was placed on licensing women. The impact of the statute, had it been
fully implemented, would have de facto granted such a monopoly. It was
physicians and surgeons who decided who might be recommended for a

81 Raach (n 70) 276, 279.
82 Guy (n 7) 529–530.
83 Ibid 531.

licence. A female herbalist who presented herself for a licence in physic would have been laughed out of the bishop's court. Guy concedes that:

> [e]nshrined in this statute is a tacit acknowledgment of the distinctive nature of the professions of physic and surgery, and that the technical expertise required by their practitioners could only be judged by those already engaged in them.[84]

Seven years later, in 1518, the foundation of the London College of Physicians by a Royal Charter created a framework for the control of physic and its practitioners based on self-regulation, and additionally bestowed on the physicians' powers to control the practice of the other health 'professions' in London. The Charter, confirmed by statute in 1522, placed the 'gentlemen' physicians at the top of the tripartite hierarchy of the orthodox medical professions, the place of honour which physicians had long claimed as theirs by right. The Act of 1522 (discussed in the next chapter) also marked a further (though far from complete) move to a more secular approach to the regulation of health care. The 1522 Act did not repeal the 1511 statute. Episcopal licensing of physicians and surgeons practising outside London endured until interrupted from 1643 under Cromwell's rule. Seventeen years later in 1660 on the Restoration of the Monarchy, episcopal licensing was also restored. Guy notes that any physician or surgeon practising outside London and its environs continued to require a Bishop's licence until the 1511 Act was formally repealed in the Statute Law Revision Act 1948.[85] In practice it seems that episcopal licensing of medical practitioners fell into disuse in the late 1700s.[86] In theory a surgeon or physician in practice before 1948 without an episcopal licence was practising illegally.[87]

Episcopal licensing extended to another important group of health-care workers, female midwives, in whom the churches before and after the Reformation in England took a great interest. Unlike the regulation of medical practitioners, which gradually migrated into the secular domain, episcopal licensing of midwives continued well into the eighteenth century when it decayed, not to be replaced by any scheme of statutory regulation until the Midwives Act 1902. The regulation of this sole female health profession and the midwife's wider role in the legal process and local government and in policing sexual morals is dealt with in Chapter 8.

84 Ibid.
85 Guy (n 7) 542.
86 Ibid.
87 Ibid.

3

'Unruly brethren': regulation and reputation

Doctors in conflict

This chapter examines the regulation of physicians, surgeons and apothecaries, and the battles between these three groups of orthodox practitioners in the sixteenth to eighteenth centuries. The Crown, Parliament and the courts were all regularly engaged in addressing the claims of the medical corporations to regulate their 'profession' and in the case of the College of Physicians to regulate the whole domain of medicine.

The tripartite division of physician, surgeon and apothecary, clearly established in many European states, and the basis of Tudor legislation regulating medical practice, was far less clear in England.[1] Robert Kerrison, an apothecary campaigning for reform early in the nineteenth century, damned the 'artificial distinctions' saying that 'Medicine and Surgery must have been always, and are now understood by one and the same person'. Physicians needed to understand anatomy and surgery. Surgeons required a grasp of physiology.[2] Pelling and Webster comment that the 'tri-partite division of labour was only imperfectly realised even in London'.[3] Outside London, R S Roberts concluded that in the provinces, 'the supposedly exclusive appellation of physician, surgeon and apothecary often bore little resemblance to the type of practice pursued'.[4] Nonetheless, whether the distinctions were artificial or not, whether the actual practice of medicine matched the legal

---

1 M Pelling *The Common Lot* (Routledge, 2013) 231.
2 R M Kerrison *An Inquiry into the Present State of the Medical Profession in England containing an Abstract of all the Acts and Charters granted to Physicians, Surgeons and Apothecaries and A Comparative View of the Profession in Scotland, Ireland and on the Continent* (Longman, Rees, Hurst, Orme and Brown, 1814) 7.
3 M Pelling and C Webster 'Medical Practitioners' in C Webster (ed) *Health, Medicine and Mortality* (Cambridge University Press, 1979) 165.
4 R S Roberts 'The Personnel and Practice of Medicine in Tudor and Stuart England: Part II. London' (1964) 8 *Medical History* 217.

framework for regulating medical practice, laws relating to the regulation of healing remained rooted in the tripartite model until the nineteenth century.

Regulation: from Church to State

Chapter 2 considered the changing role of the Church from provider of healing to regulator. The 'Act for the appointing of Physicians and Surgeons' passed in 1511 granted the Church a role akin to a Tudor version of the General Medical Council (GMC). Although the 1511 Act was passed twenty-three years before Henry VIII broke with Rome, bishops in the post-Reformation Church of England seamlessly took over episcopal licensing of physicians and surgeons. Disagreements about the purpose of the Act and the extent to which it reflects a move to secular regulation, rather than being located in canon law, do not undermine the importance of the statute.[5] A principal function of the 1511 Act was to assess whether a person practising as a physician or surgeon was fit to practise, and to drive out the array of 'unqualified competitors', traditional healers, empirics and 'quacks'. As noted in the previous chapter, the bishops shared licensing powers with the universities of Oxford and Cambridge, the 1511 Act providing that nothing in the Act should 'be prejudicial to the universities ... or any privileges granted to them'.

Subsequent legislation, while not repealing or amending the 1511 Act, moved closer to overtly secular regulation. Examining the evolution of secular regulation of medical practice, one peculiar feature of the law should be noted. Regulation in London and its environs differed significantly from regulation in the rest of the realm. Differences in regulation between the capital and the provinces were not solely the result of divergence in practice, but were embedded in Tudor laws. Local government played a larger role in regulating medical practice than at any time until recently.

The regulation of medical practice was profoundly influenced by competition between the medical corporations to which the orthodox practitioners belonged and was inextricably bound up with the history of the London College of Physicians.[6] The College was granted extraordinary powers to control not only its own members but also all other practice of physic in the

---

5 See J H Raach *A Directory of English Country Physicians 1603–1643* (Dawsons, 1962) 10; J R Guy 'The Episcopal Licensing of Physicians, Surgeons and Midwives' (1982) 56 *Bulletin of the History of Medicine* 528, 528–529; discussed above in Chapter 2.

6 G Clark *A History of the Royal College of Physicians of London* (Clarendon Press, 1964–1966).

capital and its environs. It enjoyed powers to prosecute and punish those who disobeyed its rules, powers which included imprisoning malefactors. Physicians considered themselves to be gentlemen, who having received a liberal education should have a monopoly in the 'practice of physic'. Defining 'physic' was to prove a major problem both for the College in its disputes with the surgeons and apothecaries, and for all three orthodox practitioners when they united to attack other unqualified healers, be they empirics or quacks.[7] For the moment I will consider physic to embrace diagnosis, prognosis and recommendation of remedies.[8]

In England, physicians continued to impose on themselves a prohibition on drawing blood and foreswore surgery,[9] leaving interventions such as bloodletting, amputation and other physical operations on the body of the patient to the surgeons. In 1687, the College self-imposed a further ban on physicians compounding medicines: making up medicines was the role of the apothecary. A physician would prescribe and, in theory, the apothecary made up the medicine only under the direction of a physician. The physicians distanced themselves from activities they perceived as messy manual labour or trade. The lower orders of practitioners were supposed to practise only under the supervision of the grandees of medicine, the physicians. The surgeons and apothecaries refused to kow-tow to the College, and litigation between the College and those who challenged its authority proliferated. Early in the 1600s, the College suffered a setback in its battles with the barber-surgeons in the famous *Bonham's Case*[10] but rallied and continued its fight to be the supreme regulator of medical practice. The College faced a further painful defeat in *Rose v College of Physicians* in 1703, losing its fight to prevent apothecaries providing medical advice rather than just making up medicines prescribed by a physician.[11] Defeat did not deter the College from continuing to assert its supremacy even after the enactment of the 1858 Medical Act.[12]

Exploring the regulation of medical practitioners and practice in the sixteenth and seventeenth centuries reveals what look like immense differences

---

7 H J Cook 'The Rose Case Reconsidered: Physicians, Apothecaries and the Law in Augustan England' (1990) 45 *Journal of the History of Medicine and Allied Sciences* 527, 529.

8 See *College of Physicians v Rose* (1703) 87 English Reports 806; discussed in Cook ibid 543.

9 Despite the fact that an Act of 1540 'For Physicians and their Privilege' expressly permitted physicians to undertake surgery.

10 *Dr Bonham's Case* (1609) 77 English Reports 638; 77 English Reports 646.

11 *William Rose (Plaintiff in Error) v The College of Physicians (London)* (1703) 2 English Reports 857.

12 See *Attorney-General v Royal College of Physicians* (1861) 70 English Reports 868.

between then and now in how medicine was regulated, not just in the treatments it had to offer. Different rules for licensing practitioners and monitoring practice in London and elsewhere in the realm looks odd. Even when the rules set out in legislation and case law did not differ on the basis of geography, they were not uniformly enforced. In the provinces, the tripartite structure, with each of the orthodox having its own place in the professional hierarchy, was even more blurred. The evidence indicates a 'merging of the "orders" of physician, surgeon and apothecary'.[13] The law in books was far from represented by the law in practice. So far apart the two may seem that, as we will see, historians have suggested that the letter of the law is of little relevance or interest.[14]

The notion of different orders of 'doctor' rancorously competing with each other, the idea that bishops should decide who was fit to practise appear alien to modern thinking. Differences are less than they appear. Scrutiny of Royal Charters, Acts of Parliament, and court cases demonstrate persistent themes, fundamental questions about regulating healing surviving across the centuries. To what extent is self-regulation by the medical profession reconcilable with the protection of the public? Can the welfare of patients be pleaded as justification for entrenching one preferential form of treatment over another? Is it right to accord a monopoly to any particular group of healers? Is it any more possible to define and limit the practice of medicine now than it was to define the practice of physic in 1511? Who judges responsible medical opinion?

In the *Bolam* era in the twentieth century doctors had one substantial advantage over their predecessors in early modern England. They did not have to argue that they were professionals distinct from tradesmen or artificers. By 1957, few people questioned whether medicine was a learned profession. Judges had no doubt that doctors, be they consultant physicians, surgeons or general practitioners belonged to 'a responsible body of medical men'. In 1511, it was doubtful whether any kind of doctor was regarded as a professional gentleman akin to the lawyer or clergyman. Raach suggested that since the thirteenth century university-educated physicians might be said to have joined divinity and law as a learned profession 'although it was the least important of the three'.[15] Kerrison commented that the social status of the physician might have declined; that when 'physicians were not numerous they held a rank in society next below younger branches

13 J Kett 'Provincial Medical Practice in England 1730–1815' (1964) 19 *Journal of the History of Medicine and Allied Sciences* 17.
14 Cook (n 7) 529.
15 Raach (n 5) 275.

of noble families'.[16] In-fighting between the three orthodox would-be professionals and the tactics resorted to in the war against the empirics did little to enhance doctors' claims to professional status.[17] Judicial attitudes to 'medical men' differed. Sir Edward Coke was dismissive of the physicians' pretensions. Chief Justice Holt was more sympathetic. Only after the Medical Act 1858 when one partly unified medical profession emerged did English judges more or less uniformly begin to regard medical practitioners as fellow professionals. The presence of three sorts of orthodox doctors each seeking to undermine the others created difficulty in identifying who might properly be designated a 'responsible medical man'. The physicians maintained that *they* were the repository of proper practice. The popular reputation of all the putative professions was low.[18]

Physicians and their College

The Royal College of Physicians (RCP), the lineal descendant of the London College, takes pride in being 'the oldest medical college in England'.[19] In its origins, however, the College was limited in its scope to London. Its writ did not run elsewhere in the realm. Nor was the College initially Royal. In strict law the College only became Royal retrospectively in 1960 by virtue of a private Act of Parliament, the Royal College of Physicians of London Act 1960, 160 years after the surgeons became the Royal College of Surgeons. The College had long been known as Royal. As the then librarian of the College, L M Payne, explained, a series of oversights left the strict legality of the title in doubt.[20] The adjective 'Royal' had been used on occasion from at least 1674. A new charter granted by Charles II was addressed to the President, Fellows and Commonalty of the King's College of Physicians in 1662/3. Confirmation of that charter by Parliament was never implemented. Payne suggests that the opposition of the surgeons and apothecaries blocked its progress. The Medical Act 1858 made provision for the grant of a new charter which would have established the College title as the Royal College of Physicians in England. No new charter was sought until 1960 when the uncertainty cast doubt on property transactions. That Act confirmed the

16 Kerrison (n 2) 20.
17 Pelling (n 1) 230–258.
18 C Rawcliffe *Medicine and Society in Later Medieval England* (Sandpiper Books, 1995) 113.
19 www.rcplondon.ac.uk/about-us/who-we-are/history-royal-college-physicians.
20 L M Payne 'Title of the Royal College of Physicians of London' (1960) *British Medical Journal* 123.

Royal name of the College 'as it is now known and declares to be fully valid the use of that name' before the passing of the 1960 Act.

The grant of the Royal Charter in 1518 founding the London College of Physicians was confirmed by an Act of Parliament in 1522. 'The Privileges and Authority of Physicians in London' declared that it was expedient and necessary that no person should 'be suffered to practise physic, but only those persons that be profound, sad and discreet, groundly learned and deeply studied in physick'. The statute granted the College powers to license those lawfully permitted to practise 'physic' in London, or within a seven-mile circuit around London. There were two distinct classes of licensed physicians, Fellows (elects) who controlled the College, and licentiates who were allowed to practise subject to the control of the College. The College won the right to self-regulation in London. The physicians were granted power to determine who was qualified to practise 'physic', to set standards for the licensed physicians and discipline errant practitioners. The 1522 Act did not repeal the 1511 Act (rather it supplemented the earlier legislation). Outside London, bishops retained authority to license physicians not seeking to practise in London. The 1522 Act sought to address a problem encountered by the bishops outside London in finding suitable examiners, providing that:

> [N]o person from henceforth be suffered to practise in physic, through England, until such time as he be examined at London by the president [of the London College] and three of the said elects: and to have from the said president or elects, letters testimonial of their approving and examination ...

Note though that any physician who practised outside London and the seven-mile circuit continued to need a licence from the bishop. In theory then, the College examined aspiring provincial physicians; the diocesan bishop granted successful candidates a licence to practise. Graduates of Oxford and Cambridge practising outside London were expressly exempted from the requirement to be examined by the College before being granted their episcopal licence. Surgeons also required a diocesan licence but the mode of examination remained for a time in the hands of the bishops. Although episcopal licensing fell into desuetude, recall that in strict law physicians and surgeons outside the capital continued to need an episcopal licence until 1948.[21]

The College enjoyed draconian powers to seek out and punish *mala praxis*[22] (malpractice) among its own members and to investigate and punish malpractice and unlicensed practice in physic, be the offender a surgeon or

21 Guy (n 5) 542.
22 See *Dr Groenvelt's Case* (1695) 91 English Reports 1038, 1039.

apothecary, or one of the many empiric healers. *Mala praxis* was a crime.[23] The College was accorded powers to use the criminal process in its pursuit of malefactors. Unlawful practice attracted a fine of £5 for each month of unlicensed practice and possible imprisonment.[24] One half of fines levied was to be paid to the King and the other half retained by the College.[25]

Enforcement of the College's powers to discipline their own members and to stamp out illegal practice of physic was vested in the College Censors, who combined the role of 'medical police', prosecutor and judge. The Censors have had a bad press, viewed as persecuting healers whom the College saw as lesser doctors and obsessed with infractions of etiquette.[26] They have perhaps not been given credit for efforts to protect patients from unsafe practice via the Censorial hearings. In addition to powers in relation to *mala praxis* and illegal practice, the Censors also acted as Censors of letters and morals and promulgated a 'code of ethics', just as the GMC was to do centuries later.

In 1540, the College's prospects for dominance looked rosy. Clause 2 of a further statute 'For Physicians and their Privilege' granted the College additional powers to inspect apothecaries' wares in London.[27] Four physicians 'of the best learned, wisest and most discreet' were to be chosen each year to inspect and check the quality of medicines dispensed and sold by the apothecary. The College might be regarded as a forerunner of the Medicines and Healthcare Products Regulatory Agency.

The authority vested in the London College to punish other practitioners and drive some out of business altogether significantly exceeds powers later enjoyed by the General Medical Council or other modern regulators. In the capital and its environs, regulation of a large part, if not the whole domain of healing was entrusted by the State to the College. The 1522 Act created an opportunity for the Fellows of the College to become the primary regulator of all medical practice in London. Outside London their role in examining provincial physicians to assist the bishops considering applications for licences could have opened up opportunities for a national role. The College Charter and the 1522 and 1540 Acts read literally and alone offer some evidence that the Crown and Parliament were content to defer to the physicians, accord them the status of *the* responsible body of medical men and

---

23 Ibid.
24 Powers confirmed by: STAT 1 Mariae 2 c 9 'An Act touching the Corporation of the Physicians in London' (1553) in the reign of Queen Mary.
25 S E Thorne 'Dr Bonham's Case' (1938) 54 *Law Quarterly Review* 543, 545.
26 B Woolley *The Herbalist: Nicholas Culpeper and the Fight for Medical Freedom* (Harper Perennial, 2005).
27 STAT 32 Hen 8 c 40 'For Physicians and their Privilege'.

dominion over all medical practice. No other group of practitioners could in theory challenge the mighty College. As we shall see, attitudes of 'deference' were not shared by all judges or the public. The theoretical dominance of the College was to prove temporary and largely illusory.

An obsession with social hierarchy, establishing physic as a profession for a gentleman, got in the way, hindering efforts to exercise real power. In pursuit of high social standing the College eschewed activities that could be seen as getting their hands dirty, literally or metaphorically. In a narrow interpretation of the practice of physic the College of Physicians self-imposed a prohibition on any of its members undertaking any form of surgery, including bloodletting, even though Clause 3 of the 1540 Act 'For Physicians and their Privilege' expressly provided that members of the College could practise surgery:

> [F]orasmuch as the science of physick doth comprehend, include, and contain the knowledge of surgery as a special member and part of the same ... therefore be it enacted that any of the said company or fellowship ... may from time to time as well within the city of London as elsewhere within this realm practise and exercise said science of physic in all and every his members and parts.

Nonetheless the College persisted in its narrow interpretation of physic limiting their personal practice and entrenching artificial distinctions between physic and surgery.

In 1687 the Royal College of Physicians (as it now styled itself) barred any surgeon, drug compounder or 'any other artificer' from candidacy to the College. The exercise of 'any illiberal art' was seen as prejudicial to the dignity of the College and the honour of the great universities.[28] Any licentiate of the College who engaged in the 'trade of a drug seller' forfeited his licence. In 1791, in *Chorley v Bolcot*,[29] Lord Kenyon ruled that a physician could not sue to recover his fees. The law, not only custom and professional etiquette, dictated that, like barristers, physicians' fees were honorary and not to be demanded as of right. Receiving only an honorarium was 'much more to the credit and rank of that honourable body'. Despite the certainty with which the judge declared the 'rule', Willcock expresses reservations about the longevity and reality of any such custom.[30] Insofar as physicians themselves accepted the lack of an

---

28 Entry to the College for an applicant without a degree from Oxford or Cambridge was beset by difficulty. T Gelfand 'The History of the Medical Profession' in W F Bynum and R Porter (eds) *Companion Encyclopaedia of the History of Medicine* (Routledge, 1993) 1125–1127.

29 (1791) 100 English Reports 1040.

30 J W Willcock *Laws relating to the Medical Profession with an Account of the Rise and Progress of the Various Orders* (J & W T Clarke, 1830) 111.

enforceable right to payment, they may well have regarded that 'sacrifice' as the mark of a gentleman and member of a learned profession, rather than a tradesman who sold his services for gain.[31] Pelling and Webster say that 'the College of Physicians of London in the sixteenth century is not an outstandingly impressive organisation'.[32] Porter comments 'The Royal College of Physicians of London subsided into a gentleman's club, reserved for the fashionable'.[33] With some exceptions the College showed little enthusiasm for the developments in Continental Europe within the 'anatomical Renaissance'.[34] Rather it focused on iron control of its own members and privileges 'defending only the perks and privileges of the metropolitan elite'.[35] The College sacrificed its chances to establish an effective framework for regulation of health care which both granted physicians virtually unfettered self-regulation and powers to regulate other practitioners. Nor did this sacrifice assist the aims of the physicians to assure their reputations as beneficent gentlemen.

In 1618, a further charter was granted to the College confirming their powers and privileges, and adding a new power to summon any apothecary or dealer in medicines to judge their qualifications. Apothecaries were required to testify against any unlawful practitioner or face a fine of twenty shillings. In 1662/3, Charles II issued yet another charter making structural changes within the College and re-enforcing the College's control over unlawful practice. The failure of the College to incorporate this charter was, as we have seen, the cause of the doubts about the use of the term Royal and the need for the Royal College of Physicians of London Act 1960. Despite the conferral of additional powers, in the early seventeenth century the College faced repeated challenges to its attempts to enforce and extend its powers from disgruntled physicians as well as the competing 'professions'. Disputes about the powers of the College kept the law courts busy.

Surgeons

Surgeons in Tudor England were regarded as more akin to the craftsman than the learned gentleman, because of the manual nature of their practice.

---

31 J H Baker 'Counsellors and Barristers: A Historical Study' (1969) 27 *Cambridge Law Journal* 209, 229. And see E McQuillin 'Civil Lability of Physicians and Surgeons for Negligence' (1886) 20 *American Law Review* 80.

32 Pelling and Webster (n 3) 168.

33 R Porter *The Greatest Benefit to Mankind: A Medical History of Humanity from Antiquity to the Present* (Fontana Press, 1997) 288.

34 J Sawday *The Body Emblazoned* (Routledge, 1995).

35 Porter (n 33) 354.

Porter says that surgery 'played second fiddle to physic'.[36] Yet the Master Surgeons, as we have seen, created the first 'professional' association of doctors when the Guild or Fellowship of Surgeons was set up in 1368. The Guild in London remained small in numbers, an elite group who mainly treated the aristocracy. Much everyday surgery was carried out by barbers who had their own Guilds and charters. In 1540,[37] the two separate companies of barbers and surgeons were united into one body corporate to be known as the Barber-Surgeons Company. The Preamble to the Act declared it 'needful to provide for men expert in the science of physic and surgery for the health of man's body when infirmities and sickness shall happen'. In relation to surgery and to that end the two 'mysteries' were joined in one legal entity. Strangely, though, within the new united company those admitted as barbers were forbidden in London or a one-mile circuit of the capital to practise 'any surgery, letting of blood or any other thing belonging to surgery; drawing of teeth only except'. And surgeons were similarly barred from engaging in 'any barbery or shaving' in London or its immediate environs. The companies were merged; the occupations separated.[38] The Act also responded to the needs of the surgeons for both the development of surgery and training of apprentice surgeons in anatomy by granting the new company four corpses of executed felons for anatomical dissection.

The 'marriage' of the surgeons to the barbers did the social status and academic credentials of the surgeons little good.[39] It did grant the surgeons the protection and clout of a major and powerful body corporate. And the 1540 Act established surgery as a discrete craft within the conjoined company. In 1543, a further Act of Parliament popularly known as 'The Quacks Charter' radically undermined the surgeons' attempts to assert a monopoly over surgery akin to that the College of Physicians enjoyed in relation to physic. The Act accused surgeons of having 'small cunning, yet they will take great sums of money'. Therefore, the Act made it lawful for any honest person man or *woman* with:

> [K]nowledge of the nature, kind, and operation of certain herbs, roots and waters, and the using and ministering of them to such as have been pained with customable diseases ... to minister in and to any outward sore, uncome, wound, apostemations, outward swelling or disease, baths, pulteses, and emplaisters according to this cunning, experience and knowledge.

36 Ibid 186.
37 STAT 32 Hen 8 c 42 'For Barbers and Surgeons'.
38 Woolley (n 26) 36–39.
39 Ibid 38.

Woolley comments that the Act 'effectively allowed more or less anyone to perform any surgery that did not require scalpel'.[40] He speculates that 'The Quacks Charter' was the result of machinations by the College of Physicians giving priority to downgrading surgery over the battle against the empirics.[41] In sharp contrast to the Act of 1511, in 1543 Parliament created more or less an open market for the delivery of healing outside the protected zone entrusted to the College of Physicians.

Surgery before the eighteenth century was a fairly crude discipline requiring technical skill and manual dexterity. The development of more sophisticated surgery based on greater knowledge of anatomy and more surgeons studying at universities in Scotland and mainland Europe led to a campaign to separate surgery from the craft of the barbers, in pursuit of professional status distinct from the latter. Eminent surgeons deplored the restrictions of the joint livery company. In 1745, an Act of Parliament dissolved the union of barbers and surgeons. The Company of Surgeons gained powers to dictate the required apprenticeship and training required of would-be surgeons and examine them before admission to the company. The 1745 Act expressly stated that nothing in that Act should prejudice or infringe the privileges of the College of Physicians. In 1800, King George III granted the surgeons a Royal Charter and the company became the Royal College of Surgeons. Surgeons at last gained a professional status. In the centuries before that happy day, the barber-surgeons clashed frequently with the College of Physicians which accused the surgeons of trespassing on their domain.

Apothecaries

Within the tripartite structure, apothecaries were in theory the lowest in the ranking even though they provided much of the health care in the realm. Their origins as shopkeepers tainted their social status. The name apothecary recalled their history deriving from *apotheca* meaning a place where wines, spices and herbs were stored. The term apothecary became used in England to describe a person who sold these commodities from his shop or market stall. In Tudor England, apothecaries belonged to the Grocers' Company which can itself be traced back to the Guild of Pepperers in 1118, to be joined later with the Spicers and incorporated as the Worshipful Company of Grocers in 1428. 'Specialist' apothecaries dealing principally with medicines evolved by the mid-sixteenth century and London apothecaries with

40 Ibid.
41 Ibid.

pharmacy skills petitioned on several occasions to secede from the Grocers' Company. The distinct nature of the 'medical apothecary' is illustrated in the provision in the 1540 Act empowering the College to search for and inspect 'apothecary wares, drugs and stuffs' in his properties.

In 1607, apothecaries obtained separate status within the Grocers. The Society of Apothecaries was established by Royal Charter in 1617.[42] The grocers objected. King James himself responded that grocers were 'but merchants; the mystery of these apothecaries were belonging to the apothecaries'.[43]

Their history may explain why apothecaries are sometimes regarded as ancestors of modern pharmacists. Apothecaries did much more than make up and sell medicines. Their role in most towns and villages in England was closer to that of the modern general practitioner. Apothecaries' fees, while not cheap, were less than the fees charged by physicians or surgeons. Apothecaries were prohibited from practising physic in London and the seven-mile circuit around the capital. They were forbidden to trespass on the monopoly of the College of Physicians. Diagnosis and recommendations about treatment fell within the privilege of the physicians. A physician diagnosed and 'prescribed' medicines that an apothecary would make up. Should bloodletting be ordered, a surgeon was summoned. The patient might face three sets of fees. Many families could not afford such sums and/or preferred to entrust their care to the local apothecary. The physicians continued their efforts to control the apothecaries, restricting them to the role of compounders of drugs.

Challenging the College

Challenges to the College generated numerous court cases, including three high-profile test cases. Multiple law reports of differing length and in some cases subtle differences in substance mean that what follows cannot do more than outline the principal issues in the prolific litigation.

Dr Bonham[44]

Bonham's Case is known to constitutional lawyers in England for the assertion made by Sir Edward Coke that 'when an act of parliament is against

---

42 www.apothecaries.org.history.origins.
43 Ibid.
44 Thorne (n 25) 543; Raach (n 5) 272.

common right or reason, or repugnant, or impossible to be performed, the common law will control it and adjudge such act to be void'.[45] Coke's claim that the courts could review and strike down Acts of Parliament never took root in England but was to form at least part of the basis on which courts in the USA assert the right to strike down statutes in conflict with the constitution. *Bonham's Case* is examined here as a landmark in medico-legal history. It heralded the re-entrance of another actor in the battles over control of healing, the universities of Oxford and Cambridge. Harold J Cook's account of the complex history of Bonham and the College cannot be bettered.[46]

Bonham's Case is in fact Bonham's *cases*. Proceedings were heard in the Courts of King's Bench and of Common Pleas.[47] Before looking at the cases some background is needed. In challenging the College, Bonham acted in concert with a campaign by the surgeons to challenge the powers of the physicians. Cook describes how in the 1590s the College, who had let their powers lie dormant, recovered the will to pursue those who sought to infringe the rules of the College, especially members of the Barber-Surgeons Company. The College warned the company against allowing its members to practise physic.[48] Surgeons Jenkins and Read defied the College, Jenkins 'declaring that he would exercise the art of healing as he saw fit when the need arose'.[49] After a number of hearings and legal skirmishes, both surgeons were gaoled by the College. Their lawyer issued a writ of habeas corpus and the men were freed until the case could be heard by the courts. Chief Justice Popham found resoundingly for the College, ruling inter alia that no surgeon could practise physic, and that the College had full authority to commit a man to prison. He declared: 'That no man, though never so learned a Phisition, or doctor may Practise in London, or within seaven myles without the Colledge Lycence.'[50]

Enter Dr Bonham. Thomas Bonham was (probably) a Doctor of Medicine of the University of Cambridge. He had strong connections with the barber-surgeons, and had signed a petition to Parliament seeking to extend the surgeons' rights to practise. Bonham presented himself for examination by the College in December 1605. He 'failed' the examination twice. On the second occasion in April 1606, on evidence that Bonham

---

45 *Dr Bonham's Case* (1609) 77 English Reports 646, 652.
46 H J Cook 'Against Common Right and Reason: The College of Physicians Versus Dr Thomas Bonham' (1985) 29 *American Journal of Legal History* 301.
47 Confusingly on occasion entitled the Court of Common Bench.
48 Cook 'Against Common Right' (n 46) 306–308.
49 Ibid 306.
50 Ibid.

had been practising physic in London without a licence,[51] the College fined him £5 and threatened to commit him to prison if he did not pay the fine and cease illegal practice. Bonham ignored the ruling and in October 1606 he was arrested and fined £10. In November, Bonham appeared before the College again and was offered the chance of a re-examination. He refused arguing that as a graduate of Cambridge he was lawfully entitled to prac-tise in London or elsewhere without a licence from the College. Rather than seek to placate the College, Bonham, as Cook puts it 'put on his hat and said that he would continue to practise without seeking the permission of the College and without obeying the President'.[52] The College commit-ted him to Newgate for contempt. His lawyer obtained a writ of habeas corpus from the Court of Common Pleas and Bonham walked free. The College sought advice from a committee of judges who like Popham found wholly in the College's favour. In particular, the judges endorsed the right of the College to imprison 'offenders' and held that a doctorate in medicine from Oxford or Cambridge did not exempt the doctor from the require-ment to be licensed by the College to practise in London or within seven miles thereof.

In 1608 the College successfully sued Bonham in the Court of King's Bench for £60 for a year's illicit practice. Bonham retaliated by bringing a claim against the College in the Court of Common Pleas for trespass against the person and false imprisonment, heard in 1610 and presided over by Sir Edward Coke. This suit Bonham won on a wafer-thin majority of 3 : 2.[53] Bonham's argument that, as a Cambridge graduate, he needed no licence from the College was untenable in the light of the College Charter and the confirmatory Act of 1522. While the statute of 1511 exempted doc-tors of medicine from Oxford and Cambridge practising in the provinces from the requirement of examination by the College before being granted an episcopal licence, the 1522 Act provided for no such exemption. 'The law was clear and explicit.'[54] Being a graduate of Oxford or Cambridge did not entitle the doctor to practise physic in London without a licence from the College. Bonham narrowly won his case before Common Pleas, on other grounds. The argument that in principle a doctor of the univer-sity should not need an additional licence from the College to practise in London received weighty support. The Archbishop of Canterbury, Richard Bancroft, intervened on Bonham's behalf. In his judgment Coke CJ poured scorn on the College:

51 Cook 'Against Common Right' (n 46) 308.
52 Ibid 309.
53 *Dr Bonham's Case* (1609) 77 English Reports 646.
54 Cook 'Against Common Right' (n 46) 311.

[N]o comparison was to be made between that private college and any of the universities of Cambridge and Oxford, no more than between a father and his children, or between the fountain and the small rivers which descend from it: the university is *alma mater* from whose breasts alone those of that private college have sucked all their science and knowledge.[55]

Even Coke could not evade the clear wording of the 1522 statute. He thus attacked the statute itself uttering his famous words that the common law could strike down a statute against 'common right or reason'. For the purposes of medico-legal history, it is Coke's reasons for regarding the College statutes as voidable that are pertinent. Coke said of the College Censors that they 'cannot be judges, ministers and parties'.[56] The College investigated charges of illicit practice and/or malpractice, prosecuted and judged the cases and then benefited from the fines levied on those convicted. More than three centuries later similar criticisms were levelled at the General Medical Council.[57] Coke went on to find further grounds to hold that Bonham had been unlawfully imprisoned by the College, and to rein in the powers of the College. He interpreted the 1522 Act to provide for two separate powers (1) to fine unlicensed practitioners (but only if they had engaged in illicit practice for at least one month) (2) to *fine and imprison* persons who were 'convicted' of malpractice. Moreover, even in the case of malpractice the courts of common law could strike down findings of malpractice by the College, the College not being a court of record.[58] Bonham could be fined but not imprisoned. The Court of Common Pleas fined the College £40. Harold Cook says of Coke's judgment that he sought to remove from the College the unfettered power it claimed to judge what constituted good or bad practice:

The College was not to be the only expert judge of medical practice – or rather any judge with a university education could find whether a medical case had been handled correctly or not.[59]

Edward Coke would be disappointed in his judicial heirs had he foreseen the rise of *Bolamisation*. Defeat for the College was short-lived. Cook comments: 'Within a short time the College regained its juridical confidence and acted as if Coke has never uttered a word.'[60] In *College of*

55 *Dr Bonham's Case* (n 53) 650.
56 Ibid 652.
57 See Chief Medical Officer's Report *Good Doctors: Safer Patients* (Department of Health, 2006).
58 S E Thorne 'Courts of Record and Sir Edward Coke' (1937–38) 2 *University of Toronto Legal Journal* 24.
59 Cook 'Against Common Right' (n 46) 317.
60 Ibid 322.

Physicians v Levett[61] Holt CJ ruled unequivocally that to practise in London a university graduate required a licence from the College. In 1675, the College was found to be a court of record.[62] Most damning to Coke's robust stance on accountability for poor practice, Holt CJ also rejected Coke's claim that common law judges could overrule the College's findings on what constituted malpractice. Holt charged Coke that he was 'carried away by his affection for his alma mater', the University of Cambridge.[63]

Dr Groenvelt

Bonham was not the only victim of the College's battle to control physic or, depending on your viewpoint, the only thorn in the side of the physicians. Joannes Groenvelt fell foul of the College later in the seventeenth century. As with *Bonham*, several sets of legal proceedings reached the courts and there are different reports of those proceedings. Examining even briefly all the claims and counter-claims made by the College and Groenvelt would take the whole of this chapter and more.[64] I do no more than highlight some of the most pertinent points from the cases. It will swiftly become apparent that the judges, in particular Holt CJ, demonstrated a more favourable view of the College and its powers than Coke.

Dr Groenvelt was a Dutch physician who moved to London to improve his prospects as had many of his countrymen. He became a licentiate of the London College. His battles with the College were, like Bonham, part of a more general challenge to the power of the physicians. In 1694, Groenvelt treated Susannah Withall for pains in her 'lower parts' occurring soon after the delivery of her seventh child. She complained to the Censors that the treatment left her bedridden, in excruciating pain, and unable to care for her family. Susannah did not mince her words, testifying that Groenvelt's treatment was: 'so indiscreetly, evilly, inartificially applied' and that that he had given her 'unwholesome, wicked, bad and pernicious pills and noxious drugs'.[65]

---

61 (1701) 91 English Reports 1214 and see also *College of Physicians v West* (1716) 88 English Reports 761.
62 *College of Phisitions and Cooper or Hubert* (1675) 84 English Reports 894.
63 *Case 50 Dr Groenvelt v Dr Burwell and others, Censors of the College of Physicians* (1698) 92 English Reports 967, 969.
64 H J Cook *Trials of an Ordinary Doctor: Joannes Groenvelt in Seventeenth Century London* (E-book, Johns Hopkins University Press, 1994).
65 Pleadings to the Case *Doctor Groenvelt v Dr Burwell and others, Censors of the College of Physicians* (1695) 92 English Reports 687, 691.

Groenvelt was brought before the Censors, and found guilty of *mala praxis*.[66] The woman had been severely harmed by an unorthodox prescription of a dangerous drug. The Censors mistakenly expected that the declaration of malpractice would suffice to resolve the matter. The Dutch doctor fought back and at a further hearing the Censors fined Groenvelt £20 and drew up a warrant committing him to Newgate Gaol. Groenvelt's lawyers obtained his release via a writ of habeas corpus. They attacked the legality of the warrant gaoling Groenvelt. The grounds for his release, however, were not based on the legality of the warrant but founded on a general pardon granted by the King for all but the most serious offences committed before 29 April 1695. *Mala praxis* was described by Holt as 'a great misdemeanour and offence at common law'.[67]

Freed from prison, Groenvelt sued the Censors for assault, battery and false imprisonment contending that the Censors acted unlawfully and had no authority to imprison him. Inter alia Groenvelt contended that the plea entered by the College to justify his imprisonment was insufficient. The defendants failed to give particulars of the alleged *mala praxis* i.e. the unsuitable and dangerous medicines, the College had no authority both to fine and imprison Groenvelt, the plea did not show that Groenvelt was licensed by the College, and if he was not licensed, the College could only fine him for unlicensed practice and not convict him of *mala praxis*. Groenvelt lost. Holt CJ held that the College had jurisdiction to try anyone practising physic in London for *mala praxis*. He confirmed earlier judgments that *contra Bonham* the Censors constituted a court of record and so their findings on facts could not be questioned.[68] Given that ruling, the defendants were not required to give particulars of the alleged malpractice because their findings could not be challenged. And as we have seen, Holt scornfully rejected Coke's assertion that common law judges could reject College findings on what constituted malpractice. Even if it were possible to challenge the finding 'tis not necessary to set forth the particulars of the medicines, for this Court, can make no judgment whether they were wholesome or not'.[69] The Chief Justice concurred with counsel for the College 'that none but physicians can judge ... of it for that which is good physick for one person may not be for another'.[70]

---

66 Cook (n 64) 11.
67 *Dr Groenvelt's Case* (1695) 91 English Reports 1038, 1039.
68 *Case 50 Dr Groenvelt v Dr Burwell and others, Censors of the College of Physicians* (1698) 92 English Reports 967.
69 *Dr Groenvelt versus Dr Burwell & Al* (1698) 90 English Reports 883, 885.
70 Ibid 884.

Groenvelt lost one battle. He won another. Encouraged by the College, Mrs Withall brought a civil claim against him seeking an unprecedented sum of £2000 in compensation. Her claim came to trial in 1697. The jury found for Groenvelt.[71] Groenvelt and the College continued to attack each other. The result was stalemate. As the story unfolded, the machinations of the College became apparent as did their cosy relationship with Holt. Holt had long been an adviser to the College and indeed had drafted the warrant committing Groenvelt to prison.[72] Judges and physicians appear to have enjoyed a brief honeymoon. Public opinion turned against the College.[73]

Rose v College of Physicians[74]

The decision of the House of Lords in the *Rose* case is one of the most important judgments in the history of law and healing, dealing a significant blow to the hopes of the physicians to domination of all medical practice.[75]

Mr Rose was prosecuted by the College for unlawful practice of physic. He had attended John Seale, a butcher, and had made up and administered proper medicines for him. Mr Seale disputed the bills submitted by Apothecary Rose. He complained to the College who ruled that an apothecary could only lawfully provide medicines under the direction of a physician licensed by the College. An apothecary acting independently of a physician's direction acted unlawfully and could be fined £5 for every month of unlawful practice. Rose was convicted by a jury, a conviction upheld by the Court of Queen's Bench.[76] The statute provided no appeal process. Supported by the Society of Apothecaries, Rose moved for a writ of error before Parliament. As with many landmark judgments in the common law in the sixteenth and seventeenth centuries the case formally turned on a technicality. The jury which had found Mr Rose guilty of unlawfully practising physic, found as to the facts that, while Rose provided medicines for Mr Seale without the direction of a physician, and charged Mr Seale for the medicine, he claimed no fee for advice. Therefore, Rose argued that his

71 Cook (n 64) 172.
72 Ibid 160.
73 Ibid 187–188.
74 *William Rose (Plaintiff in Error) v The College of Physicians (London)* (1703) 2 English Reports 857; see Clark (n 6) 476–479 for a full account of the case from the perspective of the College.
75 R Porter and D Porter 'The Rise of the English Drugs Industry: The Role of Thomas Corbyn' (1989) 33 *Medical History* 280.
76 *College of Physicians v Rose* (1703) 87 English Reports 806.

conviction was in error in that simply selling medicines could not constitute practising physic.

The hearing had the aura of theatre.[77] Every Fellow of the Royal College of Physicians was summoned to attend the House of Lords. Counsel for Rose and the College advanced arguments well beyond interpretation of the College Charter and statutes. Rose's counsel attacked the College's claim to a monopoly of lawful medical practice arguing that 'constant usage and practice' sanctioned the sale of medicine and the provision of gratuitous advice by apothecaries. The physicians sought to strain the interpretation of their charter and the 1522 statute, seeking to 'monopolise all manner of physic to themselves'. Were they to succeed, the social consequences would be ruinous. No medicine would be accessible without payment to a physician. Sick people would have to call the physician and pay his fee for his advice, and then summon the apothecary to sell them the medicine. This would 'be a great oppression upon poor families who, not being able to bear the charge of a fee, would be deprived of all kinds of assistance in their necessities'.[78] It would be dangerous to health, for those taken suddenly ill most commonly summoned the apothecary who, if Rose's conviction were upheld, 'should not dare to apply the least remedy without running the hazard of being ruined'.[79]

Counsel for the College countered that the College imposed on its members an obligation to treat the poor for free, and had erected dispensaries in the city to treat the poor. Every physician had a duty to visit the 'sick poor' in his neighbourhood in their own lodgings. The apothecaries' argument that the 'poorer sort of people would be lost for want of proper remedies had not the least foundation'.[80] In emergency, the College conceded that any person might lawfully do his best to treat a sick neighbour. This concession should not be allowed to permit apothecaries to 'undertake at leisure all dangerous diseases' especially as in London a skilful physician would be accessible to all. Apothecaries were not '*bred* to have suitable skill (my emphasis)'. Moreover, declared counsel for the College, it was the apothecaries who sought to exploit their patients by over prescribing whereas a 'distemper – by the discreet advice of a physician might, by one proper medicine, have been eradicated at the beginning'.[81]

---

77 M Brazier and S Ost *Medicine and Bioethics in the Theatre of the Criminal Process* (Cambridge University Press, 2013) 18–19.
78 *Rose* (n 74) 858.
79 Ibid.
80 Ibid.
81 Ibid 858–859.

The hearing in the House of Lords presented two contrasting pictures of medicine in 1703. In one, the practical, kindly apothecary provided accessible low-cost medicine to all patients in need, whereas the physician lined his pockets in service of the rich. In the other, greedy businessmen of a lower class aimed solely to maximise sales, while the gentlemen physicians devoted themselves to the vocation of healing. The House of Lords reversed the judgment of Queen's Bench, finding for the apothecaries. As was the custom of those times, no reasons are given. One can only speculate whether or not the House of Lords accepted the apothecaries' substantive arguments as well as their technical legal case.

Had the College of Physicians succeeded in convicting Rose, the development of a unified professional hierarchy with the College at its apex might have begun over a century and a half prior to the Medical Act 1858. Gelfand commented: 'The *Rose* case virtually ended the physicians' efforts to regulate other healers.'[82] Gelfand overstates the case for *Rose* ending the central role of the physicians. Outside London, the College had had little influence well before 1703. Yet even after *Rose*, the College did not abandon efforts to retain its privileges and dominance over the whole domain of medical practice. In 1861 in *Attorney-General v Royal College of Physicians*,[83] it scored a retrospective victory, thirteen years after the Medical Act 1858. In 1860 the College had amended their bye-laws of 1687 which had imposed an absolute prohibition on doctors licensed by the College to make up medicines, and thus enlarge physicians' share of the market, at the expense of the apothecaries. Fellows of the College were still barred from such activity. The College proposed to create a new class of licentiate not bound by that prohibition. This, the Society of Apothecaries argued, was creating a new class of extra-licentiates – 'purporting to allow them to act as apothecaries'.[84] The College was poaching in the apothecaries' territory. The revised bye-laws would allow admission of a new category of licentiates with a much shorter period of training who would not be restricted 'by any bye-law from supplying medicines to their patients'. The Society of Apothecaries brought an action similar to a modern application for judicial review to challenge the College's new rules. The apothecaries lost this round of the war.[85] In a complex judgment, the judge in 1861 ruled (inter alia) that ancient laws gave the College the 'whole medical domain'. The College could choose to limit their jurisdiction ceding certain sorts of practice to the apothecaries and the surgeons. The College remained entitled to claim back their territory.

82 Gelfand (n 28) 1126.
83 *Attorney-General v Royal College of Physicians* (1861) 70 English Reports 868.
84 Ibid 872.
85 Ibid 868.

If *Rose* did not mark the end of the College's fight for supremacy, what of the significance of the decision in terms of its impact on the provision of healing? The argument that *Rose* was 'an important step on the road to legitimating the services of those practitioners who served the public most, the apothecaries', is challenged in Harold Cook's powerful analysis of the case in its broader context.[86] He takes issue with two general assumptions about *Rose* (1) that *Rose* was in reality such an important step to legitimating the provision of medical services by apothecaries and (2) that it gave the apothecary the right to practise physic i.e. diagnose and prescribe but not to charge a fee for his services. The core question for Cook was 'What was physic?'

Cook places *Rose* in the context of continuing skirmishes between the College and the Society of Apothecaries. William Rose was a wealthy and influential Member of the Society, not a lone champion of access to medicine for the poor. The litigation against Rose was just one manifestation of the bad relationship between the two medical corporations. In 1694, the Society had sought exemption from taking on offices in local government which, in general, citizens were required to take their turn or pay a fine. The City authorities were unsupportive. The Society fared better with Parliament arguing that their duties to the sick were such that apothecaries should enjoy the same privilege as the physicians from such civic duties. In the teeth of opposition from the College 'An Act for exempting Apothecaries from Serving the Offices of Constable, Scavenger and other Parish and Ward Offices, and from Serving upon Juries' was passed in 1694. The opening words of the Act were especially irritating to the physicians declaring: 'Whereas the art of the apothecary is of great and general use and benefit by reason of their constant and necessary assistance to his majesty's subjects ...' The content and tenor of the Act suggested that apothecaries were medical professionals as much as the physicians.

Cook's principal argument, however, is aimed at suggestions that *Rose* was a significant change in the status quo. Well before *Rose*, apothecaries had extended their practice beyond compounding medicines. It was 'not the apothecaries who obtained legal justification of a new order, but the officers of the London College of Physicians who lost their attempt to reassert outdated legal forms'. Rose 'did not create new conditions, but rather ratified the existing order'.[87] Cook asks:

> If legal recognition of previous alterations in the medical community constitutes an important change, then the Rose case can be considered a significant

86 Cook 'Rose Reconsidered' (n 7).
87 Ibid 359.

historian moment. If, on the other hand, changes in day-to-day behavior constitute the most important developments, then the Rose case loses much of its causal significance, becoming the marker of change rather than the reason for it.[88]

Cook stresses that the apothecaries won no new rights, rather the College lost 'their attempt to reassert outdated forms'.[89] Re-characterising *Rose* in this fashion does not diminish *Rose*'s importance as a key case in medico-legal history. Had the decision been in favour of the College the continuing story of the regulation of medical practice would have been different. Cook is right to identify the gap between the law in books and the law in practice. Without such an analysis the social significance of *Rose* cannot be addressed. The bald words of legislation, and the random nature of case law, obscure dimensions of the struggle between the medical corporations.

Problems and practice: the provinces

Bonham, *Groenvelt* and *Rose* were only three of many challenges to the College in the seventeenth and eighteenth centuries. The College 'writ' ran only in London and its environs. Division into physicians, surgeons and apothecaries was unsustainable in the provinces. By 1730, outside London, many doctors described themselves as 'surgeon-apothecaries', as did the hero of *Middlemarch*, Mr Lydgate. Kett says self-descriptions by provincial practitioners were often combined as 'surgeon, apothecary and man-midwife'.[90] Outside the capital, many doctors operated as general practitioners and even if they became licentiates of the College of Physicians worked in a very different fashion to their grand London colleagues.[91]

Why did the basis for regulating medical practice in London differ from other parts of the country; is it a historical example of favouring the capital over the provinces? Roberts suggests that London was different because it 'not only had the worst epidemics and the largest agglomeration of population, but it was also the home of the court and large numbers of aristocracy, and hence of most of the highly educated physicians'.[92] Londoners were more educated and 'needed much more skill and attention'.[93]

---

88 Ibid.
89 Ibid 528.
90 Kett (n 13) 17.
91 R S Roberts 'The Personnel and Practice of Medicine in Tudor and Stuart England: Part I. The Provinces' (1962) 6 *Medical History* 363.
92 Ibid 365–356.
93 Roberts 'London' (n 4) 218.

Such arguments endorsing a London-centric approach highlight the simple fact that London was the most favourable market for practitioners. Physicians had the strongest incentive to safeguard their monopoly in the capital. Roberts indicates that the lesser role of traditional physicians may have benefited patients in the provinces.

> [E]vidence suggests that London and legislation were negligible factors, and as long as the lack of scientific knowledge precluded real and worthwhile specialism, the need of the majority of the people was for general practitioners rather than the artificially segregated grades that were imposed in London.[94]

Another factor also explains the differences in the regulation of practitioners in the provinces, the role of the craft Guilds.[95] Until 1745 and the dissolution of their union with the barbers, surgeons were subject to the customs and laws of the Guilds. Even after their divorce from the Grocers in 1617, apothecaries remained within the Guilds in their own independent Worshipful Society of Apothecaries. While Guilds in different cities had much in common, Guilds were based within their home city, and details of local regulation differed.[96] The Guilds sought to meet the needs of the local population. In many cases those needs were for accessible care from practitioners with experience and skill. The claims of the university-educated physicians cut little ice with many leading figures in local government. Kett[97] quotes the physician, Edward Harrison:

> [O]ut of the precincts of London, little attention is paid to the sources of medical degrees. They may either be the reward of severe and protracted study, or have been obtained, without previous attendance and examination, from universities where the chief care of the professors seems to be limited to the fees and perquisites of admission.[98]

The inapplicability of much of the regulatory framework governing medical practice in London, be it the result of differences in the law or simply in practice, did not mean that the provinces were exempt from attempts by the College of Physicians to exert control outside London or that they were a law-free zone. As we have seen, the 1511 Act requiring that physicians practising in the provinces obtain an episcopal licence was amended in 1522 to provide that aspiring physicians in the provinces without a university degree from Oxford or Cambridge should be examined by the College

---

94 Roberts 'Provinces' (n 91) 376.
95 A I Ogus 'Regulatory Law: Some Lessons from the Past' (1992) 12 *Legal Studies* 1.
96 Pelling and Webster (n 3) 212–215.
97 Kett (n 13) 28.
98 E Harrison *Remarks on the Ineffective State of the Practice of Physic in Great Britain* (London, 1806) 11.

before the bishop granted a licence. Roberts states that 'This clearly meant that the College meant to license all physicians outside London.'[99] That aim was never realised, principally because the College 'had no administrative machinery outside London'.[100] The College tried writing to all justices of the peace and mayors in 1556, to seek help in enforcing the legislation.[101] They tried liaising with the bishops but ultimately had no effective means of enforcing in the provinces such powers as they enjoyed within London. Difficulties in travel and communication before the nineteenth century partly explain the impotence of the College away from its base in the capital. England was unusual in having only the one College. A local College was 'common in towns throughout Italy'[102] and much of Continental Europe.

Courts in the provinces were kept as busy by 'doctors' litigating against each other as they were in London. Common informers generated business for the courts, making a living out of private prosecutions using highly dubious tactics.[103] Roberts records twenty prosecutions for allegedly unlawful practice outside London between 1512 and 1554, the majority initiated by informers. None resulted in conviction.[104] Some may have been driven by spite; others were attempts to gain redress for poor treatment. And the battle between the orthodox professionals was also played out in the provinces. Competition for business loomed large, dramatically illustrated by the suit for libel brought by Thomas Edwards against John Woolton.[105]

Edwards was first apprenticed to an apothecary in Exeter and then spent some time at Oxford University before completing his apprenticeship. Later, after proceedings had commenced, Edwards also claimed to be a licentiate of the College of Physicians and put in evidence a licence dated 17 July 1598. He opened his own business and, in or around 1602, he began to practise physic. Woolton held an MA from Oxford and was licensed as a physician in 1588. In 1603, Woolton wrote a vitriolic letter to Edwards, full of obscene language and charges of malpractice. The essence of the letter was that Edwards, an apothecary, was practising physic. To quote just one of Woolton's charges he wrote 'your master taught you not to go beyond your mortar and pestle … you ought not to minister so much as a clyster or open a vein … without licence of a physician'.[106] The letter castigated

99 Roberts 'Provinces' (n 91) 366.
100 Ibid.
101 Ibid.
102 Pelling and Webster (n 3) 167–168.
103 Ogus (n 95) 17.
104 Roberts 'Provinces' (n 91) 367–368.
105 Roberts gives a full account of the background; Roberts 'Provinces' (n 91) 371–375.
106 Ibid 372.

Edwards' treatment of Sir William Courtenay, a patient of Woolton's who had 'defected' to Edwards. A letter written to the recipient and not published to third parties could not, and cannot, form the basis of a civil suit for libel. The Court of Star Chamber accepted Edwards' claim as a criminal libel. Until its abolition in 2009,[107] a defamatory libel which can be shown to 'raise angry passion, provoke revenge and thereby endanger the peace' was a common law crime[108] even if published only to the person defamed. The offence was subject to unlimited punishment. Roberts gives a full account of how for over four years the case dragged on. Edwards added an allegation that Woolton had published his libel to others including a local physician and at least two apothecaries, joining them as defendants. Woolton made further attacks on Edwards' treatment of Sir William and other patients. At one point in the long dispute Edwards and Woolton confronted each other on a public highway, Woolton shouting at Edwards to 'go home to his pestle and mortar'.

The case was eventually heard by a commission presided over by Sir Edward Coke, who as we have seen later ruled against the College in *Bonham's Case*. Woolton faced a number of legal hurdles in seeking to justify his libel. The evidence that Edwards held a licence from the College granted before he started to practise physic was a major problem for Woolton. He responded by arguing that the licence had been unlawfully obtained and not valid. Edwards had not been examined in Latin. As an apothecary, Edwards was ineligible to be licensed at all. The President of Woolton's own College rejected Woolton's allegation saying that the Elects knew Edwards was an apothecary. He had been lawfully examined and found 'sufficiently learned to practise the Art and Faculty of Physic'. Allegations against the College of bribery or undue influence were strongly denied and Coke gave judgment in favour of Edwards. Coke ruled that the letter was a criminal libel motivated by revenge and likely to cause a breach of the peace. There was no justification for the libel. Coke declared there was no 'blemish' on Edwards' reputation 'to be an apothecary and then a physician is no disparagement, but a means to prove the better physician as an Attorney or Clerk may after prove the better judge'.[109] All the defendants were fined and damages awarded to Edwards. Woolton was ordered to stand in the marketplace in Exeter with the interrogatories from the case around his neck.

Edwards v Woolton was a victory for the plaintiff and a body blow to traditional physicians outside London. Roberts acclaims it as a cause célèbre

107 Coroners and Justice Act 2009, s 23.
108 J W C Turner *Russell on Crime* (12th edn) (Stevens and Sons, 1964) 776.
109 Roberts 'Provinces' (n 91) 374.

for the apothecaries in that Coke granted apothecaries in the provinces the right to practise physic nearly a hundred years before *Rose v College of Physicians* in 1703.[110] Is this the case in strict law? A finding that Woolton had not justified his libel against Edwards did not constitute a ruling that all apothecaries had the right to practise physic. Coke's comments that to be an apothecary before becoming a physician was to be commended are *obiter dicta*. Thomas Edwards was a licentiate of the College and perhaps the most that can be claimed is that an apothecary who was also a licentiate of the College of Physicians could lawfully practise physic in the provinces. In 1687, the College tried to close that route of entry to the practice of physic by imposing a ban on 'any surgeon, drug compounder' or 'any other artificer' from candidacy to the College. After 1687 any apothecary wishing to emulate Edwards would have to give up his business as an apothecary.

In 1703 when William Rose successfully challenged the College, no mention was made of *Edwards v Woolton*. That is not to say that *Edwards v Woolton* is not an important part of medico-legal history. The case highlights the limited effect in practice of the Tudor legislation on the regulation of medical practice and marks the stark difference in the legal framework for practice in the provinces. It might be said to mark the birth of the general practitioner as the key health professional for most patients, a role which was to endure for nearly 400 years. Of greatest interest perhaps is the disparaging language and attitude displayed by Coke in *Edwards* and *Bonham* towards the pretensions of the physicians and their College to be the 'responsible body of medical men', to be true professionals, not tradesmen. The courts in both cases showed a distinct absence of deference. The result of Coke's interventions was that 'medical practice had increasingly become a free market activity like any other'.[111]

Problems and practice: defining physic

In fighting to retain exclusive rights to practise physic, the physicians faced an enduring problem. If you seek to limit who has the right to practise, how can the physic of yesterday or medicine today, be defined in order to defend claims to exclusivity – de facto a monopoly? What sort of activity fell within the protection of practice that the College sought to defend?

Defining what constitutes an activity, which falls within practice of physic/medicine is nigh on impossible. The College sought to exclude their competitor 'professionals' from the art of physic, confining the surgeons

110 *Rose* (n 74).
111 Roberts 'London' (n 4) 229.

and the apothecaries to a limited, lower, role. Well before *Rose*, the reality of carving up practice was exposed as unworkable. The surgeons argued that it was often impossible to keep the three branches of medicine apart.[112] Assume a surgeon properly and skilfully amputated a leg, did he breach the law and violate the rights of the physician if observing his patient carefully he then determined (diagnosed) that the amputee needed a particular form of dressing and a strengthening drink and/or drugs to ease his pain? Did he violate the rights of the apothecary if he then supplied the drink and drugs?

Roberts quotes a surgeon, Richard Alison, prosecuted in 1516–17 for practising physic by way of giving his patients internal remedies (i.e. medicines). Alison, who was acquitted, contended that:

> [T]he physicians' concept of medicine was static, and the distinctions between physic and surgery archaic: a new disease like syphilis, he said, necessitated new forms of treatment which could not be classified as pertaining exclusively to medicine or surgery.[113]

Commenting on a raft of similar prosecutions, all but one of which failed, Roberts suggests that the core of the defence was that surgery embraced all medical treatment and:

> [T]he university educated physician therefore was to be regarded as a consultant for the rich rather than as a practitioner with an exclusive right to practise medicine as an arbitrarily distinct branch of the healing art.[114]

As the eighteenth century drew to a close, pressure for reform of the antiquated tripartite structure of the orthodox medical professions grew.

112 Roberts 'London' (n 4) 217.
113 Ibid.
114 Ibid.

4

The bumpy road to the General Medical Council

Becoming a profession

The nineteenth century witnessed the gradual move towards a partial merger of the orthodox professions making it easier for the legislature and the courts to identify the 'responsible medical man'. The Medical Act 1858 fell short of uniting the different cadres of medical practitioners into a single, unified medical profession. What the Act achieved was to identify practitioners recognised by the State as qualified to practise and entitled to be entered onto the Medical Register. The road to the 1858 Act was bumpy, marked by continuing litigation between the medical corporations. The only consensus among the orthodox remained their fixed abomination of the quacks and determination to drive them out of business. The courts and parliament remained the fora where the shape of medicine and the regulation of healers were hammered out. Parallel to formal encounters between law and healing, the quest by the orthodox for a social status akin to the lawyer or the clergyman persisted. And increasingly medical men acquired a stronger voice in the making of laws relating to matters such as abortion and anatomy.

Apothecaries were on the front line of calls for reform. I first examine the debates resulting in the Apothecaries Act 1815. Next, I explore the attempts by the orthodox medical practitioners to use the law courts to drive out their 'common enemy', 'quacks' and 'empirics'. Finally, I look the Medical Act 1858 itself.

A damp squib: the Apothecaries Act 1815

From early in the eighteenth century, apothecaries had become the principal providers of orthodox medical care for the majority of the population, assuming 'the function of a general practitioner of medicine'.[1] From about

---

1 S W F Holloway 'The Apothecaries Act, 1815: A Reinterpretation' (1966) 10 *Medical History* 107, 107.

1730, many apothecaries also sought a licence from the College of Surgeons to practise surgery.[2] The terms apothecary and surgeon-apothecary came to be used interchangeably.[3] In 1814, Kerrison estimated that nineteen out of twenty patients depended on surgeon-apothecaries for their health care.[4] A number of problems beset the apothecaries.

(1) Leading apothecaries admitted that standards of education and competence of apothecaries varied widely.
(2) Despite setbacks in *Rose*,[5] and *Edwards v Woolton*,[6] the College of Physicians refused to abandon its claim to control the other orthodox professions.
(3) A new group emerged to challenge the apothecaries, 'chemists and druggists',[7] tradesmen who undercut the apothecaries by selling and dispensing medicines more cheaply. While the apothecary was 'encroaching on the domain of the physician, the chemist was taking over the dispensing activities of the apothecary and even beginning to prescribe over the counter'.[8]
(4) The host of other healers continued to compete for a share of the health-care 'cake'.

Holloway details attempts to reform the law regulating medical practice generally and in particular the regulation of apothecaries. He describes how 'many reforms were advocated, several Bills drafted, numerous petitions and counter-petitions presented and innumerable amendments introduced'.[9] Apothecaries disagreed among themselves about the form which reform should take. Holloway demonstrates that the view that the 1815 Act 'marks the beginning of the process of medical reform in England is misguided'.[10] The Act was retrogressive. Read literally, it sought to restore the three

---

2 Ibid 108.
3 J F Kett 'Provincial Medical Practice in England 1730–1815' (1964) 19 *Journal of the History of Medicine and Allied Sciences* 17.
4 R M Kerrison *An Inquiry into the Present State of the Medical Profession in England containing an Abstract of all the Acts and Charters granted to Physicians, Surgeons and Apothecaries and A Comparative View of the Profession in Scotland, Ireland and on the Continent* (Longman, Rees, Hurst, Orme and Brown, 1814) 32.
5 *William Rose (Plaintiff in Error) v The College of Physicians (London)* (1703) 2 English Reports 857.
6 R S Roberts 'The Personnel and Practice of Medicine in Tudor and Stuart England: Part I. The Provinces' (1962) 6 *Medical History* 363, 371–375.
7 H Marland 'The "Doctor's Shop": The Rise of the Chemist and Druggist in Nineteenth-Century Manufacturing Districts' in L H Curth (ed) *From Physick to Pharmacology: Five Hundred Years of British Drug Retailing* (Ashgate, 2006) 79–104.
8 Holloway (n 1) 108.
9 Ibid 107.
10 Ibid.

orders of medicine, and the demarcation between physicians, surgeons and apothecaries at a time when 'the basis of separation had in fact broken down everywhere outside London'.[11]

Reformers recognised that the training, competence and quality of care offered by apothecaries varied widely. While there were a number of highly educated apothecaries, there were also many largely uneducated practitioners. The writ of the Society of Apothecaries ran only in London. The Guild system was breaking down outside London. John Mason Good[12] noted the lack of 'a competent jurisdiction within the profession itself to regulate its practice, and to *restrain ignorant and unqualified persons from practising at all* (my emphasis)'.[13] The lack of comprehensive regulation of medical education in all three orthodox professions was a major factor in calls for medical reform.

A Cromwellian Ordinance of 1654,[14] exempting veterans who had served in the armed forces, including apothecaries and surgeons[15] from the licensing powers of the Guilds, further muddied the waters. On the Restoration of the Monarchy, Cromwell's Ordinances were treated as void for lack of Royal Assent. An early Act of Parliament in the reign of Charles II in 1660 effectively re-enacted the Ordinance.[16] While concerns about education, qualifications and competence also affected physicians and surgeons, those concerns were more worrying for apothecaries seeking to escape the 'stigma of shopkeeper' while fighting off competition from the 'new shopkeepers', the 'chymists' and druggists, recognised as a fourth order of medicine by Park J in *Allison v Haydon*.[17] In the light of this new contest between apothecaries and druggists, the apothecaries' 'success' in *Rose* and *Edwards v Woolton*, declaring that apothecaries could lawfully attend and prescribe for their patients without reference to a physician, proved a Pyrrhic victory. The judgments turned on a legal technicality, ruling that the apothecary might lawfully attend and prescribe but could only do so without payment and could charge only for the sale of the medicines.

Apothecaries were accused of inflating the cost of medicines. Druggists who simply sold medicines without the hassle and cost of providing patient

11 Kett (n 3) 17.
12 J M Good *The History of Medicine, so far as it relates to the Profession of Apothecary* (1795).
13 Ibid as quoted in Holloway (n 1) 109.
14 Kett (n 3) 18.
15 Ibid 28.
16 An Act for inabling Souldiers of the Army now to be disbanded to exercise Trades 1660.
17 *Allison v Haydon* (1828) 172 English Reports 406.

care undercut them by selling much cheaper medicines. Holloway[18] exposes a weakness in the apothecaries' efforts to drive out the druggists. Given the apothecaries' desire to be regarded as general practitioners of medicine, focusing on competition from the druggist for the market in selling medicines was a backwards move. The apothecaries should rather have focused on the right to charge for attendance and patient care.

In 1793, leading apothecaries formed a society dedicated to driving out the druggists and putting their own house in order. Naming themselves the General Pharmaceutical Association of Great Britain (GPAGB), they produced evidence of the bad practice and danger to patients caused by incompetent, ignorant and greedy druggists. GPAGB presented this evidence and their proposals for reform to the medical corporations. Even their own Society of Apothecaries opposed the proposals and when a petition was presented to Parliament on behalf of GPAGB, the Society ensured it made no progress. Nonetheless, the petition had interesting features which were to become key to reforms embodied in the Medical Act 1858, including the following:[19]

(1) Statutory protection for exclusive rights for apothecaries to enjoy 'the liberty to vend pharmaceutical preparations, and compound physicians' prescriptions, anywhere in England and Wales'. Thus, they hoped, the druggists could be driven out of competition. In the event, as Holloway explains, the efforts of GPAGB to drive out the druggists merely encouraged the latter 'to put their own house in order and unite for their own protection'[20] to emerge as the forebears of modern pharmacists.

(2) Apprentices must not be taken on unless they met approved educational qualifications. Apprenticeship must last at least five years and then the would-be apothecary must be examined as to their competency.

(3) A 'competent court' should be established consisting of a number of apothecaries with '*full power to make such bye laws and regulations as may be thought most conducive to the welfare of the public and the profession* (my emphasis)'. Thus, self-regulation was qualified by a requirement that the regulators act for the welfare of the public not just the profession. Not until 2002 was the Medical Act 1983 amended to declare that the main objective of the GMC is 'the safety of the public'.[21]

GPAGB's defeat left apothecaries and general practice in a woeful state. Physic and surgery were not much better off as the Tudor model of regulation decayed. In a Bill published in 1806 the College of Physicians put

18 Holloway (n 1) 111.
19 Ibid 108.
20 Ibid 111.
21 The Medical Act 1983 (Amendment) Order SI 3135 (2002).

forward their own proposals, reviving and updating their claim to dominance: the College should have statutory powers to regulate all medical practice in England and Wales; no one would be permitted to practise medicine, surgery, midwifery or pharmacy without a licence from the College which would set the entry standards and requirements for professional conduct for each branch of medicine; a person licensed in any one branch of the profession would only be permitted to practise within that branch.[22] The College's attempt to restore and extend the old order met with little support. Two points of interest should be noted. First, the proposals extended to midwifery at the time when episcopal licensing of female midwives was collapsing and there was no express provision in place in relation to man-midwives. Second, the Bill provided for an annual list of qualified practitioners, the forebear of the Medical Register, the lynchpin of regulation after 1858.

Concurrently with the efforts of the College of Physicians to regain its supremacy, a group of eminent practitioners led by Dr Edward Harrison, and including the President of the Royal Society, set out to investigate regulatory reform.[23] Calling themselves the 'Associated Faculty' they sought evidence of the state of medical practice in England examining the extent of unlicensed practice (quackery) and the poor state of much orthodox care. In 1806, the Associated Faculty prepared an ambitious Bill 'for better regulating the Practice of Physic'. A revised version of the Bill was presented in 1808. The proposals were much wider than attempts to regulate apothecaries and druggists and extended to 'the whole field of medical care throughout the kingdom'.[24]

The Bill sought to regulate not just the three orthodox professions, but also man-midwives and female midwives, veterinary practitioners, chemists and druggists and all vendors of medicines. Proposals included provision for entry qualifications and educational requirements for each branch of the profession. These would require a university degree for physicians plus at least five years' study of physic. Surgeons and apothecaries must have served at least a five-year apprenticeship and studied at a medical school for two and one years respectively. Chemists and druggists must have served a five-year apprenticeship. A man-midwife would be required to prove that he had attended lectures in anatomy and received instruction from an experienced *accoucheur* for one year. Female midwives would have to 'obtain a certificate of proficiency from an obstetrician'. Practitioners who met the appropriate

22 Holloway (n 1) 114–116.
23 Ibid 115–119.
24 Ibid 116.

conditions would be entered on a medical register and *only registered practitioners would be allowed to practise*. Initially the practitioner would be entered in the section of the register in which he qualified. On completing further relevant educational requirements the practitioner could transfer to another branch and should he so wish to, be dually qualified. An apothecary could extend his education and experience and be licensed to practise as physician, surgeon or man-midwife. By 1808 many apothecaries were already practising as surgeon-apothecaries and man-midwives. The 1808 Bill provided that commissioners would be appointed to enforce the Act with powers inter alia to set up hospitals and medical schools. In its ambition to create a national and integrated authority enforced by appointed officers the 1808 Bill harked back to the proposals of the physicians in 1421.[25] In 2014, two centuries later, the Law Commission made recommendations for a single regulator for health and social care professionals.[26] While the government welcomed the report and conducted a consultation, as yet no action has been taken to implement the proposals.

Obsession with social status persisted. Harrison declared that he sought to restrict entry to the profession to 'youths of reputable birth and liberal education' and keep out 'mean and low persons'.[27] The Bill fell foul of that body which most actively sought social status, the London College of Physicians.[28] The College saw no need for new regulators, objected vehemently to any notion of new medical schools, and (rightly) saw Harrison's Bill as undermining the ancient, hierarchical, tripartite system of regulation to which the College was wedded.

The College also objected to proposals for the compulsory education of apothecaries. The line between the exalted physician and the apothecary was already blurred. Holloway quotes the College:

> The real design and tendency of Dr Harrison's proposal are less directed to amelioration of medical practice than to the subversion of the existing authorities in Physic and the depression of the rights, the rank and the importance of the Physician.[29]

The Associated Faculty having failed, another organisation, the Association of Apothecaries and Surgeon Apothecaries, was formed. It focused more

---

25 See above Chapter 2.
26 Law Commissions *Regulation of Health Professionals: Regulation of Social Care Professionals* (Law Com No. 345, Scot Law Com No 237, NILC No 18, 2014).
27 Holloway (n 1) 115.
28 The College of Surgeons and the Society of Apothecaries were no more enamoured of the Bill than the physicians but kept a lower profile; see Holloway (n 1) 118.
29 Ibid 118.

narrowly on the role of the apothecary and surgeon-apothecary, avoiding treading on the sensitive toes of the physicians. In a Bill of 1813, this Association's initial proposals sought common ground between the College and the reformers. In correspondence with all three medical corporations, the Association declared that they sought to avoid 'trespassing on the privileges of the chartered medical bodies'.[30] The 'chartered bodies were not impressed, treating the reformers with a coldness bordering on contempt'.[31] The Association proposed that a nationwide body be set up to regulate apothecaries, surgeon-apothecaries, midwives and compounders of medicines. The Colleges of Physicians and Surgeons, and the Society of Apothecaries would be members of that body. As with Harrison's proposals, educational standards were to be prescribed and the authority empowered to establish a medical school in London. The Colleges and the Society of Apothecaries all ultimately opposed the Bill, as unsurprisingly did the chemists and druggists. The Bill was withdrawn. In the next version of the Bill, proposals for a new national regulatory authority and a new medical school were dropped. The Colleges and the Society of Apothecaries continued to snipe at any proposals put forward. Only after several further skirmishes was the Apothecaries Act 1815 enacted.

'An Act for better regulating the Practice of Apothecaries across England and Wales'

The 1815 Act only addressed apothecaries. It was expressly founded on the Charter granted to the Society of Apothecaries by James I in 1617. Holloway suggests that founding the Act on the Charter was a ploy by the College of Physicians to remind the apothecaries of their humble origins and quash any pretentions they harboured to be part of a learned profession.[32]

The Society whose jurisdiction had previously been limited to London became a national regulator. The Act set out detailed rules relating to the powers of the Master and Wardens of the Society generally and in particular to inspection of drugs and medicines. Section 15 provided that, save for those in practice before the Act came into force,[33] no person could lawfully practise as an apothecary without a certificate of 'fitness to practise'.[34] The Act laid down conditions for the grant of a certificate requiring that the

---

30 Kerrison (n 4).
31 Ibid.
32 Holloway (n 1).
33 *The Apothecaries Company v Warburton* (1819) 106 English Reports 575.
34 S 14.

candidate be twenty-one years old, have served a five-year apprenticeship and submit testimonials providing evidence that he had a 'sufficient medical education' and was 'of a good moral conduct'.[35] Practising without a certificate was a criminal offence and to recover his fees in a court of law the apothecary must prove that he had a full certificate at the time that he treated the patient.[36] Section 23 required the Master and Wardens of the Society to publish an annual list of every person who 'shall in that year have obtained a Certificate to practise as an Apothecary'.

Section 15 revived the problems of boundaries between the different orders. A man licensed by the College of Surgeons could not lawfully practise as an apothecary though he could supply medicines 'in the cure of a surgical case', for example, when treating a broken leg. In *Allison v Haydon*,[37] a surgeon who attended and supplied medicines to a patient with typhus was held to have violated the prohibitions on practising 'physic' and practising as an apothecary without a certificate. In 1843, the Society of Apothecaries 'prosecuted' Mr Lotinga. Lotinga had treated a number of patients including Ann Pace for consumption, supplying medication to her family. The argument that Ann was a surgical case having failed, Lotinga asserted that he did not supply the medicines as a surgeon or apothecary: he sold them as a chemist. Directing the jury, Cresswell J ruled that 'a chemist is one who sells medicines which are asked for'. The defendant had acted as an apothecary selecting which medicines to supply and determining which drugs to give.[38]

At the insistence of the College of Physicians, citing the duty of apothecaries to dispense such medicines for the sick as directed by a physician, Section 5 imposed penalties on any apothecary who 'knowingly, wilfully and contumaciously refuses to make or compound' or 'deliberately, negligently, falsely or unfaithfully compound any medicine directed by a physician'. Section 28 provided that the Act did not extend to the trade or business of chemists and druggists in 'the buying, preparing, compounding, dispensing and vending Drugs, Medicines and Medicinal Compounds'. Section 5 reminded apothecaries of their origins as suppliers of medicines rather than general practitioners. Section 28 left them at the mercy of the new entrants in the competition for a share in the healing market, the chemists and druggists.

---

35 S 15.
36 S 21.
37 *Allison v Haydon* (1828) 172 English Reports 406.
38 *The Master Wardens and Society of the Art and Mystery of Apothecaries of the City of London v Lotinga* (1843) 174 English Reports 360.

The 1815 Act contained some features which offered better regulation. It applied uniformly across England and Wales. It made provision to ensure that apothecaries were educated to some degree and subject to examination of their competence. It enabled apothecaries to charge for attendance on patients. It provided a list of those duly qualified to practise, so patients could identify the qualified practitioner. From both the professional and the public perspective, however, the Act was flawed. Contrary to the hopes of the reformers the Act dealt only with apothecaries, re-enforcing the anti-quated tripartite system, the 'disappearing world' held dear by the College of Physicians.[39] It did little to address the chaos and confusion outside London leaving 'surgery and midwifery still open to every unprincipled pretender'.[40] And in the end the Act made no provision to control the chemists and druggists.

Some of the proposals bruited and defeated in the battles around the 1815 Act were revisited in debates leading up to the Medical Act 1858. The Apothecaries Act 1815 impeded progress. Meaningful, comprehensive change in the way English law regulated medical practice was delayed for over fifty years.

Outlawing quackery[41]

The one matter on which the orthodox continued to agree was the need to drive out non-orthodox healers, often described as 'quacks' or 'empirics'.[42] These derogatory terms are used interchangeably. I use 'quack' to describe those 'practitioners' who promoted and/or sold highly dubious and probably fraudulent remedies, in effect medical charlatans. I use 'empiric' to refer to unlicensed practitioners, traditional healers, such as bonesetters and herbalists, who built up experience in their field of practice and may have undergone an informal apprenticeship. Hilary Marland writes that the eighteenth century 'could be deemed as a "golden age" of quackery' and that the nineteenth century began with the survival of traditional healers as

---

39 Holloway (n 1) 129.
40 And see S W F Holloway 'The Apothecaries Act 1815: A Reinterpretation II: The Consequence of the Act' (1966) 10 *Medical History* 221.
41 A comprehensive account of the nineteenth-century campaign against unorthodox practitioners can be found in M Brown 'Medicine, Quackery and the Free Market: The "War" against Morison's Pills and the Construction of the Medical Profession, c. 1830–c. 1850' in M Jenner and P Wallis (eds) *Medicine and the Market in England and its Colonies* (Palgrave Macmillan, 2007) 238–261.
42 M J Mehlman 'Quackery' (2005) 31 *American Journal of Law and Medicine* 349.

well as numerous itinerant quacks and 'new alternative therapies' including homeopathy and mesmerism.[43]

Unlicensed practitioners and vendors of dubious medicinal products faced a sustained campaign led by orthodox practitioners to render them vulnerable to prosecution for manslaughter, charges of fraud and unlicensed practice. Contract law and libel also played a part in the battle. The common objective of the diverse means by which the law was deployed against non-orthodox healers, was to publicise the misdeeds and/or dangers of any non-orthodox healer, scare off such healers with the threat of criminal conviction and hit the quacks in the purse. In none of these objectives were the orthodox very successful. A W P Simpson suggests that the root cause of failure was that the remedies offered by orthodox doctors were not much more effective than the wares peddled by the quacks, and often just as bizarre.[44] Judges were not convinced that the licensed physician or surgeon was any better at his job than experienced empirics. The gradual development of science-based medicine and the reform of the regulation of medical practice in the nineteenth century led to a change in judicial views of medicine, more respectful of the orthodox practitioner.

The 'generals' in the war against quacks and empirics were often also prominent campaigners in the battle for reform of the orthodox professions to which they belonged. The suppression of quackery was one of the prime objectives of the Provincial Medical and Surgical Association founded in 1832 to represent the growing body of 'general practitioners' which was to become the British Medical Association in 1856. The Association campaigned extensively for medical reform. Prominent among the reformers was the founding editor of *The Lancet*, the surgeon-apothecary, Thomas Wakley.[45] Wakley was at the forefront of campaigns against quacks,[46] arguing in 1836 that '[n]ever have quacks, quackish doctrines and quack medicines, exercised a greater influence over the minds and bodies of people

---

43 Marland (n 7) 79–80. And see B Lyons 'Papist Potions and Electric Sex: A Historical Perspective on "Proper Medical Treatment"' in S Fovargue and A Mullock (eds) *The Legitimacy of Medical Treatment: What Role for the Medical Exception?* (Routledge, 2016) 51–67.

44 A W P Simpson 'Quackery and Contract Law: The Case of the Carlill Smoke Ball' (1985) 14 *Journal of Legal Studies* 366.

45 D Sharp 'Thomas Wakley (1795–1862): A Biographical Sketch' (2012) 379 *The Lancet* 1914.

46 Wakley did not confine his campaign for law reform to medical practice. Elected as an Independent Radical MP for Finsbury in 1835, he campaigned inter alia for reform of the political and criminal justice systems; see J Hostettler 'Thomas Wakley: An Enemy of Injustice' (1984) 5 *Journal of Legal History* 60.

of this country as they exert in this present epoch.'[47] He was also a passionate critic of the medical corporations.[48] He is best known for his work to
reform the coronial system.[49]

Prosecutions for manslaughter: presumption of guilt[50]

Wakley and his colleagues used coroners' inquests and the criminal process to attack the quacks. In cases where patients died after treatment from
an unlicensed healer, campaigners seeking to drive unlicensed healers and
quacks out of business first sought to obtain a verdict of manslaughter from
the coroner's jury followed they hoped by prosecution and condign punishment. The prosecution of John St John Long illustrates the tactics deployed.[51]
St John Long was an artist who claimed to have discovered a cure for consumption (tuberculosis). His 'cure' involved inhalation of certain vapours
and the application to the skin of an irritant substance producing a wound.
He treated Catherine Cashin (who probably did not have the disease). Her
family expressed concern about the suppurating wound on Catherine's
back. St John Long pronounced the wound to be 'in a beautiful state'.[52]
A few days later Catherine died after days of pain and constant vomiting.
The family sought Wakley's assistance at the inquest. Several surgeons gave
'expert' evidence of the dangers of St John Long's remedy and that it was
the cause of Catherine's death. The coroner's jury returned a verdict of manslaughter at which 'the many doctors crowded in the courtroom clapped and
stamped their feet'.[53] St John Long was indicted for manslaughter. Twenty-
nine former patients including a Marchioness gave evidence as witnesses
for the accused. On this occasion he was convicted and fined £250.[54] That
sum equates to approximately £27,000 today. St John Long was spared
imprisonment. He paid the fine 'on the spot',[55] testimony to the financial

---

47 (1836) 25 *The Lancet* 948; discussed in Brown (n 41) 238.
48 Wakley's proposal for a London College of Medicine came to nought.
49 I A Burney *Bodies of Evidence: Medicine and the Politics of the English Inquest
    1830–1926* (Johns Hopkins University Press, 2000).
50 This section draws heavily on M Brazier 'The Criminal Process and Medical
    Practitioners: Shield or Sword?' in M Henaghan and J Wall (eds) *Law, Ethics and
    Medicine: Essays in Honour of Peter Skegg* (Thomson Reuters, 2016) 7–31.
51 S Hempel 'John St John Long: Quackery and Manslaughter' (2014) 383 *The Lancet*
    1541: and see 'Extraordinary Inquest – Mr John St John Long' *Spectator Archives* 28
    August 1830.
52 Ibid 1541.
53 Ibid.
54 *R v John St John Long No 1* (1830) 172 English Reports 756.
55 Simpson (n 44) 381.

success of his 'medical practice'. One of the key arguments advanced by the prosecution, however, failed. It was argued that if a person died as a result of treatment administered by an unlicensed practitioner a 'supposition' of manslaughter arose. Summing up, Park J confirmed the view expressed by Baron Hullock in *R v Van Butchell*[56] that it made 'no difference whether the party be a regular or irregular surgeon'.[57]

Tactics of attracting publicity from an inquest deployed successfully in the first prosecution of St John Long in relation to the death of Catherine Cashin were repeated in other attacks against quacks. A particular target was James Morison. As Michael Brown recounts,[58] Morison developed a brand of pills, No. 1 and No. 2, described by him as 'The Vegetable Universal Medicine', a remedy for every ill.[59] Morison made huge profits. He also attacked orthodox medicine with a vengeance, describing surgery as a 'bastard science' and orthodox doctors as 'ignorant, incompetent, vicious and greedy'.[60] In pursuance of his battle with the orthodox, Morison advanced his own system of 'Hygeiaism'[61] contending that all disease was caused by 'obnoxious matter' in the blood. Removing this 'matter' from the blood with Morison's pills would cure disease.[62] Three prosecutions were brought,[63] not against Morison himself, but against his agents responsible for selling his 'Hygeian' remedies. The campaign against 'Hygeiaism' was carefully constructed following the template from the first St John Long case. Orthodox doctors utilised the coroner's inquest to seek to establish 'scientifically' that Morison's pills caused or hastened death followed by high-profile prosecutions for manslaughter.[64]

Joseph Webb, Morison's agent in York, was called to attend a sick apprentice and administered huge doses of the Universal Remedy. The boy's condition deteriorated and some days later a surgeon was called in who diagnosed advanced smallpox. The boy died within hours. At the instigation of the boy's mother an inquest was held. Four orthodox doctors, two physicians and two surgeons, testified that the pills had accelerated the boy's

56 (1830) 172 English Reports 576.
57 *St John Long No 1* (n 54) 760.
58 Brown (n 41).
59 Ibid 241.
60 Ibid 242.
61 Named after the Greek goddess of medicine.
62 Brown (n 41) 240–244.
63 At least nine further cases against Morison's agents resulted in verdicts by coroners' juries that the pills had accelerated death but there was insufficient evidence for prosecutions: Brown (n 41) 246.
64 Brown ibid 247.

death, one arguing that the pills directly caused the death 'by inflaming his stomach and intestines'. The coroner's jury returned a verdict of manslaughter (with one dissenter). Webb was then tried at York Assizes. Several orthodox experts testified against Webb. Only one orthodox doctor testified on Webb's behalf. Many members of the public expressed their faith in the remedy. The judge noted that the medical experts with just one exception recognised the pills as the cause of death. Webb was convicted and gaoled for six months.[65] Two other of Morison's agents, Robert Salmon and Thomas La Mott, were also convicted of manslaughter after patients died after taking large doses of Morison's pills on their advice.[66]

Victory for the orthodox was more partial than Wakley and his colleagues would have wished. A second prosecution of St John Long on broadly similar facts resulted in his acquittal.[67] In the series of prosecutions of unlicensed practitioners for gross negligence manslaughter (GNM), judges consistently rejected arguments that, simply because the accused was an unlicensed practitioner, if his intervention resulted in the death of a patient a felony was committed. Prosecutors invoked the opinion of Sir Edward Coke[68] that if a licensed medical man administered medicine to a patient without any felonious intent, yet with the result that he died within three days, that would not amount to homicide but 'if one not be of the mysterie of a physitian or chirurgion take upon him the cure of a man and he dieth of the potion or medicine this is … covert felony'.[69]

Judges preferred the opinion of Chief Justice Hale who declared it was erroneous to think that if the accused 'be no licensed chirurgeon or physician that occasioneth this mischance that then it is felony'.[70] Whether the practitioner was licensed or unlicensed, for the accused to be convicted of homicide it must be shown that he acted with gross negligence, out of grossest ignorance, or the most criminal inattention.[71] It mattered not 'whether the individual consulted the president of the College of Physicians, the president of the College of Surgeons or the humblest bone-setter in the village'.[72] The most that might be said to favour the licensed practitioner was that proof

---

65 *R v Joseph Webb* (1834) 174 English Reports 140.
66 Brown (n 41) 246–247.
67 *R v John St John Long No 2* (1831) 172 English Reports 767.
68 E Coke *Institutes of the Laws of England* Pt IV 251.
69 Were the dictum of Coke to be accepted then unlicensed practice resulting in death would constitute unlawful act manslaughter with no requirement that gross negligence needed to be established.
70 M Hale *The History of Pleas of the Crown* Vol 1 (1736) 429.
71 *R v John St John Long No 1* (n 54) 759.
72 Ibid per Garrow B at 759; and see *R v Van Butchell* (1829) 172 English Reports 576.

of gross ignorance might be easier to establish in relation to the unlicensed doctor. Summing up in the trial of Joseph Webb, Lord Lyndhurst said:

[W]here proper medical assistance can be had, a person totally ignorant of the science of medicine takes on himself to administer a violent and dangerous remedy to one labouring under disease and death ensues in consequence of that dangerous remedy having been so administered, then he is guilty of manslaughter.[73]

In refusing to favour the licensed practitioner, judges in the first half of the nineteenth century remained less than impressed by the policy arguments advanced by the orthodox practitioners seeking to suppress unlicensed practice. In *R v John Williamson*,[74] an unlicensed man had for many years acted as a man-midwife 'among the lower classes of people'. He had successfully delivered many women. Williamson was charged with murder and manslaughter after he tore away part of a prolapsed womb mistaking it for the placenta and the woman died from the tear to the mesenteric artery. Directing the jury, Lord Ellenborough stated that it was essential to any conviction for manslaughter that they were satisfied that he was guilty of criminal negligence and misconduct in respect of his care of this particular patient. Want of skill should not be presumed. The defendant's record of successful deliveries showed that he must have had some skill. Williamson was acquitted. In the first trial of St John Long, Park J reiterated that 'experience may teach a man sufficient'.[75] Judges remained sceptical of the claims to superior skills of the licensed practitioner and anxious not to create disincentives to the continuing practice of practitioners who acquired their skill from experience and whose services might be more readily accessible to the poor.

Ferner and McDowell suggest that attitudes changed after the Medical Act 1858, citing the case of *R v William Crick*[76] where a herbalist (medical botanist) was charged with manslaughter after administering a dose of lobelia which the prosecution contended caused a child's death.[77] Pollock CB expressed this view apparently favourable to orthodox medicine:

If the prisoner had been a medical man I should have recommended you to take the most favourable view of his conduct, for it would be most fatal to

73 *Webb* (n 65) 142.
74 (1807) 172 English Reports 578–579.
75 *St John Long No 1* (n 54) 759–761.
76 (1859) 175 *English Reports* 835.
77 R E Ferner and S McDowell 'Doctors Charged with Manslaughter in the Course of Medical Practice, 1795–2005: A Literature Review' (2006) 99 *Journal of the Royal Society of Medicine* 309.

the efficiency of the medical profession if no-one could administer medicine without a halter round his neck.[78]

His Lordship, however, instructed the jury to take note that it was no crime for anyone to administer medicine. A crime was committed only if the medicine were administered 'so rashly and carelessly as to produce death; and in this respect *there is no difference between most regular practitioner and the greatest quack* (my emphasis)'.[79] Pollock expressed a respect for licensed medical practitioners absent from earlier judgments but reiterated that the law which governed liability for GNM was one and the same for the qualified and registered doctor and an unqualified 'alternative' practitioner.

Quacks and fraud

Unlike Williamson and Crick, St John Long and Morison were conmen seeking to deceive the gullible. There is no doubt that unscrupulous individuals exploited vulnerable people by aggressively marketing 'remedies' that at the best did no good and at the worst caused harm, even death. Simpson commented:

> Purveyors of quack medicines, appliances and cures early learned the value of aggressive advertising. Since virtually all their wares were indistinguishably useless, success depended solely on promotion, and in the nineteenth century, quackery was advertised on a massive scale.[80]

While the criminal courts rejected arguments that there was a presumption that an unlicensed practitioner, quack or empiric, was guilty of manslaughter simply because the patient died, the judges noted that unlicensed practice could contravene Tudor legislation which sought to limit the practice of physic and surgery to licensed persons, and provided that fraudulently pretending to be a licensed person might of itself be a crime.[81] Why did the battalions of the orthodox not pursue the quacks for unlicensed practice or fraud? The near impossibility of defining practising 'physic' raised its head again. When a parent gives his child an over-the-counter medicine for a fever, or a colleague helps clean and bandage a wound after a fall, are they practising 'physic'? To this day the Medical Act 1983 does not attempt to proscribe unregistered persons from practising medicine or make practice without the licence now required unlawful. A criminal offence is committed

---

78 *Crick* (n 76) 835.
79 Ibid.
80 Simpson (n 44) 379.
81 See above Chapter 3.

only if someone falsely claims to be a registered or licensed practitioner.[82] Quacks such as Morison and St John Long made no such claims; they proudly advertised their contempt for orthodox medicine.

What about fraud? Attempts to prosecute the purveyors of quack medicine and devices for outlandish claims relating to the products they sought to sell also met with little success. Simpson examines the case of Harness's Electropathic Belt.[83] This amazing device, according to its inventor Cornelius Harness, offered cures, to name but a few, for gout, 'ladies' ailments',[84] constipation and kidney problems. In 1893, Harness and two others were charged with conspiracy to defraud. The case made little progress. The magistrate at the committal hearing refused to commit the men for trial. Evidence of the uselessness of the product was countered by evidence from many satisfied customers. The successful prosecution of Francis McConville (alias Thomas Kelly) for obtaining money by false pretences by way of selling an electric belt 'guaranteed to cure venereal disease', succeeded principally because the accused falsely claimed to be a registered medical practitioner.

The orthodox practitioners' campaign to use the criminal process to outlaw quackery was a failure. The law did not come to the aid of the medical men; judges declined to protect claims to a monopoly of medical practice. In so doing it may be argued that patient choice was respected. It was not for the State to decree that only certain sorts of remedies were permissible. The more altruistic concern of the orthodox professionals relating to the harm some of these quack remedies caused, and the evidence that even remedies harmless in themselves might cause people to delay seeking orthodox treatment, was not fully addressed. A common feature of quackery was aggressive advertising of patent medicines and extraordinary devices. The criminal law was not the only legal weapon conscripted into the service of the battle against quackery. Contract law played a role in seeking to hit the quacks in the purse. *Carlill v Carbolic Smoke Ball Company* is one contract case that no law student ever forgets. Law students know the case for its pronouncement on such arcane matters of contract as unilateral contracts and consideration. Simpson has demonstrated *Carlill*'s fascinating 'relationship to the seedy world of late nineteenth century vendors of patent medical appliances'.[85] In brief, in 1889 Frederick Roe invented a device he named the Carbolic Smoke Ball. Marketing of the Ball took place in the midst of

---

82 Medical Act 1983 ss 49 and 49A.
83 Simpson (n 44) 383–385.
84 Advertisements which may have been covert advertising of abortion services; P Knight 'Women and Abortion in Victorian and Edwardian England' (1977) 4 *History Workshop* 57.
85 Simpson (n 44) 345.

public panic about the emergence of a new and highly contagious disease, influenza. In advertisements the Carbolic Smoke Ball Co declared that a £100 reward would be paid to any person who contracted influenza, colds or any disease caused by taking cold after using the Ball in accordance with the printed directions. Crucially the company stated that many thousands of Balls had been sold as 'preventives' against influenza and 'in no ascertained case was the disease contracted by those using the CARBOLIC SMOKE BALL'. The advertisement further stated that £1000 had been deposited with the Alliance Bank 'showing our sincerity in the matter'.[86]

Mrs Carlill saw the advertisement and bought the Ball.[87] Despite following the instructions to the letter, she contracted influenza. Her husband wrote to the company claiming the reward on his wife's behalf with no success and Mrs Carlill sued for breach of contract. Hawkins J found in favour of Mrs Carlill.[88] The Court of Appeal dismissed Roe's appeal with some scorn.[89]

Simpson critically analyses the legal arguments demonstrating that there is little doubt that the judges 'stretched' principle to accommodate a finding of liability against the defendants.[90] He suggests that the judges concluded that 'the defendants had not behaved as gentlemen, and that was that'.[91] In the Court of Appeal, responding to argument that it was an insensate thing to promise such a 'reward' without means of checking claims, Bowen LJ said forthrightly:

> The answer to this argument seems to me to be that if a person chooses to make extravagant promises of this kind he probably does so because it pays him to make them, and, if he has made them, the extravagance of the promises is no reason why he should not be bound by them.[92]

The Carbolic Smoke Ball gained eternal prominence in the development of the law of contract. It had virtually no effect on quackery. No flood of further claims ensued. Simpson tracks down just one.[93]

---

86 On the back of successful advertising, sophisticated quacks made fortunes. Herbert Ingram amassed a fortune of £5 million from inter alia Parr's Life Pills; Simpson (n 44) 379–381.
87 At a cost of ten shillings, the equivalent to about £60 today.
88 *Carlill v Carbolic Smoke Ball Company* [1892] 2 QB 481.
89 *Carlill v Carbolic Smoke Ball Company* [1893] 1 QB 256 CA.
90 Simpson (n 44) 375–379. And see J D McGinnis 'Carlill v Carbolic Smoke Company: Influenza, Quackery and a Unilateral Contract' (1988) 5 *Canadian Bulletin of Medical History* 121.
91 Simpson (n 44) 379.
92 *Carlill* (n 89) 268.
93 Simpson (n 44) 370.

One final 'legal weapon' employed in both attempts to drive out the quacks and the internecine battles between the orthodox professionals was to make stinging attacks on an individual in the public domain, inviting the 'victim' to sue for libel. In this manner, the defendant could at best demonstrate that his denigration of the party under attack was justified and at worst ensure that the attack on the plaintiff received a high level of publicity. Thomas Wakley was a prime proponent of this strategy of challenging opponents to 'sue me'.[94]

The Medical Act 1858: half a loaf?

Whereas it is expedient that Persons requiring Medical Aid should be able to distinguish qualified from unqualified Practitioners ...

Thus began the Preamble to the Medical Act 1858, the outcome of over fifty years of pressure for regulation better suited to advances in medicine than the Tudor marketplace. Few reformers were happy with the Act. The Act did not create a unified profession. The Royal Colleges and the Society of Apothecaries retained a large part of their 'exalted' status. The emergent and numerous 'general practitioners' failed to achieve the representational democracy they sought. More ambitious proposals for a single regulator for all health professionals including midwives, veterinary surgeons, chemists and druggists proposed by the Associated Faculty in the debates leading up to the Apothecaries Act 1815 were ignored. Above all, the Medical Act 1858 did not even attempt to outlaw quackery. M J D Roberts suggests that relief that at last a medical reform Bill had been enacted after sixteen failed attempts since 1830[95] persuaded even that doughty proponent of reform Wakley that 'half a loaf was better than none'.[96]

Roberts comments that 'if there is a foundation of state recognition of the modern British medical profession, then the Act of 1858 is it'.[97] This is not to say that prior to 1858 the State had no concern with medicine. Tudor legislation discussed in Chapters 2 and 3 demonstrate the Crown's concern with healing. The 1858 Act created the framework for regulation of medical practitioners which despite many changes has endured, and has

---

94 W Moore 'Lancets and Libels' (2010) *British Medical Journal* 340.
95 And see I Waddington *The Medical Profession in the Industrial Revolution* (Gill and Macmillan Humanities Press, 1984) 53.
96 M J D Roberts 'The Politics of Professionalization: MPs, Medical Men and the 1858 Medical Act' (2009) 53 *Medical History* 37.
97 Ibid 37.

been the pattern for later legislation to regulate other health professionals, from nurses to opticians, and including certain practitioners of alternative medicine, for example, osteopaths. Even if the Law Commissions' proposals for a single regulator of all health and social care professions are implemented and the current Medical Act is replaced by a Health and Social Care Professions Act, many of the basic tenets of the 1858 Act will survive.

The Act marked a stepping stone from the ancient tripartite system and the domination of the medical corporations to a future in which the medical corporations retained influence, even if losing power. Examination of the Act reveals missed opportunities to develop a system of regulation more orientated to the protection of the public good and patients than defending doctors' interests.

Background to the 1858 Act[98]

The first section of this chapter demonstrated that even as the Apothecaries Act 1815 was being enacted, the tripartite division of the orthodox medical practitioners had become a legal fiction. Surgeon-apothecaries had emerged as general practitioners. In theory it was still the case that unless such a general practitioner was doubly licensed by both the Royal College of Surgeons and the Society of Apothecaries, he broke the law.[99] A surgeon acted illegally if he offered advice or provision of medicines i.e. undertook work traditionally assigned to the apothecary.[100] An apothecary broke the law if he undertook any surgery.[101] Neither surgeon nor apothecary could lawfully practise physic in London. Qualifications from the illustrious Scottish medical schools were not recognised in England. M J D Roberts notes that Queen Victoria's favourite Scottish physician, Dr Simpson, broke the letter of the law when he treated Her Majesty in London without being a Licentiate or Fellow of the College of Physicians.[102]

It gradually became apparent to all save those wholly invested in the tripartite division that the division simply did not make sense. The Select Committee on Medical Education in 1834 heard evidence from '[n]umerous witnesses ... who agreed that it was no longer possible to draw any clear distinction between medical and surgical practice.'[103] Inadequate medical

---

98 Waddington (n 95) provides an excellent account of the campaign for reform within the medical profession and the political debates preceding the Medical Act 1858.

99 Though an increasing number did seek such dual qualification: see Waddington ibid 14.

100 Ibid 13.

101 *Allison v Haydon* (1828) 172 English Reports 406.

102 M J D Roberts (n 96) 40.

103 Waddington (n 95) 11–12.

education was a primary factor in calls for medical reform. Increasingly, private anatomy and medical schools provided at least part of the aspiring students' training as did spending time in hospitals 'walking the wards'.[104]

In the clamour for change, general practitioners formed an apparently powerful lobby. In the capital, the London-based British Medical Association campaigned for:

> [A]bolition of the tripartite structure, the unification of all branches of practice and the establishment of a single controlling body which would be *elected by the whole profession* and within which all practitioners would enjoy equal status [my emphasis].[105]

The Provincial Medical and Surgical Association held its inaugural meeting in 1832. Waddington explains that the Provincial Association (unlike the London British Medical Association) was originally more concerned with 'friendly and scientific' debate than medical reform but that gradually reform came higher on their agenda.[106] In 1856, the Provincial Association extended its membership to London practitioners and (confusingly) renamed itself the British Medical Association. It is the renamed Provincial Association that is the forerunner of today's BMA.

The Colleges of Physicians and Surgeons remained largely opposed to any reform, and antipathetic to the claims of the general practitioners. Even if a member (licentiate) of one of the Colleges, the general practitioner was excluded from College Councils. The medical corporations remained locked into a system of privilege and monopoly which bore little resemblance to the actual provision of medical care.

The passing of the 1858 Act can partially be attributed to political concerns about public health, the devastating effect of epidemics of cholera and other infectious diseases, and the inadequacy of Poor Law medical care.[107] Sanitary reform became the business of the State and thus the competence and qualifications of medical practitioners was also a concern to government. In response to public health crises, a General Board of Health was established in 1854. In 1855, Dr John Simon was appointed Medical Officer to the Board, effectively the first Chief Medical Officer.[108] The Board's initial focus was primarily environmental, concerned with sanitation, clean water and decent living conditions. Simon campaigned

---

104 S W F Holloway 'Medical Education in England, 1830–1858: A Sociological Analysis' (1964) 49 *History* 299.
105 Waddington (n 95) 70.
106 Ibid 73–75.
107 M J D Roberts (n 96) 42–44.
108 S Sheard and L Donaldson *The Nation's Doctor: The Role of the Chief Medical Officer 1855–1998* (The Nuffield Trust, 2006).

for sanitary legislation and radical reform of the profession, playing a leading role in drafting the Bill introduced to Parliament by W F Cowper MP,[109] which became the 1858 Act.[110] Simon espoused the view that medical reform was not designed to protect professional interests but should be enacted in the 'service of the public'.[111] Simon's forthright opinions on medical privilege put him at odds with both the medical corporations seeking to preserve their ancient status and the general practitioners who wanted a regulatory body dominated by elected doctors. The Bill also faced trenchant opposition from those who argued that reform would impose state medicine 'at the expense of English liberties' contending that 'the country has already got a State religion and a State education and it was now about to get State physic'.[112]

The Medical Act 1858

The Medical Act 1858 brokered a compromise which enabled the medical corporations to retain their status and some of their authority while establishing a means of identifying the accredited medical 'man' and creating a framework for a more uniform system for regulating medical practice. Self-regulation survived but a body created by statute, the General Council of Medical Education and Registration of the United Kingdom,[113] soon generally referred to as the General Medical Council (GMC), became the national regulator of all the 'orthodox' medical professions, thus laying the ground for their eventual unification. The most important feature of the Act was the creation of the Medical Register identifying practitioners deemed to be 'qualified' to practise, i.e. meeting the conditions for registration set out in the Act. The Act did not proscribe or criminalise practice by unregistered healers. It protected the title of registered medical practitioner and allowed identification of those practitioners who met the criteria in the Act qualifying them for registration and the benefits registration conferred.

---

109 Waddington (n 95) 107.
110 See Waddington ibid 105–123 for an account of the unsuccessful Bills introduced in 1856 by T E Headlam MP and Lord Elcho, and the 1858 Bills sponsored by Tom Duncombe MP and a second Bill sponsored by Elcho. See also M J D Roberts (n 96) 45.
111 Ibid 40.
112 Tom Duncombe MP cited in M J D Roberts (n 96) 44.
113 The Council was formally renamed the General Medical Council by the Medical Act 1950, s 13.

Governance and the General Council[114]

The Act established a governing Council of twenty-four members. Membership provided for representation of the principal existing institutions regulating medical education and practice, that is the medical corporations and the universities across England, Scotland and Ireland. The Colleges and other stakeholders were required to nominate members of the Council. In all, the medical corporations nominated nine members, the universities eight, and six persons were to be nominated by the Privy Council. The twenty-fourth member was the President of the Council to be elected by the Council. Members representing the medical corporations were required to be registered medical practitioners under the Act. University nominees were not so required and in theory could have been lay people, as could the six Privy Council nominees. Roberts notes that it would have been possible for lay members nominated by the universities and the Privy Council to have a majority on the Council and that, while it was unlikely that the universities would choose lay representatives, it was assumed that the Privy Council would nominate laymen.[115] In the event, no lay person was appointed to the Council until 1926 when the Privy Council nominated Sir Edward Hilton Young. Not until the Medical Act 1950 was lay representation required. Effective lay membership (or lack thereof) was to be a source of controversy and public lack of faith in the GMC in the following century.[116]

Save for the election of the President by Council itself, Council membership was not by way of direct election. Members were in theory selected by their nominating body for their ability to participate in the regulation of practice and *not* to represent the interests of their own nominators or medical practitioners as a whole. The principle espoused by leading proponents of medical reform, notably Simon, that legislation should focus on 'service of the public' precluded the desire of the general practitioners that the Council should be a representative body. In Simon's judgement the General Council's duty was to regulate for the benefit of patients. Twenty-eight years later, Parliament sold the pass in the Medical Act 1886 which provided that five members of the Council should be directly elected by practitioners registered under the Act.[117] The proportion of elected members

114 E Finch 'The Centenary of the General Council of Medical Education and Registration of the United Kingdom' 1858–1958 (1958) 23 *Annals of the Royal College of Surgeons of England* 321.

115 M J D Roberts (n 96) 44.

116 Chief Medical Officer's Report *CMO's Report, Good Doctors: Safer Patients: Proposals to Strengthen the System to Assure and Improve the Performance of Doctors and to Protect the Safety of Patients* (Department of Health, 2006).

117 S 7, and see R Forbes 'The GMC Hitherto and Henceforth' (1951) 19 *Medico Legal Journal* 41.

grew incrementally and doctors came to believe that the GMC's core function was to represent, protect and campaign for doctors' interests. They demanded greater representation on the Council and at one stage withheld their fees.[118] Initially they were successful. In 1983, a bloated Council comprised 104 members with elected representatives of the profession in the majority. Success for the doctors' campaign was short-lived. The current Council comprises twelve members of whom half are doctors and half lay persons. All are appointed.[119] By the end of the twentieth century, criticism of the GMC for bias towards its own was commonplace. The Chief Medical Officer for England judged that the GMC was 'dominated by professional interest, rather than that of the patient'.[120] Had the 1858 Act been implemented differently, more in conformity with Simon's philosophy, a lay voice might have been heard much earlier, and had it eschewed direct election, the Council could have avoided capture by the professional interest at the expense of public welfare.

The Medical Register

In practice, for professionals and the public, the most important provisions of the 1858 Act relate to the Medical Register. The Register is the cornerstone of the Act and subsequent legislation regulating health workers. In the words of the Preamble to the Act the Register enabled those seeking medical care to identify 'qualified' practitioners. The word 'qualified' is misleading in that it might seem to indicate (1) that the 'doctor' in question was certified as fit to provide the care needed and (2) that all other persons practising any sort of health care were not qualified in the sense of not fit to offer that care. The Medical Act 1858 and its successors provided for a system enabling prospective patients, the courts and the public at large to identify accredited practitioners, practitioners who met the conditions entitling them to be entered in the Medical Register. Section 27 imposed an obligation on the Registrar of the General Council to maintain and publish annually, under the direction of the Council, a correct Register of all registered practitioners.

The 1858 Act did not confer on the General Council the right or obligation to determine fitness to practise. Clause 4 of the original Bill would have granted the Council power to determine what aspiring medical practitioners must study and how they should be examined. The Council, not the medical corporations, would have controlled medical education. Opposition to

---

118 See R Smith 'Profile of the GMC: 1978 and All That' (1989) 298 *British Medical Journal* 1297.

119 The GMC (Constitution) Amendment Order SI 1654 (2012).

120 Chief Medical Officer's Report (n 116) para 60.

the Bill co-ordinated by the said corporations forced Cowper to withdraw Clause 4. His attempt in a new Clause 16 to require that at the least no doctor could claim registered status unless he had been examined in both medicine and surgery also failed. Section 15 provided that every person who gained a qualification described in Schedule A of the Act was entitled to registration. Schedule A listed as such qualifications (inter alia) being a Fellow or Licentiate of one of medical corporations of England, Scotland and Ireland, or holding a doctorate or bachelor's degree from designated universities in the United Kingdom.[121] The Royal Colleges of England, Scotland and Ireland, the Society of Apothecaries, and designated universities retained largely, though not entirely, the power to determine how registered practitioners were educated and what a person needed to qualify for entry into the Register. A practitioner might train and qualify as an apothecary, surgeon or physician and that qualification entitled him to be registered under the 1858 Act.[122] A central tenet of Simon and Cowper's strategy to establish one single route to qualification was defeated. The Act's provision to recognise any United Kingdom university medical degree as sufficient to entitlement to registration (not just those of Oxford or Cambridge) indicated a nod to those who hoped for a more modern system of regulation. Section 28 required that the Colleges and other bodies report to the General Council the name of any member struck off the College lists. The Council could then (if they saw fit) direct that the name of that person be erased from the Medical Register.

At first glance, it appears that the medical corporations and the universities continued to control who was entitled to qualify as a registered practitioner and who should be barred from continuing to practise. The seeds of more radical dilution of the authority of the medical corporations can be found in Sections 18, 20 and 23 in relation to education, and Section 29 in relation to fitness to practise and medical discipline. To deal with education first, Section 18 empowered the General Council to require any of the bodies mentioned in Schedule A to provide information about their course of study and or examinations. Section 20 provided that if the Council were to determine that any curriculum and/or examination was:

> [N]ot such as to secure the Possession by Persons obtaining such Qualification of the requisite Knowledge and Skill for the Practice of their Profession, it shall

---

121 The Act removed the anomaly that practitioners entitled to practise in one part of the UK were not entitled to practise in another of the nations which comprised the UK.

122 S 17 provided that any person who was actually practising medicine in England before the Act came into force on 1 August 1858 was entitled to be registered.

be lawful for such General Council to represent the same to Her Majesty's most Honourable Privy Council.

On receipt that of such representations, Section 21 empowered the Privy Council to order that the qualification granted by the body in question for a period specified in the order no longer 'confer any Right to be registered' under the Act. The order could be revoked if and when the body satisfied the Council that their curricula had made the necessary provision for knowledge and skill required by the Council. The Council could thus override the freedom of the medical corporations and the universities to prescribe their own curricula. For example, had the curriculum set by the Royal College of Surgeons to qualify as a licentiate of the College been judged by the GMC to be inadequate to demonstrate fitness to practise, and the Privy Council had ordered that the College's qualifications for the time being no longer entitled those holding the College qualifications for registration, the licentiate could not be entered on the register. He still qualified for the College's title.

A further limitation on the powers of the medical corporations and universities to determine what entitled a practitioner to be entered on the register is found in Section 23. Should it appear to the GMC that any of the bodies entitled under the Act to grant qualifications imposed an obligation 'to adopt or refrain from adopting the Practice of any particular Theory of Medicine or Surgery as a Test or Condition of admitting him to Examination or granting him a Certificate', again the GMC was empowered to report the body in question to the Privy Council. If after due warning the body failed to comply with an order from the Privy Council, the Privy Council could revoke the offending body's power to confer on its members the right to registration. Section 23 sought to neutralise the critics of 'State medicine'. Many peers and MPs dabbled in unorthodox medicine such as osteopathy and herbalism; Section 23 retained the patient's 'liberty/responsibility to remain a free agent in the medical market place'.[123]

The Act makes no express reference to discipline. The medical corporations retained the right to discipline their own members. Section 29 described as 'half a dozen inconspicuous lines'[124] bestowed on the General Council a power independent of the medical corporations and universities to strike off the register any practitioner convicted of a criminal offence or any practitioner who 'shall after due Inquiry be judged by the General Council

---

123 M J D Roberts (n 96) 47.
124 W K Pyke-Lees *The Centenary of the General Medical Council 1858–1958: The History and Present Work of the Council* (Spottiswoode, Ballantyne & Co Ltd, 1958), quoted in R G Smith *Medical Discipline: The Professional Conduct Jurisdiction of the General Medical Council 1858–1990* (Clarendon Press, 1994) 1.

to have *been guilty of infamous Conduct in any professional Respect* (my emphasis)'. R G Smith notes that Section 29 was only mentioned once in parliamentary debate on the Act in a comment by Mr Walpole that the Council if responsible for the Register must have 'some authority to supervise and control'.[125] Section 29 became the most controversial provision of the 1858 Act and its successors.

Given that, to the annoyance of many orthodox practitioners, the Act had not prohibited unregistered practitioners from practising medicine, how did the Act 'police' medical practice? It worked on a balance of carrot and stick. By way of carrot, Section 31 provided that every registered medical practitioner was entitled to sue for any reasonable charges in respect of professional attendance and the cost of any medicine supplied. An apothecary registered under the Act could lawfully and openly charge for his time and advice. Harking back to the past, Section 31 contained a provision permitting the College of Physicians to pass a bye-law prohibiting Fellows or Members of the College from suing their patients for non-payment of fees. If any physician sought to defy the bye-law and sue for debt, the bye-law could be pleaded as a defence. The rationale of this weird renunciation of a right to recover debts lay yet again in the College's obsession with status. Gentlemen did not sell their services like mere tradesmen.[126] They were not paid, but graciously received an honorarium.[127]

Section 36 enacted that certain posts in public service such as medical officers in the military, public hospitals, lunatic asylums (*sic*) gaols and poor law doctors, could only be held by registered practitioners. Given the low pay and unpopularity of such posts outside the armed forces, this provision was less an incentive for registered practitioners to take up such a post, but rather an attempt to prevent public health authorities engaging the cheapest man they could find to do the job regardless of qualification or competence.[128]

As to stick, Section 40 made it a criminal offence for a person to 'wilfully and falsely' pretend to be registered under the Act or use any name or title implying that he was so registered.[129] Unregistered healers, quacks, empirics and alternative medical practitioners were not barred from practice. They must not claim to be 'approved' by the state in the sense of meeting the

---

125 Smith ibid 35.
126 Waddington (n 95) 122.
127 J H Baker 'Counsellors and Barristers: An Historical Study' (1969) 27 *Cambridge Law Journal* 205, 224–229.
128 K Price *Medical Negligence in Victorian Britain: The Crisis of Care under the English Poor Law c. 1834–1900* (Bloomsbury Academic, 2015) 10–12.
129 And see s 39.

requirements of the Act as a qualified medical practitioner. Section 40 operated as carrot as well as stick in that it gave registered practitioners a status that might well benefit their practice.

Reasons for rejecting criminalising non-orthodox healers so fervently desired by many reformers were largely practical. Defining practising medicine was no easier in 1858 than when the College of Physicians attempted to assert an absolute monopoly of the practice of 'physic'. What of the mother bathing her child's lacerated knee and applying a home-made remedy? There were some medical reformers who contended that a mother should be 'forbidden to administer castor oil or Godfrey's cordial to their children without [medical] sanction'.[130] Opponents of 'state medicine' took a different view regarding any limitation on the kind of healing patients might choose as undermining a free and open market,[131] a criticism echoed today in debates about consumer choice and individuals' freedom to make their own judgements about health care, just as we decide what to have for supper. Free market critics also contended state intervention would undermine people's ability to exercise self-care. Victorian critics of the 1858 Act share with their descendants a dim view of the nanny state.

Nothing in the Act prevented individuals paying for their own care opting for the healer of their choice. Only those receiving treatment from Poor Law doctors or in a public institution had no choice but to receive their care from a registered practitioner. The Medical Register at one level simply provided a reliable means of identifying practitioners deemed fit to practise orthodox medicine. Herbalists could continue to practise as long as they did not claim registered status. They were debarred from fraud not practice. Relatively few prosecutions have been brought for falsely pretending to have registered status, and this may in part be because traditional healers and practitioners of alternative medicine such as homeopathy have no desire to purport to be orthodox practitioners. Their claim is to offer a different form of healing.

---

130 M J D Roberts (n 96) 42 quoting J Chapman 'Medical Despotism' *Westminster Review*, April 1856 9 (n.s) 530, 536.
131 Roberts ibid 44.

5

Medical litigation

Doctors in court

Clinical negligence litigation commands much attention in modern medical law and generates a degree of acrimony between lawyers and doctors. Health professionals warn of a 'malpractice crisis'. Patients are not happy either with the system for compensating harm caused by medical negligence, or processes for holding health professionals to account for poor treatment.[1] None of these concerns are new.

Writing about cases from the fourteenth century, J B Post noted:

> The medieval medical practitioner, *like his fellows of every age*, was vulnerable to accusations of negligence [my emphasis]. The least fortunate, or perhaps the most negligent, might find themselves liable to public prosecution, despite some recognition that treatment was hazardous. More commonly, the doctor might face a private lawsuit from a dissatisfied patient.[2]

Carole Rawcliffe commented: 'Because of the dangers involved in even simple operations and the unpredictable effects of many drugs in common use, the medieval surgeon ran a constant risk of being sued.'[3]

It is important to note one respect in which it might appear that the medieval or early modern practitioner was less at risk than his modern counterpart. Should the patient die as a result of his negligence, no one else could sue until the Fatal Accidents Act 1846 introduced claims for dependency.[4]

---

1 M Brazier, E Cave and R Heywood *Medicine, Patients and the Law* (7th edn) (Manchester University Press, 2023) Chapter 9.

2 J B Post 'Doctor versus Patient: Two Fourteenth-Century Lawsuits' (1972) 16 *Medical History* 296.

3 C Rawcliffe *Medicine and Society in Later Medieval England* (Sandpiper Books, 1995) 42.

4 J W Willcock *Laws Relating to the Medical Profession with an Account of the Rise and Progress of the Various Orders* (J & W T Clarke, 1830).

In this chapter, I examine aspects of the history of redress for medical negligence. While much of this chapter will consider what we now style clinical negligence litigation, claims for compensation by aggrieved patients were not the only means by which healers were held to account for poor treatment. The College of Physicians' Censorial Hearings, better known for their role in pursuing rebellious practitioners such as Drs Bonham and Groenvelt, provided redress for dissatisfied patients in London.[5] And the other medical corporations offered versions of 'Alternative Dispute Resolution'.[6] After the introduction of the 'new Poor Law' in 1834[7] procedures to deal with medical negligence within Poor Law health care differed markedly from other procedures for complaints and redress in a manner unjust to both pauper patients and Poor Law doctors. I shall not deal further with the Poor Law. Kim Price's book *Medical Negligence in Victorian Britain* is a compelling analysis of a neglected area of medical law.[8] The sheer volume of case law and historical literature means that within one chapter I can do no more than introduce the questions posed by 'old medical law'. One significant matter requires especial note. *Mala praxis* (malpractice) was a crime for which a practitioner could be gaoled.

Mala praxis

Medical practitioners have recently become very concerned about the growing numbers of criminal prosecutions of doctors and nurses for gross negligence manslaughter.[9] Their predecessors had more cause to be wary of the criminal law and the risk of imprisonment. *Mala praxis* was a criminal offence even if the patient survived. In London, as Chapter 3 recounts, the College of Physicians had the authority to summon, punish and imprison any healer accused of *mala praxis*, regardless of whether they were members of the College. Powers granted by the Act of 1522 'The Privilege and Authority of Physicians in London' were confirmed by a 1553 Act in the

5 See M Pelling and F White *Medical Conflicts in Early Modern London: Patronage, Physicians and Irregular Practitioners 1550–1640* (Clarendon Press, 2003); Database: *Physicians and Irregular Practitioners in London 1550–1640*. Originally published by the Centre for Metropolitan History, London, 2004. www.british-hist ory.ac.uk/no-series/london-physicians/1550-1640.
6 See M P Cosman 'Medieval Medical Malpractice: The Dicta and the Dockets' (1973) 49 *Bulletin of the New York Academy of Medicine* 22, 23.
7 Poor Law Amendment Act 1834.
8 K Price *Medical Negligence in Victorian Britain: The Crisis of Care under the English Poor Law c 1834–1900* (Bloomsbury Academic, 2015).
9 J Vaughan, O Quick and D Griffiths 'Medical Manslaughter: Where Next?' (2018) 100 *Bulletin of the Royal College of Surgeons England* 251.

reign of Queen Mary 'An Act touching the Corporation of Physicians in London',[10] an Act which was only repealed by the Statute Law Revision Act 1948.

Outside London beyond the jurisdiction of the College, *mala praxis* was described by Chief Justice Holt in 1695 as 'a great misdemeanour and offence at common law'.[11] Writing in 1765, Blackstone concurred with Holt. It is unclear whether Blackstone is expressly addressing criminal liability for he immediately goes on to say that a patient harmed by medical neglect has a civil claim for damages, then described as an action on the case, in the same manner as for 'any other personal wrongs and injuries'[12] and he locates this statement in Volume III of his *Commentaries* which deals with civil, not criminal, matters. Writing in 1830, Willcock divided malpractice into four categories; wilful, avaricious, negligent and ignorant. He says of negligent malpractice that it is 'generally regarded as the subject of a civil action rather than criminal prosecution' 'yet were a very gross case to come under the consideration of the court there is no doubt that it would be treated as a great misdemeanour whether it was a licensed or unlicensed practitioner'.[13] What Willcock meant by gross, whether he alluded to especially gross *conduct* on the part of the practitioner, or a particularly gross *outcome* (i.e. the death of the patient) is not clear. He goes on to say 'it has been justly observed that in the most serious case of this kind the offence of itself will defeat the civil remedy by destroying the only person who would be entitled to sue.' In highlighting the inability of the deceased's family or anyone else to bring a claim for compensation for loss caused to them by the fatal negligence of the defendant, a state of affairs not remedied until 1846 by the Fatal Accidents Act, it may be that Willcock is addressing cases where it was the fatal outcome which moved *mala praxis* from the civil to the criminal sphere in the form of gross negligence manslaughter.

Litigation crisis: medieval 'style'?

US judge B Abbott Goldberg wrote that 'some of our present problems [with medical litigation] replicate those of the thirteenth and fourteenth

---

10 STAT 1 Mariae 2 c 9.
11 *Dr Groenvelt's Case* (1695) 91 English Reports 1038, 1039.
12 W Blackstone *Commentaries on the Laws of England* Book III (Oxford University Press, 2016) Chapter 8 'Of Wrongs and their Remedies: Respecting the Rights of Persons'.
13 Willcock (n 4) 89.

centuries'.[14] I start by setting the scene from those distant centuries, a scene depicting a 'medieval litigation crisis':

> Grossly inflated claims for damages were a standard feature of legal life, but sometimes juries felt such sympathy for those who had experienced pain and mutilation that they recommended generous settlements.[15]

Of the three orthodox medical professions, the surgeons lived in the greatest fear of litigation. There are very few reported cases of actions against physicians. The vulnerability of the surgeon is unlikely to be because surgeons were less competent than physicians or apothecaries, nor did physicians enjoy any immunity from suit. Willcock stated that the 'physician is responsible for his want of skill, as well as the surgeon or apothecary'.[16] He dismisses as erroneous two arguments advanced by physicians. First, physicians contended that as (like barristers) their fees were honorary, a physician was not 'responsible'. Willcock expresses grave doubt about the argument that fees were purely honorary and makes it clear that even were there no contract physicians could still be liable in an action on the case, a claim that we would now describe as an action for negligence. Second, Willcock rejects the claim that the physicians' profession is to judge the disease and the remedy and that the law holds no man responsible for an error in judgement. The crucial question was whether the error was negligent.[17]

The differences in vulnerability to litigation between physician and surgeon lie at least in part in causation and difficulties of proof.[18] Should a physician attend, sniff the patient's urine, consider his astrological chart and advise on diet and medicines, proving that the diagnosis and/or prescription were incompetently given *and caused* the harm of which the patient complained was challenging. Unless the physician prescribed a toxic or unwholesome medicine, a claim against a physician would be likely to be based on a plea that the physician had proffered incompetent advice and as a result the plaintiff had suffered the loss of a chance of recovery: i.e. had the defendant provided proper care the patient would have been more likely to recover. Such cases of loss of a chance remain difficult to establish in the twenty-first century.

---

14 B Abbott Goldberg 'Horseshoers, Doctors and Judges and the Law on Medical Competence' (1978) 9 *Pacific Law Journal* 107, 113.
15 Rawcliffe (1995) (n 3) 142.
16 Willcock (n 4) 106.
17 Ibid.
18 Ibid.

A rare example from 1388 of an action against a physician is *Skyrne v Butolf*.[19] The defendant, described as a 'leech', undertook to 'cure' the plaintiff of ringworm, and applied medicines to the plaintiff. The plaintiff claimed that the medicines were 'contrary to the disease' making him worse not better, forcing him to seek another leech to cure him. There is no record of the outcome of the case.

Claims against surgeons were more straightforward. Proving that a surgeon bungled an amputation of the leg below the knee and as a result the patient later lost the whole leg was much easier. There is substantial evidence that surgeons were extremely anxious about claims by patients; anxieties not solely prompted by fears of being sued in the common law courts. Rawcliffe addresses religious factors in play. A medieval surgeon whose patient died in the course of surgery might fear that the Church would hold him to be an accessory to murder, or mutilation where the patient survived but horribly injured.[20] Ecclesiastical censure was as much to be feared as any attempt at secular redress. It seems that the religious concerns waned over time but acted as a deterrent to surgeons seen to be taking risks solely for gain, a stance perhaps to be commended. Less helpfully, the spectre of the disapproval of the Church resulted in surgeons becoming unduly risk averse and practising defensive medicine. The wise counsel of the cleric Robert Courson was often ignored. He advised that while surgeons should avoid unnecessarily dangerous procedures especially in the hope of financial gain, the surgeon was 'duty bound' to carry out procedures with a reasonable chance of success.[21]

The combination of factors which made surgeons concerned about litigation resembles arguments that litigation today is damaging medical care and promoting defensive medicine. A malpractice suit could be ruinous, especially as many surgeons made relatively modest incomes.[22] In 1405, London surgeon Nicholas Bradmore was ordered to pay damages of £4 (approximately £2451 in today's money) to a plaintiff who sued him for injuring his thumb.[23] Surgeons complained that 'duplicitous' patients used allegations of negligence to avoid payment and blacken the surgeon's name.[24] In this

---

19 J Baker (ed) *Baker and Milsom Sources of English Legal History: Private Law to 1750* (2nd edn) (Oxford University Press, 2010) 405.
20 Rawcliffe (1995) (n 3) 71–74.
21 Ibid 71.
22 Rawcliffe (1995) (n 3) 141–142; and see C Rawcliffe 'The Profits of Practice: The Wealth and Status of Medical Men in Later Medieval England' (1998) *Social History of Medicine* 1.
23 *Select Cases in the Court of King's Bench under Richard II, Henry IV and Henry V* ed G O Sayles (Selden Society) LXXXVIII 1971 162–163.
24 Rawcliffe (1995) (n 3) 141–142.

respect a significant difference between the medieval and the twenty-first century surgeon is that in the majority of cases, the relationship of surgeon and patient was contractual. A dissatisfied patient could opt not to pay the surgeon's bill placing the onus on the doctor to initiate legal proceedings to recover the debt. The defendant patient would defend non-payment and possibly counterclaim alleging that the surgeon had treated him negligently. Rawcliffe suggests that the cost of taking patients to court was a major factor in the perception of crisis held by many surgeons.[25]

It is impossible to prove conclusively one way or the other if claims brought by patients were often dishonest or frivolous, if there was a crisis, as opposed to simply an uncomfortable state of affairs for practitioners. The surgeons and the Guilds to which they belonged certainly took actions prompted by perception of crisis. Their objective was to keep surgeons and disputes about surgical practice out of the common law courts. The Fellowship of Surgeons and the London Barbers banned members from taking each other to the common law courts without the permission of the masters or wardens.[26] The surgeons' dirty linen was not to be washed in public. Deterring surgeons from internecine warfare does not of itself appear unreasonable but could be seen as an attempt to cover up poor practice, the forerunner of the conspiracy of silence which in the mid-twentieth century made it extremely difficult for a patient to find a medical expert willing to testify on their behalf. From 1435, London surgeons were required to consult the masters and wardens before taking on any especially risky case and were heavily fined if they broke the rule.[27] This measure may be seen as common sense and beneficial to surgeons and patients. Less patient-friendly were practices whereby surgeons required to be paid in advance. The surgeon shifted the onus to the patient to initiate legal proceedings to recover money paid and any compensation for injury rather than the doctor having to sue for debt when his fees went unpaid after the operation.

A further measure to avoid litigation in 1394, described by Post[28] and Rawcliffe,[29] was to require that before surgery the patient and his family undertook to relieve the surgeon of any legal responsibility for the consequence of the surgery 'for the stane' (bladder stones) even if the patient died. In what I assume is the same case cited by both historians, the patient and the surgeon were both barber-surgeons. Asking a patient and family to exempt a doctor from any liability in advance of treatment looks highly

---

25 Ibid.
26 Ibid 137.
27 Ibid 71.
28 Post (n 2) 296.
29 Rawcliffe (1995) (n 3) 141.

unethical at first sight and today would contravene consumer protection regulations. Further consideration prompts a somewhat different judgement. Without antibiotics, anaesthesia or modern instruments the surgery was highly dangerous. Without surgery, the patient suffered excruciating agony. The patient begged his colleague to attempt the operation.[30] The case may be seen as akin to current controversies relating to innovative treatment in relation to which it has been argued that fear of litigation deters medical practitioners from undertaking innovative surgery or therapy, even with the patient's consent and where no other treatment option would appear to be likely to succeed.[31]

Alternative dispute resolution (ADR) is frequently discussed today as a cheaper and more effective means of resolving disputes about care between patients and health professionals. The craft Guilds were 'almost without exception'[32] determined to establish ADR to resolve disputes between craftsmen and clients as well as between Guild members. Guilds regulating surgeons (and apothecaries) shared that determination. Rawcliffe notes that malpractice suits were often referred to a panel of expert surgeons for arbitration. She goes on to add that while lay plaintiffs might well fear bias, the Guilds were ready to find against members shown to be incompetent or 'unduly' venal.[33]

The mists of medico-legal history

While there is evidence that claims pursued by dissatisfied patients were frequent in the medieval and early modern era, thorough critical analysis of the cases is difficult, save for expert legal historians. It is a difficulty which applies to other areas of 'old law' especially abortion law discussed in Chapter 9. I address the problem here because it is most acute in relation to medical negligence case law. Searching for case law, the first difficulty encountered is the random nature of law reporting and an approach to reporting which results in a product which bears little resemblance to a modern law report. Even where reports of cases are more easily accessible, they are not wholly reliable. Once a report is identified, the reader will often find the report is written predominantly in Norman French with insertions

30 Ibid 71.
31 N Hoppe and J Miola 'Innovation in Medicine Through Degeneration in Law? A Critical Perspective on the Medical Innovation Bill' (2014) 14 *Medical Law International* 266.
32 Rawcliffe (1995) (n 3) 137.
33 Ibid 137–139.

of Latin and some medieval English. If the reader can master the languages, the script itself may be hard to decipher. Finally, the key role that procedure played in the common law until the abolition of the forms of action in the Common Law Procedure Act 1852 and the Judicature Act 1873 impedes a clear exposition of principle in many judgments.

Early law reports

The earliest 'law reports' are found in Plea Rolls of the Court of Common Pleas (the King's Court which heard most civil claims). Post explains that the Plea Rolls are definitive and:

> [D]espite the vagaries of medieval spelling and the stilted formulae of law Latin the interest of the litigants and the professionalism of the clerks ensured a high degree of consistency and accuracy.[34]

The Plea Rolls only recorded the claim and the defence with no discussion of the points of law or even the full judgment. The Rolls might be said to be a list of proceedings with little information on the content of those proceedings. For more details the reader must turn to the Year Books. The Year Books offer more information about legal arguments and judgments but vary immensely in detail and reliability. Post comments:

> Names of persons and places, and similar details of fact were not wilfully corrupted, but they were secondary to the legal points involved, and were often reduced to initials, changed in error, or omitted altogether.[35]

Winfield gives a full account of the challenges of using these ancient documents and warns:

> The form and purpose of the earlier Year Books are so unlike those of a current law report that the term is misapplied to them, unless we give it a meaning no more definite than a partial narrative of a legal proceeding.[36]

For the non-specialist the English Reports are a boon providing a reprint of previously reported cases and bringing together a huge number of case reports from other sets of reports from 1220 to 1867. The English Reports are now available both in print and online but as Dwyer points out searching the rather poor index and using the online access is far from easy and

---

34 Post (n 2) 297.
35 Ibid.
36 P H Winfield 'Early Attempts at Reporting Cases' (1924) 40 *Law Quarterly Review* 316, 316.

cannot be guaranteed to be comprehensive.[37] Dwyer identifies other problems. The original choice of cases to be reported was random and very much up to the individual reporter. The amount of detail varies. The decision on what to reprint was a 'commercial one separate from the reporter's original basis for choosing which cases to reprint',[38] and the quality of reports prepared before 1750 was variable.[39]

Problems of access and content, not to speak of constraints of time, mean that a comprehensive analysis of individual cases is rarely feasible and that the possibility of error in the reports is high. Law reports, including very early reports, do provide, however, more than sufficient material from which both to identify the emerging obligations imposed on medical practitioners, be they physicians, surgeons, apothecaries or other healers, and to offer a picture of medical litigation across the centuries.

Procedure ruled supreme

The common law of England was dominated by rules of procedure to the extent that development of substantive principles of law gave the 'look of being gradually secreted in the interstices of procedure'.[40] Practically, in terms of claims against medical practitioners, should a plaintiff wish to escape the local courts,[41] he needed to obtain a writ to remove his claim from the local courts to the King's courts of common law. To obtain such a writ he must identify the right form of action and serve the right writ. Select the wrong form of action or fail to comply with some other rule of practice and your case was lost. When a case went to trial much of the argument and the judgment focused on procedure, not the merits of the claim. The forms of action dominated common law until abolished by the Common Law Procedure Act 1852.

The forms of action did not sit comfortably with the real issues in play in relation to medical litigation, and despite Lord Atkin's injunction that when the 'ghosts of the past stand in the path of justice ... clanking their medieval chains the proper course for the judge is to pass through them undeterred',[42] Atkin's ghosts still bedevil modern medical law. The earliest writ in medical negligence cases was trespass *vi et armis et contra pacem regis* (by

---

37 D M Dwyer 'Expert Evidence in the English Civil Courts 1550–1800' (2007) 28 *Journal of Legal History* 93.

38 Ibid 95–96.

39 J Baker *An Introduction to English Legal History* (5th edn) (Oxford University Press, 2019) 194–195.

40 H Maine *Early Law and Custom* (1883) 389.

41 Goldberg (n 14) 113.

42 *United Australia Ltd v Barclays Bank* [1941] AC 29.

force and arms and contrary to the King's Peace). Despite the language of force, trespass *vi et armis* soon came to embrace any direct physical interference with another person, what we now call battery. Trespass *vi et armis* thus addressed certain sorts of harm inflicted by medical practitioners, for example, a surgeon acting to amputate a leg without consent or operating grossly incompetently. The key point was whether the injury was directly inflicted on the plaintiff. The distinction between trespass and negligence evolved much later.[43] Imaginative lawyers sought to squeeze a case into trespass. The King's courts developed a further writ of trespass on the case, also described as the action on the case, or just case. To limit confusion, I refer to trespass *vi et armis* as trespass, and trespass on the case as the action on the case. The action on the case lay in relation to injury and damage inflicted indirectly. If the incompetent surgeon wrongly did not amputate a gangrenous leg, or an apothecary supplied unsuitable or contaminated medicines, the patient's redress lay in the action on the case.

One crucial difference was that while in trespass all that needed to be proven was that the defendant unlawfully interfered with the person of the plaintiff, in the action on the case, the plaintiff had to prove that the acts or omissions of the defendant caused them injury creating problems of causation which endure in modern claims for clinical negligence. Thus, in claims relating to 'informed consent' the descendant of trespass *vi et armis*, the tort of battery, was seen by patients as a better option than negligence, the 'child' of the action on the case.[44] The patient suing in battery did not have to prove that, had he been adequately informed, he would not have consented to treatment. Having limited the scope of battery to cases where there was such a lack of disclosure that there was no information at all about the nature or purpose of proposed treatment, or consent was vitiated by fraud,[45] modern judges sought to develop the law to recognise and protect patient autonomy within the tort of negligence. They found themselves forced to modify, even distort, the usual principles of proof of causation.[46] Another 'ghost' of the forms of action remains to haunt us. The words 'battery' and 'trespass' carry connotations of deliberate wrongdoing motivated by intent to harm,[47] contributing to the opinion held by some medical practitioners today that the profession is unfairly treated by the law.

---

43 P H Winfield 'The History of Negligence in the Law of Torts' (1926) 42 *Law Quarterly Review* 184.
44 T K Feng 'Failure of Medical Advice: Trespass or Negligence' (1997) 7 *Legal Studies* 19.
45 *Chatterton v Gerson* [1981] 1 All ER 457.
46 *Chester v Afshar* [2004] UKHL 41.
47 A Maclean 'The Doctrine of Informed Consent: Does It Exist and Has It Crossed the Atlantic?' (2014) 24 *Legal Studies* 386, 399.

Only relatively recently did a distinction emerge between intentional torts of trespass to the person and the tort of negligence. One other matter of procedure should be noted before examining historical case law, and that is the role of the jury. Almost every 'old' case relating to litigation between patients and their healers was heard by judge and jury.[48] As with criminal cases today, the judge directed the jury on the law and questions of fact and assessment of damages were left to the jury. In 1965, in *Ward v James*[49] the Court of Appeal finally ruled that only in the most exceptional circumstances should a personal injuries claim be heard by a jury. Judges alone would decide such claims. Two consequences ensue from the abolition of a role for the jury. First, it may be the case that juries were more likely to be swayed by sympathy with the patient and were not too concerned with legal niceties.[50] Second, in cases where the hearing was before judge and jury, it is harder to elucidate the points of principle from a direction to a jury, than from a modern judgment.

Long ago

Identifying the first lawsuit that might be seen as ancestor of clinical negligence claims is way beyond my skills. It can be said with certainty that it was *not*, as once claimed, *Walden (or Dalton) v Mareschal* in 1369.[51] The 'patient' in that case was a horse and the defendant a horse-doctor whom it was alleged had negligently killed the plaintiff's horse.[52] Cases from the fourteenth century which do relate to human patients offer those 'first glimmers of the modern law of the quality of medical care'.[53] Goldberg quips that a degree of flippancy in the Year Books encouraged humorous analogies between surgeons and horse-doctors.[54] The analogy highlights a persistent theme in clinical negligence – is there any difference between the standard of care between the human and the horse-doctor just because one treated people?

---

48 Note that *Bolam* itself was heard by judge and jury and that the (in)famous principle it was said to embody derived from MacNair J's direction to the jury: *Bolam v Friern Hospital Management Committee* [1957] 1 WLR 582.
49 [1965] 2 WLR 623. CA.
50 H Teff 'The Standard of Care in Medical Negligence – Moving on from Bolam?' (1988) 18 *Oxford Journal of Legal Studies* 473, 474.
51 Baker (n 39) 351.
52 Goldberg (n 14) 115.
53 Ibid.
54 Goldberg (n 14) 117.

Early reported cases relating to negligent treatment of humans include *The Oculist's Case* in 1329 (Eyre of Nottingham).[55] The action was heard by the King's Justices on circuit and concerned a claim that the defendant had undertaken to 'cure' the patient of an eye condition. Alas in the attempt he 'destroyed' his eye. No full account of the resolution of the case appears to survive. Procedural objections were as ever raised, but Ibbetson notes that the court seems to have been concerned with the substantive issue of whether a doctor could be liable at all. He quotes Denum J's reluctance to hold doctors or other 'men of occupation' – 'men of mystery' – liable for professional incompetence.[56] Ibbetson identifies a case from 1363/4, *Broadmeadow v Rushenden*.[57] John Broadmeadow and his wife alleged that the defendant surgeon had undertaken to treat the wife's injured arm, but did so so negligently that she lost her hand. The jury returned a verdict for the defendant. Goldberg[58] and Willcock,[59] while giving the case different names, note another case from 1374 on similar facts to *Broadmeadow*. The same case under yet a third name is addressed by Baker and Milsom who adopt Kiralfy's identification of the case as *Stratton v Swanlond*.[60] The plaintiffs alleged that a surgeon, Morton, had undertaken to cure the wife's injured hand. The defendant's negligence resulted in making the hand 'so much worse that she is now maimed'. Defects in the pleadings, the failure to plead the place where the undertaking to treat was given, resulted in the loss of the claim in trespass. The crime of maim is addressed in Chapter 7.

Retainers and contracts for services

Most people in late medieval England in need of medical care arranged such care when necessity arose and domestic remedies had failed. Rich and noble families and the great institutions retained the services of their own medical advisers, pre-eminently though not exclusively physicians. The retained practitioner, like his legal colleagues, was paid an annuity in return for promising and providing medical care as required by his patron in a contract for his services. The first duty of a retained doctor in noble or ecclesiastical

---

55 Baker and Milsom (n 19) 381.
56 D Ibbetson *A Historical Introduction to the Law of Obligations* (Oxford University Press, 1999) 45.
57 (1364) Baker and Milsom (n 19) 400.
58 Goldberg (n 14) 115–117 '*Un home post bre de Trespass sur son cas devers un J mort surgeon*'.
59 J W Willcock (n 4) s p ccxxi '... *v J Morton*'.
60 Baker and Milsom (n 19) 402.

service was to his patron. Patrons were often lax about payment.[61] Royal bills often went unpaid. The benefit to the physician may have been the ability to advertise his connections rather on the lines of modern businesses competing to claim their company is 'By Appointment to His Majesty'. The amounts paid to retained practitioners varied greatly.[62] Legal proceedings arising from disputes about the terms of the retainer are among the earliest recorded cases addressing medical negligence and the duties of medical practitioners.

Post describes two cases from the fourteenth century.[63] Discovering and interpreting what Post described as the 'traces' of medieval medical litigation is challenging. As we have seen, even ascertaining the names of the parties can be problematic. Post's first case related to an action brought by a physician whom Post identifies as Master Geoffrey Dauratus. Master Geoffrey sued the abbot of St Peters, Gloucester, for arrears in the payment of the annuity agreed in 1298. The 'contract' stated that the plaintiff was to be paid four marks twice a year for his services in 'medical treatment'. The agreement provided that the plaintiff would carry out treatment 'faithfully whenever so requested by [the abbot] in case of urgent need'. The abbot would meet reasonable travel expenses. The defendant abbot contended that the contract was void because Master Geoffrey had failed to carry out his duty to attend when the abbot fell ill. He became ill in a town 'only eight leagues' from where the plaintiff was at the time. He sent for Master Geoffrey who 'did not bother to attend (*ad ipsum Abbaten venire non curavit*)'.[64] The plaintiff argued 'rather half-heartedly'[65] that he had not been summoned and that, if he had, no expenses had been sent with the messenger as the contract required.[66] The verdict cannot be traced though Post concludes that the plaintiff probably succeeded. This is despite the fact that the judges honed in on the distance Master Geoffrey would have had to travel, the Chief Justice commenting that eight leagues was not far to journey and so advance payment of travel costs was not needed. Post comments that this case was 'treated as little different from numerous other examples of retained advisers, usually lawyers' who sued for non-payment of an agreed annuity.

---

61 Rawcliffe (1995) (n 3) 141.
62 Rawcliffe (1998) (n 22): note though that payments were often made in kind and that where the physician was also a cleric he might be rewarded by the grant of a living.
63 Post (n 2).
64 Ibid 297.
65 Ibid 298.
66 A plea by the defendant that expenses had been sent was ruled out of time.

Post's second case concerned one of the most eminent physicians of his time, Master Simon Bredon.[67] Simon Bredon was a cleric as well as a physician. In 1361 he was retained as a medical adviser by a priory at Lewes. Post sets out the 'deed of appointment' granting Bredon £20 a year, and free accommodation if wanted in return for 'good and praiseworthy service and counsel to us and our monastery performed and to be performed henceforward'. In 1365, Bredon started legal proceedings to recover unpaid sums of £30 due under the deed, and £100 in damages. The monastery's defence was that Bredon had not performed his obligations under the deed. In 1364, the prior fell ill and summoned Bredon to attend him and undertook to meet his expenses. The defence stated Bredon was at the time in practice about twelve leagues (eighteen miles) away. Bredon refused to attend or send any advice or medicines and the priory cancelled his appointment.

Post painstakingly pieced together the proceedings. Certain factual matters were pleaded, that Bredon himself was ill and could not travel, and that the annuity was not for medical services but rather for resigning a living wanted by the priory. My concern is with the judges' analyses of the deed and what they tell us about the obligations of physicians. First, Bredon argued that unless there was a specific obligation to travel, the physician was only bound to provide medical services in the place where he pursued his practice. Second, he contended that the message seeking aid did not say what the illness suffered by the prior might be, and third (extraordinarily) that nothing in the deed specified that the plaintiff's services should be medical. That final claim was dismissed cursorily. Cavendish CJ said simply that if you retained a lawyer the assumption was that his duty was to provide legal services and if you engage a physician the assumption was that he undertakes to provide medical services. In relation to travel one of the judges (Finchden) noted that a legal adviser was not required to travel to the client unless the agreement expressly so required. Finchden also suggested that no lawyer would be required to advise without some indication of the matter on which his advice was sought. The Chief Justice distinguished the doctor from the lawyer.

> Illness is so privy that only a physician can diagnose; the physician is bound to counsel and aid his patient; since the patient cannot himself diagnose in order to notify the physician, nor because of illness, travel to him, the physician has to travel to the patient.[68]

Illustrating his argument that illness was 'so privy' Cavendish noted that diagnosis depended on 'inspection of urine', a task a layman could not

---

67 Post (n 2) 298–300 and see Rawcliffe (1995) (n 3) 114.
68 Post (n 2) 300.

undertake nor presumably could the 'specimen' have been sent with the messenger to Master Bredon. There was also some discussion of about the standard of competence a physician might be held to, Bredon's counsel saying no man could be expected to perform services outside his competence. Exactly what was demanded of the physician depended on 'the nature of the grant'[69] (the deed of appointment). The interpretation of the 'contract' proved difficult and the case dragged on ultimately resulting in victory for the prior.

The cases of these two physicians, both of whom sued to recover monies due to them under the agreement by which they were retained as medical advisers to the defendants, conflicts with *Chorley v Bolcot* (1791)[70] which 'confirmed' that in law as much as professional etiquette the fees of a physician were honorary and not to be demanded as of right. Masters Geoffrey and Bredon were in effect suing their ecclesiastical clients for debt. It may be that critics of *Chorley v Bolcot* were correct in their doubts as to the honorarium-only rule enjoying any antiquity.[71]

Alternatively, a distinction could be made between resorting to the courts to recover unpaid fees and bringing an action for breach of a specific contract to retain the services of the physician or barrister. In a comparatively modern case, *Veitch v Russell* in 1842,[72] a physician sued to recover disputed payments for expenses and treatment in relation to his attendance on the defendant. The court held that while physicians like barristers had no legal claim to their fees they were 'not disabled from entering into a special contract',[73] a contract of retainer. Suing for fees as such would 'do wrong to his reputation.' The distinction was tricky to establish in practice, as the judgments in *Veitch v Russell* demonstrate.

Surgeons and apothecaries had no such inhibitions and when fees were unpaid, they resorted to legal actions against their patients to recover the debt. The question of medical negligence arose in defence of the action. The patient would respond that the improper (that is negligent) treatment constituted a good defence to the practitioner's claim for his fees. In *Kannen v M'Mullen*[74] a surgeon-apothecary sued to recover unpaid fees for treating the defendant having both provided medical advice and supplied medicines. Expert witnesses called by the defendant testified that the plaintiff had administered 'medicines perfectly inconsistent with each other' but

69 Ibid.
70 (1791) 100 English Reports 1040 (discussed above in Chapter 3).
71 Goldberg (n 14) 111.
72 (1842) 12 Law Journal Reports 13.
73 Ibid 16.
74 (1791) 170 English Reports 87.

conceded that the progress of illness could never be entirely predictable. Directing the jury Lord Kenyon said:

> In a case where the demand is compounded of skill and things administered, if the skill which is a principal part is wanting, the action fails because the defendant has received no benefit.[75]

It was then for the jury to determine whether or not the plaintiff had 'misconducted himself' i.e. been negligent.[76] In the event, the jury found for the plaintiff and awarded him the 'money charged for medicines'. Directing the jury, Lord Kenyon added that had the defendant summoned a physician and the physician had prescribed the medicines to be supplied by the apothecary, the plaintiff would not have been liable for the diagnosis and choice of remedy. Only if the apothecary made up the medicines improperly would he be responsible for any ill effects of the medicines supplied. If the medicines were improperly prescribed, liability lay with the physician.

Kannen v M'Mullen emphasises the continuing importance of procedure and onus of proof. It was argued that Lord Mansfield had earlier ruled that when a surgeon or apothecary sued to recover fees, improper treatment could never be a good defence because the plaintiff doctor would not have notice of such a charge of negligence, as he would if the action were initiated by the defendant patient against him. Lord Kenyon ruled that where 'plain and certain misconduct' appeared, such misconduct was a good defence though seeming to suggest that the jury must have no possible doubt as to that misconduct. The central role of the jury is highlighted. The jury, not the judge, determined questions of fact and the credibility of the parties.

The action on the case and the genesis of the duty of care

Given that, after the closure of the monastery hospitals, medical care was predominantly a matter of contract law,[77] it was not necessarily the patient being treated by the medical man who contracted with the practitioner. The 'head of the household' would contract with the chosen healer to treat his family and servants. The parish might contract for the care of a pauper. The common law doctrine of privity of contract ruled that a third party cannot sue on the contract to enforce obligations undertaken in that contract. A series of cases established that where the practitioner injured the patient

---

75 Ibid 87.
76 The word misconduct in modern usage connotes more than negligence and suggests some element of deliberate wrongdoing involving intent to harm, or recklessness.
77 As to Poor Law medical care after 1834 see Price (n 8).

negligently, the patient had a remedy in an action on the case, case law which laid the foundations of present law governing the duty of care owed by health workers to their patients.

In *Everard v Hopkins*[78] the plaintiff sued a 'common chyrurgeon' (surgeon) who had undertaken the cure of his (nameless) servant, for which service the plaintiff promised to pay five marks. The servant had been injured by a cart wheel. The plaintiff alleged that the defendant was not 'onely careless of the cure ... but he had also applied unwholsome medicines'. The servant had suffered more pain and was unable to work for a year. While much of the argument centred on a dispute about whether the pleadings were in the correct form, substantive questions relevant to understanding the emergent obligations of medical practitioners were addressed. Did the servant have a claim against the surgeon if the latter were shown to be negligent and did the master have any claim for the losses caused to him by the inability of the servant to perform his duties? Coke CJ first made it clear that the servant 'cannot have an action upon this agreement, but he may have an action on the case for his supplying of unwholesome medicines to him'.[79] Privity of contract prevented the servant suing on his master's contract. The undertaking by the surgeon to treat his injury created a duty of care to the servant, independent of the contract. The master could claim for loss of the injured man's services under the agreement. The case came to no definitive judgment. The Court of Common Pleas 'inclined to be of opinion for the plaintiff' but errors in the pleadings precluded a judgment. The law report concludes that in the event the parties agreed a settlement.[80]

Everard v Hopkins established that patients in receipt of medical treatment were owed a duty regardless of whether they had contracted to engage the doctor's services. It is notable for other reasons too. Counsel for the plaintiff, George Croke, cited precedents from arcane sources such as 'The Old Book of Entries Title Physicians and Chyrurgeons', precedents that further demonstrate that medical negligence claims have a long history. The argument addressing the question of duty invoked case law relating to careless conduct by blacksmiths and drew analogies with carpenters suggesting that in 1614 the judges had no special regard for surgeons; they were just one form of skilled artificer.[81]

The emergence of what is now styled a duty of care to patients regardless of payment is further illustrated in *Pippin and Wife v Sheppard*.[82]

---

78 (1614) 80 English Reports 1164.
79 Ibid 1165.
80 Ibid 1166.
81 Goldberg (n 14) 118–120.
82 (1822) 147 English Reports 400.

At common law a married woman could not sue or be sued: her legal personality was subsumed into her husband's.[83] When a wife suffered injury from alleged medical negligence any action had to be brought jointly, hence *Pippin and Wife*. Damages could be awarded for both the injury to her and any loss to her husband occasioned by the loss of his wife's services.

The plaintiff engaged the defendant surgeon for reasonable reward 'to treat, attend to and cure' serious injuries suffered by his wife. He alleged that the careless and incompetent treatment administered to the wife aggravated and inflamed the original injury, placing her at risk of her life and forcing her to submit to painful surgical operations. The defence largely rested on matters of pleading and disputes about the contract between the husband and the surgeon. The court found for the plaintiff; the action was not 'brought or founded on the contract, but on the damage done to the individual by the negligence, improper treatment and unskilfulness of the defendant'. Richards LCB and Graham B stressed that only the person injured can recover damages for that injury. Garrow B invoked policy. He declared that to accept the arguments for the defence would have 'most mischievous consequences' saying:

> In the practice of surgery particularly, the public are exposed to great risks from the number of ignorant persons professing a knowledge of the art, without the least pretensions to the necessary qualifications, and they often inflict very serious injury on those who are so unfortunate as to fall into their hands.[84]

Were the defendant's arguments to be accepted, he continued:

> [W]ould be to leave such persons in remedyless state. In cases of the most brutal inattention and neglect, patients would be precluded frequently from seeking damages by course of law, if it were necessary to enable them to recover that there should have been a previous retainer, on their part, of the person professing to be able to cure them. In all cases of surgeons retained by any of the public establishments, it would happen that the patient would be left without redress for it could hardly be accepted that the governor of an infirmary should bring an action against the surgeon employed by them to attend the child of poor parents who may have suffered from his negligence and inattention: and are they to be without a remedy ...[85]

The question of to whom a duty of care might be owed arose again in *Gladwell v Steggall*.[86] The plaintiff was a girl aged ten who sued via her

---

83 Baker (n 39) 522.
84 Ibid 409.
85 Ibid.
86 (1839) 132 English Reports 1283.

prochein ami (next friend). She complained of a pain in her knee while working in the fields with her father and went home. Her mother sent for the defendant, a surgeon-apothecary who was also a clergyman. It was alleged that the defendant treated the girl so incompetently that her general health suffered and she underwent great suffering. At the trial, the defendant's counsel argued that his bill for services was made out to the plaintiff's father and so a claim that the plaintiff 'employed' him was not made out. The jury found for the girl. The defendant then obtained a *rule nisi*, a procedure to remove the legal argument to a higher court. Chief Justice Tindal, with whom the other judges agreed, ruled that the action was not 'framed as in an action on a contract'. In action ex delicto (i.e. a claim in negligence), the duty was owed by the defendant who undertook the care of the patient to the person suffering bodily injury.[87] The word 'employment' used in *Gladwell v Steggall* did not mean employed under any sort of contract be it for service or services but rather that the defendant agreed to treat a patient who 'assented to his attendance'.[88]

Standard of care

Once a duty to a patient whom the medical practitioner had undertaken to treat was established, the scope of the duty had to be addressed. A number of reports state that the defendants 'undertook the cure' of their patient. Speaking of 'cure' not 'care' erroneously suggests that in an action on the case the doctor guaranteed to treat the patient successfully. There is little evidence that this was ever so.[89] The duty imposed was a duty to treat the patient with proper care and skill. An action lay against a surgeon according to the general rule:

> [T]hat in all cases where a damage accrues to another by the negligence, ignorance, or misbehaviour of a person in the duty of his trade or calling, an action will lie ... *as if a farrier kill my horse by bad medicines, or refuse to shoe, or prick him in the shoeing* [my emphasis].[90]

Two important points should be made. First, the need for factual evidence of negligence in the case in issue; negligence could not simply be inferred from evidence that the defendant was a poor surgeon. And second, the test for a surgeon and by analogy any other medical practitioner was no different to the test for the farrier (the horse-doctor).

87 Ibid 1284.
88 Ibid per Vaughan J.
89 Winfield (n 43).
90 *Seare v Prentice* (1807) 103 English Reports 376.

Care not cure

In *Seare v Prentice*[91] the plaintiff was a shoemaker who suffered a broken arm and a dislocated elbow falling from his horse. He was first treated by the defendant surgeon who thought that the arm was not broken, applied vinegar and bound up the arm. The defendant was described in the report as 'a village surgeon'. About ten days after the fall, the defendant and another surgeon set the arm, the fracture by then presumably patent. The plaintiff's state was such that he could not work. Two months later, the plaintiff consulted Mr Kingston who described the plaintiff as 'being a cripple in his arm'. Mr Kingston carried out a further operation which he described as 'a very fine cure'. Kingston considered that the plaintiff's state before he himself took over his care was due to the defendant's negligence, saying that 'an apprentice boy might have known better' and he 'recommended that the plaintiff bring an action'.

At trial before Heath J the jury found for the defendant. It is reported that this was 'much to the Judge's satisfaction; who intimated that the vaunting language of the witness Kingston must have diminished his credit with the jury'. The question before the Court of King's Bench related to whether evidence of lack of skill was sufficient to prove the plaintiff's case. Heath J had withdrawn allegations of lack of skill from the jury, finding that the evidence of Mr Kingston did not impute unskilfulness, but attributed the damage to the plaintiff to negligence and carelessness, directing them that 'unless negligence were proved they could not examine into the want of skill'. The judge further commented that he struggled to state what degree of skill would be required of a 'village surgeon'. The court ruled that on the facts of the case, there were no grounds to upset the judge's ruling. Lord Ellenborough CJ made it clear that, if properly pleaded, want of skill was a proper ground to find a surgeon liable just as the 'farrier who undertakes to cure my horse must have common skill at least in his business'. A surgeon would be liable for 'crassa ignorantia ... for having rashly adventured upon the exercise of a profession without the ordinary qualification of skill'.

Hancke v Hooper[92] re-affirmed that a medical practitioner was not subject to an obligation to produce a 'beneficial result'. The plaintiff was a whitesmith (metal worker). He went to the defendant surgeon's shop and asked to be bled which he said would ease a disease in his head and had helped him before. One of the defendant's apprentices started the procedure. On seeing the blood flow rather more rapidly than usual he sent for his master, the defendant. The defendant ordered the apprentice to stop the

---

91 Ibid.
92 (1835) 173 English Reports 37.

bleeding and bound the arm. The plaintiff claimed that as a result of the 'improper' bleeding his arm swelled up and bruised, he lost an unnecessary amount of blood so that he was too ill to work and had to spend £30 on subsequent treatment, presumably with another surgeon. The plaintiff contended that the apprentice bled him from an improper vein, one too close to a tendon and that the apprentice may have nicked the filament of a nerve. His counsel argued that it was doubtful if the bleeding should have been performed at all and the defendant was to blame for allowing so delicate an operation to be performed by an apprentice who had not completed his education. The apprentice in fact had served the defendant for two years, worked with other surgeons, spent some time in hospitals and attended anatomy lectures. Three surgeons testifying for the defendant stated that what occurred was 'an accident which might occur to the best surgeon and did not shew the slightest want of skill'. This view was shared by one of the witnesses for the plaintiff.

In his direction to the jury Tindal CJ made several important points in relation to the obligations of medical practitioners. The defendant was responsible for the acts of his apprentice. The test of liability was whether the injury could be proven to be the result of lack of skill on the part of the apprentice. Only if some fault could be ascribed to the apprentice was the master liable. A surgeon does not become an actual insurer; he is only bound to display sufficient skill and knowledge of his profession. If from some accident, or some variation in the frame of a particular individual, an injury happens, it is not a fault of the medical man.[93] Finally the judge went on to state that the plaintiff had not asked the apprentice about whether bleeding was a proper and useful remedy; 'he took that on himself, and only required the manual operation to be performed'.

Common practice: responsible opinion

The principles governing claims for 'medical negligence' brought under the appellation 'action on the case' before 1852[94] were no different to any other claim relating to injury caused by a defendant whose occupation entailed holding himself out as having special skills. There was then as now no separate legal action for medical negligence. Goldberg notes that Holdsworth in his *History of English Law*[95] 'simply lumps surgeons with smiths, horse-doctors, innkeepers, vintners, butchers and carriers'.[96] Holdsworth saw no

93 Ibid 38.
94 Common Law Procedure Act 1852.
95 W Holdsworth *A History of English Law* (5th edn) (1942).
96 Goldberg (n 14) 110.

justification for treating the surgeon more favourably than the farrier. Any notion that credible medical opinion could not be questioned,[97] or that 'the standard of medical care was a matter of medical judgment',[98] is largely absent from the older case law on claims for medical negligence.

Lanphier and Wife v Phipos,[99] decided in 1838, indicates a marginally more favourable judicial attitude to surgeons, recognising their professional status. In 1835, the plaintiff – wife, Mrs Lanphier – was out walking with a friend, Mrs Jones, and Mrs Jones's little daughter, when she was frightened by a cow, turned round to escape the cow and fell on her right wrist. Mrs Jones and the child fell on top of her. When Mrs Lanphier arrived home her husband sent for the defendant who practised as a surgeon-apothecary. The defendant said that he thought that the small bone in the arm was broken so put splints on and bound the arm from below the elbow to the wrist, leaving the hand hanging down. Before the defendant arrived to treat Mrs Lanphier, her arm was already very swollen and over the next seven weeks or so the inflammation spread but at each visit the defendant expressed the view that the injury was 'doing very well'. Mr Lanphier became very concerned. His wife had lost the use of her hand, she could not dress herself or use a knife and fork. He dismissed the defendant and Mr Vandenburgh attended. By the time of the trial Mr Vandenburgh had died. Evidence of his practice was given by his son. His father had sent some lotions and put on longer splints to support the hand. The treatment reduced some of the inflammation but Mrs Lanphier still had little use of her hand. His son reported that Mr Vandenburgh was of the opinion that the splint had not been properly placed and in addition to the fracture of the small bone there was a dislocation of a bone in the hand. Directing the jury, Tindal CJ set out what was to become a classic test for professional liability:

> What you will have to say is this, whether you are satisfied that the injury sustained is attributable to the want of a reasonable and proper degree of care and skill in the defendant's treatment. Every person who enters into a *learned profession* undertakes to bring to the exercise of it a reasonable degree of care and skill. He does not undertake, *if he is an attorney, that at all events you shall gain your case, nor does a surgeon undertake that he will perform a cure; nor does he undertake to use the highest possible degree of skill. There may be*

---

97 *Bolam v Friern Hospital Management Committee* [1957] 1 WLR 582. Subsequent case law distorted McNair's direction somewhat by overlooking the judge's imposition of a condition that the evidence should be responsible: see M Brazier and J Miola 'Bye-Bye Bolam: A Medical Litigation Revolution?' (2000) 8 *Medical Law Review* 85.

98 *Sidaway v Bethlem Royal Hospital Governors* [1985] 1 All ER 643, 649.

99 (1838) 173 English Reports 581.

persons who have higher education and greater advantages than he has, but he undertakes to bring a fair, reasonable and competent degree of skill, and you will say whether in this case the injury was referred to the want of such skill in the defendant [my emphasis].[100]

The jury found for the plaintiffs and awarded Mr and Mrs Lanphier damages of £100. The Chief Justice's direction in its reference to the standard demanded of a member of a *learned* profession and equation of the surgeon with the attorney indicates a higher status for the medical man than earlier cases 'lumping' the surgeon with blacksmiths and innkeepers. Much though being classified as belonging to a profession may have pleased the surgeons, practically it had little effect. From the report, the 'expert' evidence strongly favoured the defendant. Giving evidence for the plaintiffs, Mr Calloway of Guy's Hospital and Mr Tyrell of St Thomas's described the defendant's conduct as injudicious especially in letting the hand hang down. A year before the hearing, a surgeon appointed by the court, Mr Luke of the London Hospital, examined the plaintiff's arm (in the company of the Mr Vandenburgh) and 'gave it as his opinion that there had not been any mismanagement on the part of the defendant'. Mr Luke also testified that Mr Vandenburgh agreed with him and that they had so informed the plaintiffs. Three other surgeons, after hearing Mr Luke's evidence, testified that in their opinion the defendant was not to blame. Counsel for the plaintiffs appealed to the jury's own judgement of the facts. Most tellingly Serjeant Wilde argued:

> When a judge gives leave for a surgeon to attend and examine a wound, it is not intended that questions should be asked, and that the cause should be tried in the patient's parlour.[101]

Medical men, including surgeons, might be admitted to the ranks of the learned professions. They did not set the standard of care.

A second point to note from the Chief Justice's summing up is his statement that a surgeon does not *'undertake to use the highest possible degree of skill. There may be persons who have higher education and greater advantages than he has* (my emphasis)'. The standard to be met was not that of the best surgeon in the realm but the average reasonably competent practitioner. It is not clear from the report if this statement relates to the question of whether the defendant was licensed to practise and what sort of training he had received. Counsel for the plaintiffs argued expressly that if a man practised as a surgeon, it was irrelevant whether 'he belongs to

100 Ibid 583.
101 Ibid.

the College of Surgeons or not'. There is nothing in the report to indicate whether Mr Phipos was a member of the College. It may be that in his reference to men of greater skill and education Tindal CJ alludes to a distinction between elite surgeons of the College and those trained as apothecaries and not licensed by the Surgeons, or men practising surgery with no formal 'qualifications'. Given the time and effort expended by the medical corporations seeking to establish and expand their powers to control practice, it is somewhat surprising that the question of a formal licence to practise rarely surfaces in claims for medical negligence. In *Seare v Prentice*,[102] the trial judge had expressed himself as at a loss to direct the jury what degree of skill should be required of a 'village surgeon', a description suggesting a more or less wholly self-trained or at least informally trained practitioner. Lord Ellenborough's response that anyone embarking on surgery will be held to the standard of care demanded of any surgeon undertaking the procedure in question is confirmed in *Ruddock v Lowe*[103] and *Jones v Fay*.[104]

Informed consent

The cases discussed so far in this chapter related to allegations of incompetent or unskilled treatment. *Slater v Baker and Stapleton*[105] (decided in 1767) also addressed what is now called informed consent. An action on the case was brought against a surgeon, Mr Baker, and an apothecary, Mr Stapleton. The plaintiff had broken both bones in one of his legs and engaged the two defendants to 'cure' the fractured leg. Initially another (unnamed) surgeon set the fracture. That surgeon testified that after a month the leg was healing well, a callous (bony healing tissue that forms around the ends of broken bone) had formed and while there was a 'little protuberance' it was well within what might be expected. Breaking the leg again and disuniting the callous to straighten the leg would, the original surgeon claimed, have been 'very dangerous'. An apothecary, Mr Latham, who had attended the plaintiff for nine weeks, gave evidence that when the plaintiff went home the bones were well united. A lay female witness testified that when he first came home the plaintiff could walk with crutches.

Once home the plaintiff sent for the second defendant, the apothecary Stapleton, to remove the bandages from his leg. Mr Stapleton asked to call in the first defendant, surgeon Baker, to assist him. Baker attached a heavy

---

102 *Seare* (n 90).
103 (1865) 176 English Reports 672.
104 Ibid 675.
105 (1767) 95 English Reports 860.

instrument with teeth to the plaintiff's leg, a device designed to extend and straighten the leg. On their third visit, Baker took the plaintiff's foot in his hands and Stapleton took the leg on his knees. The leg 'gave a crack' and the plaintiff cried out saying that the defendants had 'broke what nature had formed'. Baker told him he 'must go through the operation of extension' and Stapleton added that they 'had consulted and done what was for the best'. The plaintiff claimed that his leg was thereafter permanently damaged and caused pain. One of his servants swore that before the 'operation' Mr Slater could put his foot on the ground.

At the trial before Lord Chief Justice Wilmot, the plaintiff alleged that the defendants had ignorantly and unskilfully broken the callous causing him permanent injury. The surgeon who had first set the leg gave evidence that having been instructed in surgery by his father, he considered disuniting the callous after it had healed to be very dangerous. The apothecary Latham who had first treated the plaintiff said that 'he had known such a thing done as disuniting the callous but only where the leg was set very crooked'. Three surgeons testified as 'expert' witnesses. The first stated that in cases of crooked legs compression not extension was the correct remedy, and he had no idea what Baker's 'instrument' might be, but he gave Baker a good character reference as the first (chief) surgeon at St Bartholomew's Hospital. The second expert testified that if the callous was hard, extension was not proper and if it was not hard 'he would not have done it without the consent of the plaintiff'. He too testified to Mr Baker's eminence. The third expert said that if the patient could put his foot on the ground, he would not have disunited the callous even if the plaintiff had asked him to do so. Counsel for the defendants relied on Mr Baker's good character and argued there was no evidence to inculpate Mr Stapleton. He had not professed any skill relating to the leg; the responsibility for the decision to disunite the callous rested with the surgeon alone.

The jury found against both defendants and awarded Mr Slater damages of £500. The judge pronounced himself well satisfied with the verdict. The defendants sought to have the verdict set aside. They contended that Baker:

> [R]eads lectures in surgery and anatomy, and is celebrated for his knowledge in his profession as well as his humanity; and to charge such a man with ignorance and unskilfulness upon the records of this Court is most dreadful.[106]

Counsel went on to say there was no evidence of ignorance or want of skill by Mr Baker, and that such evidence as there was only indicated that the callous was broken without the plaintiff's consent, in which case the claim

---

106 Ibid 862.

should not have been brought as an action on the case but via trespass *vi et armis*, i.e. that the defendant directly and unlawfully interfered with the person of the plaintiff. The defence sought to play a procedural trump card. The plaintiff's claim should be rejected as it did not conform to the forms of action.

The defendants' arguments received short shrift from the judges. Without hearing from the plaintiff's barristers, they found for the plaintiff. The judges turned the pleas to Mr Baker's good character against him. They could not 'conceive why he acted in the manner he did'. They said that 'many men very skilful in their profession have frequently acted out of the common way for the sake of trying experiments'. Proof of skill in the exercise of his profession in general did not mean that there could not be particular cases when a practitioner acted rashly and unskilfully. The evidence from surgeons was that it was improper to disunite the callous without consent and 'contrary to the usage and law of surgeons'. It was 'reasonable that a patient should be told what is about to be done to him, that he may take courage and put himself in such a situation as to enable him to undergo the operation'. As to the plea that the claim should have been brought in trespass, more than a century before the abolition of the forms of action, the court refused to 'look with eagle's eyes to see whether the evidence applies exactly or not to the case'. The plaintiff obtained a verdict he deserved. It appeared to the court that 'this was the first experiment made with this new instrument, and if it was it was a rash action, and he who acts rashly acts ignorantly'.

Slater v Baker and Stapleton is an amazing case. Goldberg's 'glimmers of modern medical law' shine brightly. In their disdain for the argument that Baker was eminent and thus not negligent, the court exhibited a healthy scepticism of deference. In their readiness to overlook procedural niceties, the judges showed a desire to ensure that victims of medical misconduct gained justice. In classifying failure to inform as an action on the case, the seeds were sown for decisions such as *Chatterton v Gerson*[107] and the location of debate on informed consent in the tort of negligence. In the value placed on patient consent the court foreshadowed the judicial endorsement of patient autonomy in modern cases such as *Chester v Afshar*[108] and *Montgomery v Lanarkshire Health Board*.[109] And the condemnation of rash experiments equally foreshadowed the development of stringent rules for consent in relation to clinical trials. *Slater* stands out as evidence that eighteenth-century judges showed little deference to medical brethren.

107 [1981] QB 432.
108 [2004] UKHL 41.
109 [2015] UKHL 11.

Two caveats should be noted. Counsel's decision to appeal to Mr Baker's standing in his profession and the community suggest that at least the elite surgeons were acquiring a somewhat protected status. And in holding Baker liable the court itself appealed to the 'law and usage of surgeons'. The experimental nature of Baker's treatment of Slater loomed large in the judgment. Had the defendants called expert testimony supporting the procedure, not just lauding the eminence of the man, might the outcome have been different?

Expert testimony

By the latter half of the twentieth century, medical negligence litigation could be characterised as trial by expert. Prior to the decision of the House of Lords in *Bolitho* in 1998,[110] McNair J's direction to the jury in *Bolam* (1957) de facto handed decisions as to whether the defendant fell below the requisite standard of care to the medical professionals who were called as expert witnesses. Pre-twentieth-century cases, as we have seen, also featured experts testifying to the practice of the profession and offering their opinion whether the defendant had fallen below the standard of care and skill required. The judges do not appear from the reports to have been strongly supportive of, and certainly not subservient to, their 'learned brethren'; Mr Kingston was criticised for his vaunting language in *Seare v Prentice*. Testimony to Mr Baker's exalted status in the surgical profession in *Slater v Baker and Stapleton* cut little ice with the judges. But was the evidence proffered by practitioners such as the much-criticised Mr Kingston in *Seare v Prentice* or the medical witnesses in *Lanphier v Phipos* expert evidence as we know it today? The distinction between evidence of fact and opinion was not clear cut, nor was it clear what the role of the expert was supposed to be.

Dwyer, examining the use of expert evidence in the civil courts from 1550 to 1800,[111] notes that it has been generally considered that the judgment of Lord Mansfield CJ in *Folkes v Chadd*[112] established that the opinion of experts who had no personal knowledge of the case was admissible in evidence. Yet as she continues, expert evidence had been admitted in criminal cases since at least the fourteenth century, and in civil matters since the sixteenth century.[113] She traces developments in the use of experts in the different civil courts and the earlier and greater use of experts in the criminal

110 *Bolitho v City and Hackney Health Authority* [1998] AC 232.
111 Dwyer (n 37).
112 (1782) 99 English Reports 589.
113 Dwyer (n 37) 93–94.

courts. Most pertinently for a study of medical malpractice claims, Dwyer identifies the emergent specialisms within the medical profession giving the example of male obstetricians. She quotes Lord Mansfield from *Folkes v Chadd* that in 'matters of science the reasonings of men of science can only be answered by men of science'.[114] Mansfield echoed Holt CJ in *Groenvelt* in suggesting that judges and juries cannot evaluate medical practice.[115]

The emerging role of experts is highlighted by Stein, Guzelian and Guzelian.[116] Their survey of forty-nine reported cases (1800–1900) showed that patients won sixteen cases and the defendant doctors thirty-three. In the eight cases where only the plaintiff patient called an expert, the patient won. In the twelve cases where only the defendant called expert testimony the practitioner won. When both parties proffered expert evidence, the score was Patients 8 : Doctors 21.[117] From 1817 to 1828 all the cases in the survey were won by the patient. From 1828 to 1862 the result was a draw. After 1866 'practitioners effectively never lost again in the cases'.[118] Stein et al suggest that their figures 'are consistent with the hypothesis that judges and juries were highly deferential to expert opinion'.[119] Insofar as any conclusion can be drawn from the relatively small number of cases, a change in the 'power' of expert testimony and its impact on juries appears to have grown as the century progressed. Bell and Ibbetson single out the Medical Act 1858 as a crucial factor in the increasing success of the defendant doctors over the century. They suggest that the Act, in particular the creation of the Medical Register and the General Medical Council, effectively endorsed the competence of a registered practitioner.[120] Stein et al go further suggesting that the 1858 Act (which they call the Medical *Reform* Act) 'had a stark effect of immunizing doctors from malpractice liability'.[121]

As medical treatment became more complex, and increasingly based on scientific development, attention by judges and juries to the evidence given by practitioners in the relevant specialty was unremarkable. Ignoring such evidence, being influenced only by the eminence of the defendant or the sad state of the patient, would be a failure to adjudicate justly. A lay jury

---

114 *Folkes* (n 112) 159.
115 *Dr Groenvelt versus Dr Burwell & Al* (1698) 90 English Reports 883, 885.
116 M Stein, C Guzelian and K Guzelian 'Expert Testimony in Nineteenth Century Malapraxis Actions' (2015) 55 *American Journal of Legal History* 194.
117 Ibid 203–204.
118 Ibid 206.
119 Ibid 205.
120 J Bell and D Ibbetson *European Legal Development: The Case of Tort* (Cambridge University Press, 2014) 88–89.
121 Stein et al (n 116) 206.

presented with only one party backing their case with expert opinion was likely to ask why, and be readier to assume that the party with an expert had the better case. The changing 'success' rates over the nineteenth century may have been coloured by the greater social status and respect gradually accorded to medical practitioners.

Whether judges and/or juries became 'highly deferential to expert opinion' can only be itself a matter of opinion. The secrets of the jury room remain hidden. Alfred Swaine Taylor writing in 1865 suggested that faced with competing evidence 'the default legal standard should be to absolve the medical practitioner under attack; he was after all a trained and presumably competent professional'.[122] The question of what is meant by deference is tricky.[123] Respect for the knowledge of practitioners, their informed opinion, is wholly appropriate. Blind deference, compliance or submission to the opinion of the 'medical man' just because he was such was to blight medical law for much of the twentieth century.

---

122 A S Taylor *The Principles and Practice of Medical Jurisprudence Vol 1* (1st edn) (Churchill, 1865) 502.
123 S Devaney and S Holm 'The Transmutation of Deference in Medicine: An Ethico-Legal Perspective' (2018) 26 *Medical Law Review* 202.

6

Human life, common law and Christianity

Christian tradition

Chapters 2–5 primarily considered questions arising from themes of identification, regulation and responsibility of healers. In the following chapters I turn to address questions principally related to what would now be described as bioethical questions and in particular the use of human bodies, from the womb to the grave. Chapter 2 examined the relationship of law, healing and religion in the late medieval and early modern eras, highlighting the role played by the Church in delivering and regulating health care. This chapter explores the influence of Christianity in shaping secular laws relating to moral dilemmas in medicine. The common law has long addressed debates about the nature of human life, beginning and ending human lives. Christian tradition undoubtedly played a part in forming English common law relating to the protection and value of human life, especially in the context of homicide. What is perceived to be the persistent influence of Christian theology in shaping the law on matters of life and death is decried in a country where fewer and fewer people practise that faith.

Attributing prohibition of assisted dying, suicide and abortion to religious dogma enables those campaigning to change the law to argue that principles of law based on belief that only God enjoys 'the power to give or take life' cannot be sustained in a secular society.[1] I suggest that religion was one factor but not perhaps the major factor in the formation of legal principles applicable to the value of life. '[P]ragmatic considerations', which Glanville Williams stated were the foundation of much of the law of murder, are also present in those 'killings' which he argued are expressions of 'a philosophical attitude'.[2] Examining the history of the laws touching on human life applied to healing and biomedical science,

1 E Jackson and J Keown *Debating Euthanasia* (Hart, 2012) 37.
2 G Williams *The Sanctity of Life and the Criminal Law* (Alfred A Knopf, 1974) x.

the tangled roots of 'medical law' create knotty problems. 'Medical law' often draws on principles initially developed by the courts and the legislature to curtail violence and unrest, principles not always easily, or appropriately, applicable to the dilemmas about human life posed by healing and medicine. In looking at theological influence on laws related to healing, the very particular nature of the relationship between the State and the Church of England from the Reformation to well into the nineteenth century must be taken into account. The conflict between the Anglican Church and Roman Catholicism was political as much as theological. On a practical level the Church enjoyed an effective and nationwide system of local administration.

'Sanctity of life': ancient or modern?

Many bitterly contested questions of bioethics and law today focus on the nature and value of human life. In debates on abortion, the reproductive technologies, the treatment of neonates, assisted dying and euthanasia, there is little common ground between philosophers, lawyers, health professionals, pressure groups and families who are drawn into high-profile controversies. 'Sanctity of life' is often invoked as a fundamental precept of English law. Put briefly, appeals to 'sanctity of life' usually classify any act deliberately designed to end an *innocent* human life as morally wrong. 'Sanctity' is perceived as underpinning the common law in its prohibition of abortion, infanticide and murder, including self-murder (until 1961).[3] Proponents of 'sanctity of life' are likely to oppose any dilution of prohibitions against deliberately ending human life at any stage of development. Legislation such as the Abortion Act 1967, and decisions of the courts relating to end of life beginning with *Airedale NHS Trust v Bland*,[4] are perceived as sanctioning 'murder'. Proposals to decriminalise abortion or permit any form of active euthanasia fall foul of the red line defended by the adherents of 'sanctity'.

The use of the word 'murder' is strongly contested by those fighting for 'liberalisation' of antiquated laws which take insufficient account of personal autonomy. Opponents of liberalising the law to respect autonomy and value quality of life above quantity play 'sanctity of life' as a trump card. John Keown, a doughty protagonist of what he prefers to call *inviolability of life*, asks bluntly '[s]hould the law allow doctors intentionally to kill their patients?'[5] Ironically proponents of liberalising the law also use

---

3 Suicide Act 1961.
4 [1993] AC 789 HL.
5 Jackson and Keown (n 1) 83.

'sanctity of life' as their trump card.[6] They argue that a concept founded on religion, in effect on the teachings of Christianity, has no place in modern society.[7] Religion dominated and distorted the law as it addressed the value of life and was, and is, a pervasive and inappropriate influence on English medical law today.

Before examining the substantive relationship of the common law and sanctity of life, a puzzle arises. In academic debates and in judgments of the courts in the twentieth century the phrase is ubiquitous. In *Airedale NHS Trust v Bland*, the House of Lords was asked to rule whether or not it was lawful to withdraw artificial hydration and nutrition from a young man in a permanent vegetative state. Lord Goff declared that:

> Here, the fundamental principle is the principle of the sanctity of life – a principle long recognised not only in our own society but also in most if not all civilised societies throughout the modern world.[8]

He went on to say that the principle while fundamental was 'not absolute'. Goff and his fellow Law Lords, countless other judges in subsequent cases, academics with hugely divergent views on the nature and value of life, assume the longevity of the catchphrase 'sanctity of life'. Depending on which side of a conflict on beginning or ending life they stand, they may then agree with Lord Goff that the 'fundamental principle' may be qualified. Defenders of the 'fundamental principle' attack any suggestion that the principle is not absolute. Save for Keown, the naming of the concept is rarely contested. Yet I have not found any reference to the three-word phrase 'sanctity of life' in English case law or academic literature before the nineteenth century, and sparse use of the term until later in the twentieth century. References to *sanctity* abound. A person may be lauded for the sanctity of the way they lived their lives. In Chapter 10, we see how the law sought to protect the sanctity of the graveyard. 'Sanctity of life' makes a late appearance in discourse relating to the nature and value of life, invoked in nineteenth-century campaigns to abolish capital punishment.[9] By the end of that century, when proposals that medical practitioners should be permitted to end the lives of terminally ill or severely disabled patients began to be advanced, medical professionals and religious leaders who were opposed to any form of euthanasia invoked 'sanctity of life' as the principle which they maintained

---

6 See J F Keenan 'The Concept of Sanctity of Life and Its Use in Contemporary Bioethical Discussions' in K Bayertz (ed) *Sanctity of Life and Human Dignity* (Springer, 1996) 1–2.
7 Williams 'Sanctity' (n 2).
8 *Bland* (n 4) 863–864.
9 See C Spear *Essays on the Punishment of Death* (Self-published, Boston, 1844).

confounded the case for letting doctors kill.[10] George Khushf[11] identifies a paper by John Bonnell[12] in 1951 as the first academic paper to use the term within its current meaning. In the same volume, Keenan notes:

> Surprising too is the fact that the concept's origin has not been recorded nor its development narrated though often noted to be used without any exactitude ... more surprising is the fact that we do not seem to know where the term comes from, what it roots are why it has been appropriated elsewhere.[13]

Appeals to 'sanctity of life' per se seem to be relatively modern.

Do words matter? In judgments of the courts, in legislation, in theological, philosophical and legal debates dating back to at least the thirteenth century, the notion that human life is intrinsically valuable is articulated, and Christian doctrine is prayed in aid of the value of human life.

Assault on sanctity

In 1957, Glanville Williams published *The Sanctity of Life and the Criminal Law*, an incisive assault on the role of 'sanctity of life' in English criminal law, an assault focused on his analysis of the history of 'sanctity' and the common law. Williams wrote in the preface:

> Much of the law of murder rests on pragmatic considerations of the most obvious kind. Law has been called the cement of society and certainly society would fall to pieces if men could murder with impunity. Yet there are forms of murder or near murder the prohibition of which is rather the expression of a philosophical attitude than the outcome of social necessity.[14]

Williams gave as examples of such killings, infanticide, abortion and suicide. Prohibition of such killings, he argued, can only be justified, if at all, on 'ethico-religious or on racial grounds'.[15] Glanville Williams characterised much of the law relating to the value and protection of human life (as it stood in 1957) as driven by theology, in particular the teaching of the Roman Catholic Church. In a commemorative issue of the *Medical Law Review* published a year after Williams's death, Professor A T H Smith wrote of *Sanctity of Life* that: 'It is a tactic throughout to show that, very

---

10 C Bell 'Has the Physician ever the Right to Terminate Life?' (1896) 14 *Medico-Legal Journal* 463; H Stephen (1899) 5 *Law Quarterly Review* 188.
11 George Khushf 'Sanctity of Life: A Literature Review' in Bayertz (n 6) 273–308.
12 J S Bonnell 'The Sanctity of Human Life' (1951) 8 *Theology Today* 194.
13 Keenan (n 6) 1–2.
14 Williams 'Sanctity' (n 2) ix–x.
15 Ibid x.

frequently, our practices have their origin in a Judeo-Christian tradition to whose tenets not all subscribe.'[16]

Depicted as essentially theological dogma, 'sanctity of life' became an easy target for Williams and others to attack. In her debate with Keown, Emily Jackson wrote that a principle based on the 'idea that God alone should have the power to decide the moment of an individual's death' was an anomaly in a secular society.[17] In a robust counter-attack on Williams, twenty-one years after his death, Keown and Jones set out to distance the concept of 'sanctity of life' from religion, arguing that Williams was mistaken in characterising the concept as essentially theological and that to boot he misunderstood the relevant theology.[18] Keown and Jones eschew the word sanctity preferring to describe the concept as *inviolability of life*. Keown acknowledged that 'sanctity has distracting religious overtones'.[19] Inviolability, he maintains, is embedded in the common law and crucial to any understanding of human rights.

Before turning to the history of Christianity and the common law, it should be noted that Christian, especially Roman Catholic, doctrine relating to sanctity of life is not limited to questions about ending life, such as abortion and assisted dying. Hazel Markwell and Barry Brown wrote of Catholic doctrine in 2001:

> Fundamental to Catholic bioethics is a belief in the *sanctity of life*, the value of a human life, as the creation of God and a gift in trust, is beyond human evaluation and authority [my emphasis]. God retains dominion over it. In this view we are stewards, not owners, of our own bodies and accountable to God for the life that has been given us.[20]

For people who regard human lives and bodies as a 'gift' from God, that all-embracing definition of sanctity of human life informs virtually every personal decision which they make about their own bodies, and the views they hold about developments in medicine. In the context of secular law-making, consideration of such an all-embracing approach to sanctity makes Jackson's point even more pertinent. Can it be acceptable to found law on the basis of Divine law when many people do not believe in the Divinity? And how should Parliament or the courts discern the will of the Almighty?

16 A T H Smith *Commentary* (1998) 6 *Medical Law Review* 263.

17 Jackson and Keown (n 1) 37.

18 J Keown and D Jones 'Surveying the Foundations of Medical Law: A Reassessment of Glanville Williams's *The Sanctity of Life and the Criminal Law*' (2008) 16 *Medical Law Review* 85.

19 Jackson and Keown (n 1) 89.

20 H Markwell and B Brown 'Bioethics for Clinicians: Catholic Bioethics' (2001) 165 *Canadian Medical Association* 189, 189.

I do not attempt to answer questions posed above or jump into the choppy waters of the conflict about the role in law of sanctity/inviolability of life. Rather, subsequent sections of this chapter trace the relationship between Christianity, medicine and biomedical law in an attempt to gain insight into the history of the relationship of law, religion, medicine.

Christianity and common law

The significant role played by Christian tradition in the formation of the common law generally is almost universally accepted. Until 1858, the common law judges were all of necessity Christian. From the Reformation until 1858 adherence to Christianity as propounded by the Anglican Church was mandatory for law-makers, be they judges, members of parliament or university teachers. The Test and Corporations Acts 1661–1673 required all office holders to swear oaths which inter alia abjured crucial tenets of Roman Catholic doctrine such as transubstantiation and also to be in communion with Church of England. The requirement to be in communion with Church of England was removed in the Sacramental Test Act 1828 allowing non-conformist dissenters to hold office, including judicial office. The 1828 Act retained the requirement that a prospective office holder abjure transubstantiation. In the following year, the Roman Catholic Relief Act 1829 finally repealed such provisions, opening up the Bench and Parliament to Catholics but retaining the requirement that office holders profess the Christian faith, excluding Jews from the Bench until the Jews Relief Act 1858.

Leading jurists from medieval times onwards attested to their personal adherence to Christian faith,[21] taking for granted the close relationship between Christianity and law. The avowed Christianity of the law-makers looks like ammunition for Williams which supports his argument that principles of law developed by Christian judges and jurists were little more than religious evangelism. The picture is more complicated. William Blackstone epitomised the evangelising Christian jurist, just the sort of judge, legislator and scholar whom Williams would decry. Jeremy Bentham described Blackstone as 'the professed champion of religious intolerance'.[22] Blackstone published four volumes of his *Commentaries on the Laws of England* between 1765 and 1769.[23] Book IV entitled *Of Public Wrongs* (criminal law) was published in 1769. Blackstone drew heavily on the work of earlier jurists, notably Coke, Hale and Hawkins. In his essay on Blackstone,

---

21 M Hill and R H Helmholz (eds) *Great Christian Jurists in English History* (Cambridge University Press, 2017).

22 W Prest 'William Blackstone's Anglicanism' in Hill and Helmholz ibid 213.

23 W Blackstone *Commentaries on the Laws of England* (Oxford University Press, 2016).

'William Blackstone's Anglicanism', Wilfred Prest critically examined Blackstone's fervent adherence to Christianity in the form of the established Church of England.[24] Prest records a speech by Blackstone in the House of Commons on the expulsion of John Wilkes where Blackstone declared that 'opposing the Gospel was opposing the common law of this Kingdom'.[25] In Blackstone's 'Introduction' to his *Commentaries on the Laws of England*, assertions such as 'Man considered as a creature must be subject to the laws of his creator'[26] seem to reinforce the case for suspecting that the author's account of the common law was primarily driven by religion. Similar broad and general references to the Divine are to be found in the writings of earlier jurists. Yet Blackstone drew a line between divine and human laws, accepting that certain sorts of 'wickedness' carried out in private were beyond the reach of the law unless they violated 'public decency'.

Before addressing Blackstone's account of crimes directly pertinent to medico-legal history, Blackstone's more general examination of the basis of criminal law and its roots in Christian religion in *Of Public Wrongs* is instructive. Blackstone said simply 'for christianity is part of the laws of England'.[27] The context of his statement merits interest for it is made in a chapter (Chapter 4) expressly devoted to '*Offences against God and Religion*'. That focus on crimes *against religion* bolsters Williams's condemnation of 'old' law made by judges who equated Christianity to the law of the land.

The case is less straightforward. Blackstone divided offences against religion into eleven 'species'. I place the crimes he addresses into three principal categories.

(1) Attacks on Christianity. The first part of his Chapter 4 addressed 'apostacy' and heresy. The apostate had to be shown to have once embraced the true religion. The heretic had to be shown to have denied some of Christianity's essential doctrines '*publicly and obstinately avowed* (my emphasis)'. Blackstone also addresses the tussle between the King's courts and the ecclesiastical courts over jurisdiction and punishment, calling for certainty and expressing unease with secular engagement with 'religious' crimes. In his assessment of apostasy and heresy, Blackstone's acute hatred and suspicion of Roman Catholicism is patent.

(2) Protecting the security of the state. The second part of Chapter 4 addresses criminal offences designed to protect the established Anglican Church, for example, offences of reviling the ordinances of the church

24 Prest (n 22) 234.
25 Ibid 239–230.
26 Blackstone *Commentaries* (n 23) Book I 33–35.
27 Ibid Book IV 58.

and Sabbath-breaking. Blackstone set out, and critically examined, the laws against 'papists' and the lesser restrictions on Protestant dissenters. The crimes outlined derived little from Christian doctrine and were rather formulated to protect the security of the state and the delicate balance between Church and State. 'Papists' were perceived as threats to Church and State. Offences against the Established Church were declared to 'strike at our national religion, or the doctrine and discipline of the Church of England in particular'.[28]

(3) 'Anti-social' behaviour. A third category consists of a random grouping of offences of immoral/anti-social behaviour, for example, drunkenness, lewdness and having an illegitimate child, but also included blasphemy and witchcraft. Of these crimes, Blackstone said that while a spiritual court might punish sin for the sake of reforming the sinner, the secular courts correct more 'for the sake of example than private amendment'.[29]

While Blackstone expressed vehement attachment to the Divine Creator, his conception of the role of secular laws is as much motivated by the need to protect the state and the good order of the populace. In an era in England when Church and State were so closely intertwined, Blackstone's offences against religion were equally offences against the Crown. He makes it clear that there is a line to be drawn between private morality and public wrongdoing. Of sexual misconduct, he said, for example, that public lewdness might be punished as a secular crime but the 'temporal courts ... take no cognizance of the crime of adultery otherwise than as a private injury'.[30]

Thou shalt not kill (or euthanise)

In attempting to assess more direct effects of Christianity on the common law regarding the nature and value of human life, laws relating to homicide take centre stage. In discussing homicide, Blackstone makes only one point directly relating to healing, noting the disagreement between Coke and Hale as to whether if a healer gave his patient a 'potion or plaister' and that treatment resulted in the patient's death, if the healer were not a '*regular*' (orthodox) physician or surgeon, it 'is manslaughter at least'.[31] Such a presumption of responsibility for fatal malpractice on the part of the irregular practitioner was (as explained above in Chapter 4) consistently rejected by

28 Ibid 38.
29 Ibid 39.
30 Ibid 64.
31 Ibid 197.

judges in the nineteenth century. In this chapter, I deal with deliberate killing (murder) rather than reckless or negligent homicide (manslaughter), seeking to discern English law's historical valuation of human life, the influence of Christian doctrine in the formation of secular laws on homicide and their application to matters of modern medical law in a secular society.

Absent express laws (in Blackstone's time or ours) which set out specific rules in the context of health care, principles have to be abstracted from the general common law. At the start of Chapter 14, 'Of Homicide', Blackstone described homicide as the offence of 'taking away that life which is the immediate gift of the great creator'. Elsewhere in that chapter his emphasis is different. Homicide was not only a wrong against the victim. An unjustifiable and inexcusable killing risked the public peace, might give rise to private vengeance and thus was an offence against the King as well. Justifiable or excusable homicide must be distinguished from felonious homicide. Blackstone cited Coke[32] in stating that laws protecting human life embraced every human, aliens, Jews and outlaws as much as 'the most regular born Englishman, except he be an alien-enemy in time of war'.[33] Coke and Blackstone recognise an obligation to protect all human lives regardless of status or nationality or the means by which life was ended. Given the nature of society in eras in which Church and State were so closely intertwined, Christian teaching unsurprisingly played a role in the general development of the laws on homicide protecting human life, but not necessarily a dominant role. In a medico-legal context recognition that every human had a claim not to be killed takes us no further than to say medical practitioners must not kill a patient, just as I must not kill my neighbour however irritating or undeserving she may be. I cannot lawfully take her life from her. Or more accurately I cannot take her life without justification. Should she attack me with a carving knife openly threatening to kill me I may defend myself, if need be, with fatal force.

R v Dudley and Stephens[34] illustrated the value the common law attached to innocent human life, addressing what was to become a central question in the context of euthanasia: whether necessity can be a defence to murder. The crew of a sinking yacht, Richard Parker, the 'cabin boy', and his adult shipmates, Thomas Dudley, Edwin Stephens and Edmund Brooks took refuge in a life boat with little food or water. After about three weeks all four men were close to death by starvation. Dudley proposed to Stephens and Brooks that they cast lots to see who should be killed and eaten. Brooks refused to

---

32 E Coke *Institutes of the Laws of England* Pt III 50.
33 Blackstone *Commentaries* (n 23) Book IV 131.
34 [1884] 14 QBD 273.

take part. Dudley and Stephens killed Parker. The survivors then 'fed upon the body and blood' of the hapless Parker. The men were rescued some days later. Dudley and Stephens were charged with murder. They sought to argue that necessity justified the killing in that inter alia had they not fed upon the boy they would probably have died before being rescued and that the boy's weakened state meant it was likely that he would have died first in any event.

The Divisional Court ruled that 'necessity' did not justify killing the cabin boy, Parker, to prevent his shipmates from dying of starvation. The exact ratio of *Dudley and Stephens* is disputed, but holding that duress was no defence to murder, the House of Lords in *R v Howe*[35] interpreted *Dudley and Stephens* to mean that necessity of any kind save self-defence was no defence to murder.

Giving the judgment of the Court of Queen's Bench in *Dudley and Stephens*, Lord Coleridge CJ briefly addressed a number of questions of law and procedure before focusing on what he considered to be 'the real question in the case'. Might you 'to save your own life ... lawfully take away the life of another, when that other is neither attempting nor threatening yours, nor is guilty of any illegal act whatever towards you or anyone else?' Rejecting a defence of necessity, Coleridge delved back to the thirteenth century and the writings of Bracton, embarking on an examination of the arguments advanced by the pre-eminent jurists of succeeding centuries, and ultimately founding his own judgment primarily on Hale. Hale admitted a defence to safeguard a man's own life but stated that 'if a man be desperately assaulted and in peril of death, and cannot otherwise escape unless to satisfy his assailant's fury he will kill an innocent person' he will not be acquitted of murder.[36] Coleridge rejected arguments in support of a broader defence of necessity dismissing what he describes as the 'only real authority of former time', Lord Bacon, who maintained that 'Necessity carrieth a privilege in itself'. Bacon spoke of a necessity of conservation of life so that a man is not guilty of felony or larceny if he steals food to avert hunger. Nor:

> [I]f divers be in danger of drowning by the casting away of some boat or barge, and one of them get to some plank, or on the boat's side to keep himself above water, and another to save his life thrust him from it whereby he is drowned this is not se defendendo nor by misadventure, but justifiable.[37]

Coleridge noted that Bacon cited no authority for his proposition, and suggested it may have derived from canon law. If Lord Bacon meant to state

---

35 [1987] 1 AC 417.
36 M Hale *History of the Pleas of the Crown* (1736) Vol I, 54.
37 *Dudley and Stephens* (n 34) 283.

that a man could save his own life by killing an innocent and unoffending neighbour that 'certainly is not the law of the present day'.[38]

The circumstances which led to the killing of the cabin boy are very different to the case advanced now to permit doctors to comply with a patient's request for voluntary euthanasia. The cabin boy did not choose his death. His shipmates deprived him of a life which as far as we can know still had value to him. *Dudley and Stephens* remains instructive when tracing the influence of Christianity on the law and human life. Coleridge dismissed Greek and Roman scholars lauding a duty to die for others as 'heathen ethics'. He pronounced that: '[I]t is enough in a Christian country to remind ourselves of the Great Example whom we profess to follow.' He called in aid the devil.

So spake the fiend, and with necessity, The tyrant's plea, excused his devilish deeds

Taken in isolation these invocations of God and the devil appear to signal that the rejection of the accused men's plea of necessity was simply dictated by God 'the Great Example'. Looked at as a whole, the appeal to divine authority played a lesser role. Lord Coleridge stated clearly that 'law and morality are not the same ... yet the absolute divorce of law from morality would be of fatal consequence'. He noted that 'the weaker, the youngest, the most unresisting was chosen. Was it more necessary to kill him than one of the grown men? The answer must be "No".'[39] Appeals to religious doctrine were unnecessary. Coleridge expressed sympathy with the men's terrible temptation. He stated that if their case was accepted there would be no safe path for judges to tread. He commended the prerogative of mercy. In the event sentence of death was commuted to six months' imprisonment. Emphasising the difficulty of drawing the line in relation to necessity, *Dudley and Stephens* foreshadows a key argument of opponents of changing the law on euthanasia. In the exercise of the prerogative of mercy, the case resonates with the oft-expressed views of those same opponents who contend that current law protects patients from coercive pressures enabling doctors to focus on good end-of-life care. It prohibits euthanasia but permits flexibility in its interpretation. As Baroness Finlay put it, 'it is a law with a stern face and a kind heart'.[40]

---

38 Ibid.
39 Ibid 287.
40 M Brazier and S Ost *Medicine and Bioethics in the Theatre of the Criminal Process* (Cambridge University Press, 2013) 87–88.

Euthanasia: a gentle death?

Debates about decriminalising physician-assisted dying occupy ample space in textbooks on modern medical law. Books and articles devoted to 'Debating Euthanasia' abound. In the last century, starting with the Voluntary Euthanasia (Legalisation) Bill 1936,[41] several Bills were introduced in Parliament to permit, at their request, some form of assistance to end the life of patients afflicted by incurable or terminal illness, or intolerable suffering.

Before the nineteenth century, the 'euthanasia debate' seems muted. Stolberg identifies two German doctors ready to endorse active euthanasia around 1800 and practise what they preached.[42] Before he discovered a cure for rabies, Louis Pasteur resorted to active euthanasia to save patients from a grisly death from rabies.[43] Mercy killing was not unknown, but was shrouded in secrecy.[44]

While there was little discussion of euthanasia in a medical context, theologians and philosophers lauded Judaeo-Christian rejection of classical notions of the acceptability of helping to terminate certain lives, even a duty to end one's own life if in disgrace or a burden on the community. In ancient Greece and Rome involuntary euthanasia was practised. Infanticide, exposing unwanted and/or deformed infants, was lawful. Medieval priests stressed the teaching of the Christian Fathers that life was God's gift, a gift only He could reclaim. Not only was prematurely ending that life sinful; suffering should be accepted as a form of martyrdom in the imitation of Christ. The value of life as preached by Christian clergy may have been so deeply embedded in their congregations' minds that few people dying in pain would think of requesting help to die. Fye cites Charles Tidy, a London physician and author of a book on medical jurisprudence writing in 1882: 'The law knows of no such principle as that involved in the term "Euthanasia".'[45] Hastening death even by minutes was murder.[46]

---

41 T Helme 'The Voluntary Euthanasia (Legalisation) Bill' (1991) 17 *Journal of Medical Ethics* 25.

42 M Stolberg 'Two Pioneers of Euthanasia around 1800' (2008) *Hastings Center Report* 19–22.

43 F Biotti-Mache 'Euthanasia: Elements of Language and History' (2016) *Etudes sur la mort* 17, vi.

44 W B Fye 'Active Euthanasia: An Historical Survey of Its Conceptual Origins and an Introduction to Medical Thought' (1978) 52 *Bulletin of the History of Medicine* 492, 501.

45 C Tidy *Legal Medicine* (Smith Elder, 1882) 1 279 cited in Fye ibid 501.

46 *R v Paine* (1880) cited in Tidy ibid.

Even before 1800, the occasional voice expressly addressed the question of medical practitioners helping to end a life of suffering. Francis Bacon, Lord Chancellor from 1618 to 1621, wrote:

> I esteem it the office of a physician not only to restore health, but to mitigate pain and dolours; and not only when such mitigation may conduce to recovery, but when it may serve to make a fair and easy passage. For it is no small felicity (...) that same *Euthanasia*.[47]

In 1870, the essayist Samuel Williams, wrote that:

> [I]n all cases of hopeless and painful illness it should be the recognised *duty* of the medical attendant, whenever so desired by the patient ... to put the sufferer at once to a quick and painless death; all necessary precautions being adopted to prevent any possible abuse of such duty.[48]

Williams expressed scorn for claims that there was anything sacred about human life 'apart from the use made of it by its possessor'.

The near invisibility of medical practitioners until later in the nineteenth century in the context of 'euthanasia', be it in public debate or evidence of practice, may be traced to a number of factors. In England until the nineteenth century, unless you were from the highest rank in society, the presence beside the death bed of any orthodox medical man was rare. Many of the dilemmas relating to the care of patients whose illness prompts them to seek help to die are products of the success of modern medicine. Problems of artificially prolonging life did not arise when there were no means to do so. Shorter lifespans meant fewer people lived to suffer from the ravages of cancer or the major neurogenerative diseases. Before the advent of antibiotics, traumatic injury killed swiftly. Effective means to hasten an easier death were not accessible till the mid-nineteenth century. There was little any 'doctor' could do until medical science improved understandings of disease, and provided effective analgesia and anaesthesia. At the start of the nineteenth century, the aspiring medical professionals were still divided into the three orders, and as we have seen, often at war with each other. There was no united 'voice' to speak for medicine, and medical 'professionals' did not command any especial authority. In 1858 the Medical Act initiated the first stage of unification. At about the same time the authority of the Church began to ebb. Gradually euthanasia became a medical matter in England and the USA.

An account of a Medico-Legal Congress in New York in 1896 represents debates between practising doctors of the time. Some argued that in

---

47 F Bacon *Bacon's Advancement of Learning* cited in Biotti-Mache (n 43) v–vi.
48 Extract from Samuel Williams 'Euthanasia'; see Fye (n 44) 498.

extreme cases of incurable illness, doctors should have the 'right' to terminate life, and admitted to putting theory into practice.[49] The arguments
advanced in favour and against permitting medical euthanasia are similar
to those deployed today. Active and passive euthanasia are not clearly distinguished. Proponents of law reform emphasised the cruelty of leaving
incurable patients in agony and the lack of other means to relieve suffering. Opponents countered with fears of abuse, killing the patient not in his
interests, but to benefit others. They may not have used the phrase slippery
slope but the concept of extending 'euthanasia' desired by the patient to
people who were considered to be a burden to family or community was
integral to the 'antis'. Some of the case histories recounted by Dr Clark Bell
from the Congress in New York are patently non-voluntary euthanasia.[50]
A number of medical professionals appear to assert that doctors should
decide when assisting a patient to die was legitimate, a stance endorsed
by Lord Dawson of Penn in 1936 in debates on the Voluntary Euthanasia
(Legalisation) Bill.

> This is a matter the guidance of which properly lies within the medical pro-
> fession itself: a profession very sensitive to its own honour and for the welfare
> and feelings of those whom it serves.[51]

Lord Dawson, it might be noted, hastened the death of King George V so that
the King's death could be announced in the morning edition of *The Times*
rather than 'less appropriate evening journals'. The medical professions
were deeply divided. No specialist group of 'end of life' practitioners akin to
the obstetricians emerged in the nineteenth century to medicalise end-of-life
care as abortion was medicalised from 1803 to 1861. The strong personal
faith of a number of eminent medical practitioners may have contributed to
the low profile of practitioners in debates on physician-assisted dying until
late in the nineteenth century. The Manchester physician, Thomas Percival,
promoted a model of the physician as a Christian gentleman. Percival
invoked God 'our Maker' at several points. Condemning infanticide and
abortion he argued that extinguishing the

> first spark of life is a crime of the same nature both against our Maker and
> society, as to destroy an infant, a child or a man; these regular and successive
> stages of existence being the ordinances of God, subject alone to his divine
> will.[52]

---

49 C Bell 'Has the Physician ever the Right to Terminate Life?' (1896) 14 *Medico Legal Journal* 463.
50 H Stephen 'Murder from the Best of Motives' (1889) 5 *Law Quarterly Review* 188.
51 House of Lords Deb Vol 103 Column 484, 1 December 1936.
52 T Percival *Medical Ethics* (J Johnson, 1803) 79.

Proponents of permitting doctors to assist patients to end their lives dismissed 'divine will' as a 'theocratic world view' the patient may not share.[53] Opponents called in aid 'sanctity of life' and claimed that effective safeguards against serious abuses would not be feasible. It is difficult to disagree with Fye when he says that controversy over 'active' and 'passive' euthanasia 'more than a century ago continues today with little likelihood of resolution in the immediate future'.[54]

Suicide: against God and the King?

Until the enactment of the Suicide Act 1961 English law decreed that both successful and attempted suicide constituted felonies, giving rise to complex questions about law, the value of life and Christianity. Decriminalising suicide did not of itself indicate that the law condoned, much less approved, suicide. Assisting suicide remains an offence, becoming the focus of numerous attempts to bring about law reform to decriminalise physician-assisted dying.

The common law provided that an individual could not choose to end his life himself and thus could not authorise another, physician or not, to end his life for him. In considering law's engagement with healing and its application to end of life, a key question is *why* the common law made suicide a crime. If the secular courts were driven exclusively or primarily by religious doctrine, prohibition of suicide and assisting suicide rest on shaky ground. Describing suicide as self-murder (*felo de se*) Blackstone stated that:

> [T]he law of England wisely and religiously considers that no man hath a power to destroy life, but by commission from God, the author of it: and as the suicide is guilty of a double offence; one spiritual in invading the prerogative of the Almighty and rushing into his immediate presence uncalled for: the other temporal, against the King, who hath an interest in the preservation of all his subjects, the law has therefore ranked this among the highest of crimes making it a peculiar species of felony, felony committed on oneself.[55]

The property of the successful suicide was forfeit to the Crown. The rationale for secular punishment for a choice to end one's own life is difficult to discern. It is clear that by the Middle Ages suicide was 'a crime in the

---

53 Helme (n 41) 28.
54 Fye (n 44) 502.
55 Blackstone *Commentaries* (n 23) Book IV 189–190.

eyes of English secular law'.[56] The sin against God in rejecting the gift of life was patent and punished as a mortal sin in the eyes of the Church.[57] The offence against the king is vaguer.[58] Gwen and Alice Seabourne comment that authors addressing medieval law and suicide have often dismissed it as 'either a harsh regime which is driven by unforgiving religious precepts or a royal revenue raising exercise'.[59] In his passionate attack on laws which he saw as driven by incoherent appeals to religion and sanctity of life, Glanville Williams wrote that:

> The object of the king's judges was to enrich their master and the readiest argument to this purpose was that suicide was a felony. Since every felon forfeited his goods to the king, it only had to be decided that suicide was a felony to divert the forfeiture from the immediate lord to the royal coffers.[60]

He added that the judges' task was 'of course, facilitated by the ecclesiastical view of suicide a mortal sin'.[61]

Seabourne and Seabourne in their study of suicide and medieval law acknowledge that suicide 'does not fit easily into a theory of felony as an offence against the king's peace or public order, or a theory of royal intervention as a replacement for blood feuds'.[62] They find little evidence to support the case made by Pollock and Maitland that suicide was originally a parasitic offence and the secular courts first intervened in suicide to punish those who killed themselves to escape judgment for a prior offence.[63] Acknowledging that the Crown had a financial interest in the forfeiture of a suicide's property, they reject the view that revenue was the only concern of the Crown and secular law.[64] Noting that attempted suicide, while a grave sin, was not clearly a secular crime in the medieval era the authors flag up as possibly significant that 'no overt link was made between mayhem and suicidal self-wounding'.[65]

In sum, such evidence as there is about why the secular courts intervened in suicide indicates a plurality of reasons, of which the sin against God

---

56 C L Wright 'The English Canon Law Relating to Suicide Victims' (2017) 19 *Ecclesiastical Law Journal* 193.

57 Ibid.

58 R de Groot 'When Suicide Became Felony' (2000) 21 *Journal of Legal History* 1.

59 G Seabourne and A Seabourne (2000) 21 *Journal of Legal History* 21, 22.

60 Williams 'Sanctity' (n 2) 273.

61 Ibid.

62 Seabourne and Seabourne (n 59) 24.

63 Ibid.

64 Ibid 37–38.

65 Ibid 127.

so prominent in Blackstone's work is but one. One other matter should be noted. 'Passive suicide', for example, self-starvation, was not treated as a felony. Seabourne and Seabourne suggest this may have been for practical reasons or that 'there was perceived to be a genuine theoretical distinction between active and passive suicide'. They find no evidence on which to base any conclusion as to which view is right. Arguments about any distinction between active and passive measures to end life continue seven centuries later.

Whatever the original reason for the medieval courts to condemn suicide as a crime in secular as well as canon law, the law by the sixteenth century was clear. Suicide and attempted suicide were felonies. Courts faced an avalanche of cases arising from suicide. Nearly all dealt with forfeiture and the financial consequences to the suicide's family, so are of little help in exploring the grounds motivating criminalising suicide. One exception is the judgment of the Common Bench in *Hales v Petit*.[66] The plea brought by the widow of Sir James Hales, himself a former judge of the Common Bench, related to rights to property and forfeiture. The coroner's jury had found that Hales drowned himself 'not having God before his eyes, but seduced by the art of the devil'.[67] Suicide is described as:

> [A]n offence against nature, against God and against the King. Against nature because it is contrary to the rules of self-preservation, which is the principle of nature, or every thing living does by instinct of nature defend itself from destruction and then to destroy one's self is contrary to nature, and a thing most horrible. Against God it is a breach of His commandment, *thou shalt not kill*; ... Against the King in that he has hereby lost a subject ... one of his mystical members. Also he hath offended the King, in giving such an example to his subjects, and it belongs to the King, who has the government of the people to take care that no evil example be given them, and an evil example is an offence against him.[68]

Judging the spiritual offence of their one-time colleague, the court invoked the Ten Commandments and the intervention of the devil, suggesting that Hales may have been bewitched. Theological considerations loom large. Two other grounds for condemnation by the secular courts speak of the loss to the king and the evil example to others. The deceased is described as 'a subject of the king... one of his mystical members'. The subject was not free to dispose of his body as he wished but must hold his body ready for the service of the King. In the next chapter, I explore how fealty to the monarch

66 (1561) 75 English Reports 387.
67 At 390.
68 At 400.

limited sovereignty over one's own body and whether, in our modern era, a degree of responsibility to the community constrains our freedom to do what we will with our bodies.

Even a brief look at the roots of suicide as a felony uncovers a variety of motivations. Prohibition of suicide cannot be dismissed as wholly a religious tenet insupportable in an age when most of the population does not adhere to Christianity or any other faith. Other grounds for treating suicide as self-murder, however, are equally unlikely to command support in the twenty-first century. Utilising the tragedy of suicide to generate state revenue will have small appeal. Responsibility to others taking account of the impact of suicide on other people may resonate more favourably with society today but in the context of suicide or assisted suicide in the face of serious illness or disability it does not follow that choosing to end life is irresponsible.

Who or 'what' is human? 'Monstrous births'

The injunction endorsed by Church and State not to kill the innocent was limited to humans.[69] In 1628, Coke described the crime of murder:

> Murder is when a man of sound memory, and of the age of discretion unlawfully kills ... any reasonable creature in *rerum natura* [today rendered *anglice* as 'in being'] under the King's peace with intent to kill or cause grievous bodily harm.[70]

Coke emphasised that the protection of the common law extended to any such creature within the realm: '[M]an, woman, childe, subject borne, or alien person or otherwise attainted of treason, felony or *praemunire*, Christian, Jew, heathen, Turk or any infidel.'[71] What was meant by 'reasonable creature'; what was entailed in the requirement that the creature should be *in being*? Much of the debate arising from Coke's definition has focused on abortion, addressing whether a fetus in utero is yet *in being*. Chapter 9 addresses that question, considering the complexity of the 'born alive' rule. This chapter reflects on what is meant by *reasonable creature*. Does it mean no more than that the creature was of human parentage? Were any biological humans excluded from the definition?

---

69 Strangely to modern thinking non-human animals could in some cases be indicted for crime; P Beirnes 'The Law is an Ass: Reading E P Evans' The Medieval Prosecution and Capital Punishment of Animals' (1994) 2 *Society and Animals* 27.
70 Coke *Institutes* (n 32) Pt III, 50.
71 Ibid.

From the thirteenth century, English jurists have debated the existence and limits of a category of 'legal monsters'.[72] The original context in which monsters were distinguished from 'man' related (as does so much of the common law) to laws of inheritance. A 'monster' could not inherit. The medieval jurist Bracton wrote '*Quia partus monstrousus est cum non nascitur ut homo*'. Deformity, even gross deformity, did not equate to monstrosity. As Sharpe points out hermaphrodites were not classified as monsters.[73] Coke stated that a hermaphrodite being both male and female could inherit 'according to that kind of sex which doth prevail'.[74] The aberration from the norm had to be extreme and focused on appearance. Blackstone wrote that a 'monster, which hath not the shape of mankind, but in any part evidently bears the resemblance of brute creation hath no inheritable land'. And not being man, the monster could be killed as could any beast.[75] The rationale for exclusion of monsters from the protection of the law lay in the belief that the monster was the progeny of intercourse between a woman and a beast, a non-human animal. The perversion of the act which created it justified its exclusion from humanity. While presumably rejecting both the notion of the monster as punishment for sexual sin, and the possibility of inter-breeding between human and non-human animals, Glanville Williams was content to conscript medieval monsters into service of his contention that severely disabled neonates could be killed saying: 'It seems probable ... that a creature that is clearly a monster in the old-fashioned sense could lawfully be put to merciful death.'[76] The very term 'monster' applied to a newborn infant, however severely impaired they may be, does not sit well with society today. Yet when the Court of Appeal was asked to rule on the lawfulness of the surgical separation of conjoined twins born in Manchester, surgery which would inevitably lead to the death of the weaker twin, Mary, it was unsuccessfully argued that Mary should not be considered a 'reasonable creature' but rather a 'monster'.[77]

'Monsters' (*monstra*) fascinated medieval thinkers.[78] Conjoined twins attracted particular interest. Were the twins one or two individuals? Were there one or two souls present? Crucially should the infant(s) be baptised as one or separately as two children? Scholars debated whether having two

72 A N Sharpe 'English Legal Monsters' (2009) 5 *Law, Culture and the Humanities* 100.
73 Ibid 105, 122.
74 Coke *Institutes* (n 32) Pt I 8a.
75 Blackstone *Commentaries* (n 23) Book II 246–247.
76 Williams 'Sanctity' (n 2) 22.
77 *Re A (children) (Conjoined Twins: Surgical Separation)* [2001] Fam 174.
78 I Resnick 'Conjoined Twins, Medieval Biology, and Evolving Reflection on Individual Identity' (2013) 4 *Viator* 343.

heads or two hearts indicated separate personality: debates which resonate to some extent with modern bioethical discourse on personhood. Whether the conjoined twins should be classified as monsters at all provoked disagreement.[79] The Court of Appeal in *Re A* unanimously rejected arguments that Mary was a monster denied the protection of the law. Robert Walker LJ said forcefully:

> It hardly needs to be said that there is no longer any place in legal textbooks, any more that there is in medical textbooks, for expressions (such as 'monster') which are redolent of superstitious horror. Such disparagingly emotive language should never be used to describe a human being, however disabled or dysmorphic.[80]

Rejecting the language of monstrosity does not mean that the concept of a biological human falling outside the protection of the law is of historical interest only. Brooke LJ left the door ajar saying he had 'no hesitation in accepting the submission' of the amicus curiae that:

> [T]he criminal law's protection should be as wide as possible and a conclusion that a creature in being was not reasonable would be confined only to the most extreme cases, of which this is not an example.[81]

It is difficult to envisage what sorts of gross deformity in an infant conceived of human parents would constitute Brooke's 'most extreme case'.

Louis Waller discussed what is meant by reasonable creature.[82] He states that 'traditionally "reasonable" has meant human – no more and no less', but goes on to say that Coke uses the term 'in its older sense of having the faculty of reason, that is, that quality which distinguishes human beings in general from other living beings in general'.[83]

The conundrum of what makes an entity legally human cannot simply be dismissed as a footnote in history. Scientific developments on the horizon have revived the importance of considering what is meant by human, what qualifies an entity to enjoy human rights. In the twenty-first century the question may not be whether a creature biologically human is a 'monster', and thus not 'legally human', but rather whether an entity not biologically human should be legally human. How for example will the law classify Artificial General Intelligence (AGI), or Synthetic Biological Constructs

---

79 Well-illustrated in the Special Issue of the Medical Law Review 'The Conjoined Twins Case' (2001) 9 *Medical Law Review* 201.

80 *Re A* (n 77) 243.

81 Ibid 213.

82 L Waller 'Any Reasonable Creature in Being' (1987) 13 *Monash University Law Review* 37.

83 But see Sharpe (n 72) 121–124.

(commonly known as Androids), in the event that such entities share or exceed normal human cognitive capacity?[84] Realisation of these possibilities for the creation of such novel entities will revive medieval debates. They are not born of human parents. They may not have the shape of a human. In the case of AGI they may have no conventional physical shape. Will 'reason' suffice to admit them to the community of reasonable creatures?

Re A addressed a host of other thorny questions requiring the Lords Justices to engage with history, and attempt to adapt 'old law' to modern advances in neonatal surgery.[85] The law on necessity loomed large forcing a radical reinterpretation of *Dudley and Stephens* while seeking to ensure that the judgment did not open the door to endorsing assisted dying.

The Court was anxious to emphasise that it was 'a court of law, not of morals'.[86] Walker LJ stated that 'ultimately the court has to decide this appeal by reference to legal principle, so far as it can be discerned and not by reference to religious teaching or individual conscience'.[87] The judges misled themselves. The questions asked were moral questions. No legal principle could be discerned without addressing the prior moral questions. The continuing influence of Christian doctrine on the value of life permeates the judgments. Evidence that Christianity still had a role to play was illustrated in the permission granted to the Roman Catholic Archbishop of Westminster to make submissions to the court. No secular bioethicist, no religious leader of any other faith shared the archbishop's privilege. Christian teaching framed the underlying question of Mary's disputed fate. Simply canvassing the option that Mary enjoyed the same intrinsic value as any 'other' unimpaired infant, and that the twins' parents were limited in their freedom to decide how 'their' infants should be treated, assumed that Mary had a claim to such a value. In ancient Greece and Rome, she could have been killed at her father's behest. Contemplating interference with the parents' choice presumes that infants are not the property of the parents. In antiquity, the stronger twin, Jodie, could have shared her sister's fate. The moral question for the Greek or Roman father was not, was he lawfully permitted to euthanise his child, but was it his duty to do so?

From Bracton to Blackstone, from Blackstone to *Bland*, English law has struggled to answer questions about the value of human life. While answers to those questions were influenced by Christian doctrine, in most instances invocation of Divine Will was not the only factor driving the common law.

---

84 D R Lawrence and M Brazier 'Legally Human? "Novel Beings" and English Law' (2018) 26 *Medical Law Review* 309.

85 See *Re A* (n 77).

86 At 155 per Ward LJ.

87 Ibid 257.

It is tempting to dismiss historical case law and jurisprudence as one of Lord Atkin's ghosts of the past 'standing in the path of justice clanking their medieval chains whom judges today should pass through undeterred'.[88] Yet could modern judges, legislators or scholars do any better? One small step might help. 'Sanctity of life' has been conscripted as a catchphrase bandied about by all sides in debates on matters of life and death. Euthanising the phrase might assist clarity of thinking.

88 *United Australia Ltd v Barclays Bank* [1941] AC 1, 29.

7

Your living body: 'temple of the soul'

Whose body?

> The body ... whether in life or death is of central concern to most people's understanding of the moral issues raised by modern biomedicine and modern medical practice.[1]

The everyday language of property used when discussing the body suggests that we 'own' the flesh we inhabit and its parts.[2] Or at least, we control what can be done to the body and what we choose to do with *our* bodies. An ancestor living in the sixteenth century consulting a surgeon about an injured leg would complain of the injury to *her* leg, just as I would today. Should the injury be so acute that amputation below the knee was advised, my ancestor writing to her sister might well say of the now separated part that *her* lower leg had been given to the surgeon to dispose of. Language can mislead. Our ancestress's body was not exclusively hers. Ours may not be wholly ours.

This chapter explores aspects of the history of English law and the living human body. I do not deal with questions of ownership and permitted uses of separated body parts from the living. A rich and extensive literature addresses body ownership.[3] After noting the ambivalent attitudes to physical bodies in late medieval and early modern eras, I examine the extent to which, in centuries past, English law granted individuals sovereignty over their living bodies.

A confusing picture emerges. Most people take it for granted that their bodily integrity will be legally protected and that capacitous adults enjoy the

---

1 A V Campbell *The Body in Bioethics* (Cavendish, 2009) 2.
2 A Grubb ' "I Me, Mine": Bodies, Parts and Property' (1998) 3 *Medical Law International* 299.
3 M Quigley *Self-Ownership, Property Rights and the Human Body* (Cambridge University Press, 2018).

right to use their body as they judge fit. The right to say no to any interference with one's body is the most basic aspect in a claim to sovereignty over that body. In the context of healing, before the twentieth century certain categories of patients enjoyed significantly greater rights to bodily sovereignty than patients in the later *Bolam* era. A surgeon treating a man with a fractured arm was required to explain what the proposed treatment would entail. Until the onset of the short age of deference in the late nineteenth and twentieth centuries, in claims against medical men concerning consent to medical (primarily surgical) interventions, judges largely affirmed the right of the adult man and unmarried woman, *feme sole*, to determine whether or not to consent to any proposed surgery or treatment. The choice of what should, or should not, be done belonged to the patient and no privilege justified the doctor overriding his wishes or withholding information from him. Married women were less fortunate. While sharing the same rights vis-à-vis the surgeon as their husbands, married women were subject to the control of their husbands in deciding what healing to seek for injury or illness. Although not subject to medical patriarchy, wives were, until surprisingly recently, subject to marital patriarchy. The powers which husbands enjoyed in respect of wives and children went further and granted men quasi-proprietorial rights. In England, laws which endorsed male authority over women's bodies and choices have at long last been consigned to history. Yet ghosts of those laws remain to haunt aspects of medical practice and medical law.

They join another ghost, the ghost of maim (or mayhem), an ancient criminal offence which limited what any subject of the Crown could have done, or do, to their bodies. Re-attired as 'public interest' by the House of Lords in *R v Brown*,[4] 'old law' continues to frame limits of permissible interventions in the body. A group of men were convicted of assault after engaging in consensual sado-masochistic practices. They appealed. The Law Lords ruled that the 'victim's' consent alone was insufficient to render any infliction of actual bodily harm lawful. The 'harm' must be justified in the public interest. Surgery often entails a degree of infliction of harm well above the threshold of harm which the individual can authorise and so make lawful.[5] Surgeons avoid the dock thanks to the 'medical exception'.[6]

Recognition of a right to say no to the surgeon advising amputation of a limb amounted to less than conferral of a right of sovereignty over anyone's

---

4 [1994] 1 AC 212, HL (discussed more fully below).
5 Discussed in R B Gibson 'No Harm No Foul? Body Integrity Disorder and the Metaphysic of Grievous Bodily Harm' (2020) *Medical Law International* 73.
6 S Fovargue and A Mullock (eds) *The Legitimacy of Medical Treatment: What Role for the Medical Exception?* (Routledge, 2016).

body. Even men and *femes soles* enjoyed only limited sovereignty over their bodies. Maim, in placing limits on what the inhabitant of the body could choose to do with or to 'his' body, signalled that in a metaphorical sense your body was not solely yours but a gift from God and partly also the 'property' of the Crown.

Human bodies: temples of corruption

The wealth of literature on canon and common law addressing what could lawfully be done to the corpse (discussed in Chapter 10) may lead the reader to conclude that for Church and State the treatment of the living body was of lesser importance. Chapter 2 examined the concerns of the medieval Church that physicians for the body should not take priority over physicians of the soul, addressing fears that when a priest-physician had both the care of body and soul he would be tempted to neglect the soul. Living bodies were not ignored. The biblical question 'Do you not know that your body is a temple of the soul?'[7] indicated that the body should be treated with the respect due to such a temple both by its 'owner' and others. Mutilation was a violation of respect. Fear of ecclesiastical censure inhibited surgeons treating patients. Surgeons worried that in amputating a diseased limb, they might be accused of mutilation, and that should the patient die, be regarded by the Church as an accessory to murder.[8] Yet that same Church endorsed penitential practices such as flagellation and wearing belts which bit into the skin and caused suppurating wounds. Secular law was equally self-contradictory. The crime of maim prohibited certain levels of self-harm, while in late medieval and early modern England the law provided for an abundance of cruel and inhumane punishments inflicted on the body of the hapless 'criminal'. Whipping, branding, chopping off body parts, such as ears, were common and often a public spectacle. When the convict was sentenced to death, hanging, drawing and quartering were the usual refinements on judicial execution. Other variations on lethal but lawful torture included boiling and burning to death. Centuries before the secular state abolished corporal and capital punishments, Canon 18 of the Fourth Lateran Council 1215, the same canon which prohibited clergy of the higher orders from practising the art of surgery, also banned all clerics from any involvement with 'a sentence involving the shedding of blood' or writing any letter relating to such punishments. Such matters were for

---

7 1 Corinthians 6.19.

8 C Rawcliffe *Medicine and Society in Later Medieval England* (Sandpiper, 1995) 71 (discussed above in Chapter 5).

the secular authorities. The Church did not seek to stop the ghastly parade of bodily punishments; rather, it distanced itself from any public messy involvement with blood and guts.

Some of the contradictions in lay and ecclesiastical laws about what could be done to bodies derived from contradictions in attitudes to bodies, exemplified in the contrast between St Paul in his letter to the Corinthians depicting the body as temple of the soul, and St Augustine. The latter expressed contempt for bodies saying that 'The corruptible Body is a burden to the Soul.'[9]

'Your' body: your right to say no to the 'doctor'

The same questions about the human body, the integrity of the body and most importantly, *who* is entitled to decide what may be done to his or her body, have persisted across the centuries. The common law protected bodily integrity, and any contact lacking consent from the person touched constituted the tort of battery and in some instances the crime of assault. Holt CJ summed up the principle in 1704 in *Cole v Turner*: 'The least touching of another in anger is a battery.'[10] Two hundred and fifty years later, a patient's right to say no became diluted when, applying the *Bolam* test[11] to determine what information patients should be given when consenting to treatment, the courts privileged medical professionals, adopting the reasonable doctor test to judge what patients should be told about the risks, benefits and alternatives to the treatment proposed.[12] English judges eschewed the jurisprudence of 'informed consent' developed in the USA and many Commonwealth jurisdictions. In judgments handed down on a range of matters concerning medical care, medical paternalism was endorsed by judges in England.

By the new millennium, the courts had gradually retreated from *Bolam* and support for medical paternalism. The privilege accorded to medical professionals to determine how much information patients should be given when asked to consent to treatment, exemplified in *Sidaway v Royal Bethlem Hospital*,[13] gave way to judicial endorsement of patient autonomy

---

9 See Augustine *De Civitate Dei* trans Henry Bettenson (Penguin, 1972) II XIII 16 (525) quoted in J Sawday *The Body Emblazoned: Dissection and the Human Body in Renaissance Culture* (Routledge, 1996) 17.
10 *Cole v Turner* (1704) 87 English Reports 907.
11 *Bolam v Friern Hospital Management Committee* [1957] 1 WLR 582.
12 *Sidaway v Royal Bethlem Hospital* [1985] 1 All ER 643 HL.
13 Ibid.

and dignity in *Chester v Afshar*[14] and *Montgomery v Lanarkshire Health Board*.[15] The Supreme Court in *Montgomery* ruled that patients should be provided with the information about proposed treatment which, in the circumstances of the case, a reasonable person in the patient's position would be likely to regard as significant, or information of which the doctor is or should be aware is of significance to the particular patient. Summing up the philosophy adopted by the Court, Lord Kerr said that patients are 'now widely regarded as persons holding rights, rather than as the passive recipients of the care of the medical profession. They are also treated as consumers exercising choices.'[16] Lord Kerr appeared to herald a *Brave New World*. In reality, *Montgomery* restored 'old law'.

Patients contemplating proposed surgery were better protected before the late nineteenth century than when *Bolam* reigned. Judges affirmed the need for consent based on information about the procedure proposed. In *Slater v Baker and Stapleton*[17] (discussed fully in Chapter 5), it was said that it was 'reasonable that a patient should be told what is about to be done to him, that he may take courage and put himself in such a situation as to enable him to undergo the operation'. Professional status as a licensed surgeon or physician conferred no right to overrule the competent patient. Medical men were not privileged to decide what should be done for the patient and, as Chapter 5 also indicates, judges showed little deference to the surgeons or apothecaries. As importantly, the contractual framework of most doctor/patient relationships operated to ensure a greater equality of power between the medical practitioner and his paying patients. Catherine Crawford, in her study of thirty-four lawsuits between patients and practitioners, states that patients:

> [C]ould expect not to be neglected, deceived about their condition, or misled about the nature of a treatment…The courts can also be seen protecting patients against bullying and treatment without consent.[18]

Female bodies

Eighteenth-century judges might appear less paternalist than their twentieth-century peers in upholding a right to patient autonomy. Appearances are deceptive. Protection of patients' rights to determine for themselves whether

---

14 [2004] UKHL 4.
15 [2005] UKSC 11.
16 *Montgomery v Lanarkshire Health Board* [2015] UKSC 11.
17 (1767) 95 English Reports 860.
18 C Crawford 'Eighteenth Century Patients' Rights and the Law of Contract' (2000) 13 *Social History of Medicine* 381, 408.

or not to agree to treatment was less than comprehensive. It is only a slight exaggeration to say that until late in the nineteenth century legal protection of bodily integrity itself was the prerequisite of adult men, spinsters and widows. Until the Married Women's Property Acts of 1870 and 1882, married women could not own property. Any property or income a wife brought to the marriage or acquired during the marriage vested in her husband.[19] When a woman wed, her independent legal personality was suspended for the duration of the marriage. The common law provided that 'By marriage the husband and wife are one person in law.'[20] For all practical purposes, that person was the husband.[21] A married woman could not enter into a binding contract, nor could she sue or be sued in tort. An unmarried woman, single or widowed, a *feme sole*, enjoyed in theory the same rights as any man. Quite apart from the social stigma of spinsterhood, laws on inheritance resulted in few unmarried women having an independent income. The married woman, a *feme covert*, was dependent on her husband to remedy any wrong against her. She could not contract for medical services on her own behalf. Any suit against a practitioner alleging lack of consent was remediable only if the husband brought a claim jointly with his wife. Compensation awarded belonged to the husband, who could also claim damages for any loss to him such as loss of his wife's services,[22] including her sexual services (loss of consortium). Not until 1935 and the Law Reform (Married Women and Tortfeasors) Act were married women granted the same rights as men and their unmarried sisters to bring a claim for damages independently on their own behalf. Indeed, the extent of the legal incapacities which were imposed on married women in England led to Parliament passing an Act in 1554 declaring that on the marriage of Queen Mary Tudor to Philip of Spain, the Queen would remain for all legal purposes a *feme sole,* an unmarried woman![23]

Married women were not alone in lacking the same protection as most adult men of their right to decide what medical treatment to agree to or refuse. Minors (until 1969 any person under 21) also lacked capacity to enter into a contract or bring an action for damages independently.

---

19 By custom, in the City of London married women could retain their income; *La Vie v Phillips* (1765) 96 English Reports 329; *Clayton v Adams* (1796) 101 English Reports 727.
20 W Blackstone *Commentaries on the Laws of England* (Oxford University Press, 2016) Book I 442.
21 J Baker *An Introduction to English Legal History* (5th edn) (Oxford University Press, 2019) 522.
22 Ibid 527–528.
23 J M Richards 'Mary Tudor as "Sole Quene": Gendering Tudor Monarchy' (1997) 40 *The Historical Journal* 893.

Being an adult domestic servant did not, as such, result in any formal legal incapacity. When a servant became ill, it would often be his master who arranged and contracted for medical services and, in practice, controlled what should be done. Crawford comments of married women, minors and servants, that ' "Subject" patients such as these possessed few legal rights on their own account.'[24]

While 'medical patriarchy' may have been rejected, English law endorsed patriarchy in relation to medical care within the household: the domestic patriarch was a husband, father or master. The husband and head of the household who held the keys to access to the courts, and who would have contracted for the treatment required by wife, child or servant, was de facto a patriarch in this field of family life as in all others.

The paucity of rights retained by married women and, in particular, any 'right' to bodily integrity is graphically illustrated by rights once conferred on husbands to chastise and detain their wives. Blackstone commented that in polite society chastisement had long been obsolete but still claimed that it was an ancient common law right.[25] The second 'right', to confine a wife in a manner such that were she any other adult would amount to false imprisonment, was securely settled in law until *R v Jackson*[26] in 1891 when the Court of Appeal held that a husband had no right to restrain the liberty of his wife. Perhaps the most startling and obnoxious incapacity imposed on married women was that a wife could not refuse her husband sexual intercourse without good reason and thus a husband could not be guilty of rape. Not until 1991, in *R v R*,[27] was the married woman at last granted the right to say no to marital intercourse.

The incapacities once imposed on wives continued to influence medical decision-making long after the Law Reform (Married Women and Tortfeasors) Act 1935 granted married women independent access to justice. Until 1988, the Medical Protection Society's model consent form for all surgical procedures contained a clause to be signed by the patient's spouse that he/she confirmed they consented to the proposed surgery. A note advised that where the surgery affected sexual or reproductive functions it was particularly desirable to obtain a counter-signature from the other spouse.[28] The British Medical Association's *Handbook on Medical Ethics* gave similar guidance describing spousal consent as a 'matter of courtesy.'[29] Spousal

24 Crawford (n 18) 382.
25 Blackstone *Commentaries* (n 20) Book I 445.
26 [1891] 1 QB 171.
27 [1991] 1 AC 599, HL.
28 I Kennedy and A Grubb *Medical Law* (2nd edn) (Butterworths, 1994) 709–712.
29 M Brazier *Medicine, Patients and the Law* (1st edn) (Penguin, 1987) 267.

consent while appearing to be a general 'courtesy', seems to have been regarded as the perquisite of husbands more than a right of both partners. Kingdom commented that:

> Appealing to this more general right may in turn be a less than innocent practice, if the alleged general right is identified covertly or not, with a man's, or worse a husband's, right to reproduce.[30]

Bodies as property: wives, children and servants

In debates on developments in modern medicine, especially reproductive technologies, issues relating to people (not just parts) as property arise. Property models are endorsed by some bioethicists and medical lawyers in a number of contexts, such as gamete donation and surrogacy. Other commentators are wary of invoking a property model.[31] No current commentator writing on law or bioethics in the United Kingdom advances a case for endorsing the literal ownership of one human person by another, nor that an adult and competent person should have their right to make independent decisions about medical treatment subject to another's will. Wives are not their husbands' property in the twenty-first century, but it is humbling to recall that until relatively recently English wives, children and servants might well be viewed as property. Writing in 2001, Davies and Naffine cite jurist Matthew Hale[32] who suggested that a wife 'was an object of sexual property, a physical being over whom he exercised exclusive rights of use and possession'.[33]

A husband bringing a claim in battery jointly with his wronged wife was, as we have seen, entitled to claim damages on his own behalf for loss of her services, as well as compensation for her injuries on her behalf. At common law, a man's rights to the services of wife, children and servants[34] gave rise to several torts allowing a man to seek compensation from a defendant who

---

30 E Kingdom 'Consent, Coercion and Consortium: The Sexual Politics of Sterilisation' (1985) 12 *Journal of Law and Society* 19, 24.

31 Campbell (n 1).

32 M Hale *The History of Pleas of the Crown* Vol 1 (London Professional, 1971; reprint of 1736 edition) 515 cited in M Davies and N Naffine in *Are Persons Property? Legal Debates about Property and Personality* (Ashgate, 2001) 80.

33 Ibid.

34 A claim for loss of a servant's services could lie when, for example, the defendant's negligence rendered the servant unable to work. Other actions lay if a servant was enticed away from his master. In *IRC v Hambrook* [1956] 1 QB 154, the Court of Appeal held that the action only lay in relation to 'menial' servants living within the household.

interfered with those rights.[35] Similar rights were accorded to fathers for loss of services of a minor child and, indeed, the rape or seduction of a daughter. The aggrieved father was required to prove that as a result of the rape or seduction *he* had suffered some defined loss of the daughter's services, but once some quantifiable loss to the father had been proven additional compensation could be awarded to reflect 'the dishonour and injured feelings caused by the sexual misconduct'. Daughters until of age were paternal 'property'. Their mothers remained so for the duration of the marriage.

Husbands enjoyed extensive rights to the services of their wives including sexual services, the right to consortium. A husband could sue any third party who 'stole' his wife's affections, damaged her ability to provide her services in the household, or otherwise interfered with his right to consortium. He could also seek damages for adultery against his wife's male lover in divorce proceedings. It might be argued that if one party in a marriage suffered an injury which resulted in additional expenditure to replace contribution to family life which the disabled spouse could no longer provide, there was, on the face of it, no logical objection to allowing such claims. Should the disabled spouse have undertaken all the child care and food preparation before they suffered injury as a result of the defendant's negligence, compensating the family for the cost of a nanny and cook seems eminently reasonable. The House of Lords in *Best v Samuel Fox and Co*,[36] held that an action for loss of services or consortium was an action limited to husbands. His right derived from his proprietary interest in his wife.

Even one of the most conservative judges of his time said of such actions that 'ideas which had come down from the days of serfdom and villeinage lingered on'.[37] The surprising fact is that it is only just over forty years since the last vestiges of male 'ownership' of members of his household were abolished by Parliament.[38] Not until 1982 were these last remnants of a husband's proprietary rights abolished by Section 2 of the Administration of Justice Act 1982. When I married in 1974, had I been injured in a road accident, my husband could have sued the defendant to recover the cost of paying for a cook. I enjoyed no such reciprocal right to claim for a replacement washer-up.

35 Baker (n 21) 489–492; *Clerk & Lindsell on Torts* (16th edn) (Sweet and Maxwell, 1989) 947–948.
36 [1952] AC 716 HL.
37 *Jones Bros (Hunstanton) v Stevens* [1955] 1 QB 275 at 282 per Lord Goddard CJ.
38 The Law Reform (Miscellaneous Provisions) Act 1970, s 5 abolished actions for harbouring and enticing wives, children and servants and claims for seduction of a daughter. S 4 abolished claims for damages for adultery.

Bodies: the protection and safeguard of the King

Even the favoured categories of men and single women did not enjoy an unfettered right to decide what could be done to their living bodies. The common law crime of maim, or mayhem as it is sometimes styled, limited the choices which individuals could make about their body and demonstrated that ultimately sovereignty over the bodies of the King's subjects rested with the Crown. The history of the law relating to voluntary euthanasia, suicide and abortion (discussed in Chapters 6 and 9) needs to take account of the common law which denied any subject absolute freedom to do as they wished with their bodies. The 'old law' has become the anvil on which the legality of novel treatments and the limits of bizarre bodily practices are hammered out. In that process, medical practitioners have, in many cases, effectively been granted the power to determine the limits of what we can do to our bodies.

Maim encompassed consensual and self-harm as well as an uninvited assault by another party. If a man shot himself in the foot, that self-harm could constitute maim. 'My body, my choice' did nothing to advance arguments about abortion or suicide. Claims that just because the womb you were seeking to evacuate by inserting some crude instrument was *your* womb, or the body whose existence you were seeking to terminate by cutting your wrists was *your* body, were insufficient. Absent a sufficient justification for the violation of the body, such acts of self-harm might fall foul of the law without reference to the consequences. Moreover, in those cases which fell within ambit of maim, you could not authorise another person to violate your body without due cause. As we shall see later, in *R v Brown* Lord Mustill maintained that the common law crime of maim was obsolete.[39] It is by no means certain that he was right. And even if the crime is dead, its ghost lives under the guise of 'public interest'.

The origins of maim derive from the criminal law to prevent and punish violence, and maintain public order. Sir Edward Coke wrote of maim, 'Life and members of every subject are under the protection and safeguard of the King.'[40] Thus, the King's courts punished certain attacks and infliction of injury committed by one person against another as 'an atrocious breach of the King's Peace, and an offence tending to deprive him of the aid and assistance of his subjects'.[41] Expressed in that manner, the criminalisation of maim might be perceived as benevolent protection by the Sovereign

---

39 [1994] 1 AC 212, 262.
40 E Coke *Institutes of the Laws of England* Pt I 127.
41 Blackstone *Commentaries* (n 20) Book IV 206.

of his subjects; protection from injury, protection from violation of bodily integrity. Maim fell short of the latter for not all physical assaults causing bodily injury were maims. Hawkins described maim as limited to 'cutting off or disabling a man's hand or finger, or striking out his eye or foretooth or castrating him are said to be maim, but cutting off his ear or nose only disfigures him'.[42] Blackstone defined maim as 'depriving him of such parts of which in all animals abates their courage, are held to be mayhems'.[43] An attack which cuts off one's nose seems to be somewhat peremptorily dismissed. The exclusion from maim of injury which only disfigured did not mean that 'lesser' attacks fell outwith the criminal law. Assaults, batteries and wounding were separate misdemeanours; maim was reserved for the most serious harms.[44] Coke and Hawkins state that, at any rate from the time of their *Commentaries*, most maims were not felonies punishable by death, but grave misdemeanours punishable by imprisonment and fines. Castration, it was suggested, had 'anciently' been classified a felony and so 'punishable by death'.[45] Coke wrote of maim that of all offences less than felonies 'this is the worst'.[46]

The odium attached to maim and limitation of the sort of injuries which could constitute maim, is explicable when the purpose of maim is explored. Hawkins stated that maim was committed in relation to 'hurt of any part of a man's body whereby he is rendered less able in fighting either to defend himself or annoy his adversary'.[47] Blackstone declared that maim was also a public wrong (a crime) because the crime may deprive the King of the 'aid and assistance of his subjects'.[48] Coke said that to constitute maim the offending act should weaken the victim so as to 'disable him to do the King service'.[49] At any rate, in previous centuries a one-eyed or one-legged man would make a poor soldier. A missing nose would not so impair the victim. Consent to having a foot chopped off did not justify the maim. Victim and perpetrator both committed maim and should the unwilling conscript maim himself, he committed the misdemeanour. His offence was to deprive the Crown of fighting men. Escaping military service was not the only ground for prosecution. Coke recalled the case of *Wright*:

---

42 W Hawkins *A Treatise on the Pleas of the Crown* Vol I, 111.
43 Blackstone *Commentaries* (n 20) Book IV 206.
44 Ibid 136.
45 Hawkins *Pleas of the Crown* (n 42) 108.
46 Coke *Institutes* (n 40) 127a. 127b.
47 Hawkins *Pleas of the Crown* (n 42) 108.
48 Blackstone *Commentaries* (n 20) Book IV 206.
49 Coke *Institutes* (n 40) Pt I 127, 127bt.

And in my circuit... in the county of Leicester one Wright a young strong and lustie rogue... to make himself impotent by to have more colour to begge or be relieved without putting himself to any labour caused his companion to strike of his left hand an both of them were indited.[50]

Hawkins stated that it was an offence to maim oneself 'to have more specious pretence for asking for charity or to prevent his being impressed as a sailor or inlisted as a soldier'. In setting limits to what a person could choose to do with and to his body, maim imposed public interest constraints on unfettered sovereignty over his body. That the constraints focused on military fitness in an age when England was almost continuously at war is unsurprising. The extension to self-harm to aid a man begging for alms, or seeking parish charity, signals a broader purpose in the scope of maim. The law limited the subject's sovereignty over his body at the point when self-harm or consensual injury imposed a loss or burden on the community, be it the loss of a fighting man or a 'fraud' to obtain charity.

How is maim relevant to healing? There must have been many thousands of surgical operations performed in England before the nineteenth century which disabled the patient as a fighting man. There do not seem to be recorded cases of prosecutions for maim of either orthodox surgeons, or unlicensed empirics, even though one of the most common surgical interventions was amputation of a diseased or damaged limb. The absence of criminal charges is explained by the tacit acceptance of the medical exception without which the practice of surgery would have been largely impossible. In 1878, Stephen wrote that he could find no authority for such exception but that none was needed as '[t]he existence of surgery as a profession assumes the truth [of the exception]'.[51]

Sterilisation, women and maim

What about women? Could a woman commit maim by way of self-harm or collusive injury? The emphasis on fit to fight seems to exclude women from maim, given its evolution in times when the very thought of females in the armed forces would have been risible. Disabling herself to become a more credible beggar or beneficiary of public assistance was something which women could attempt as much as any man.

A particular question relating to both men and women is sterilisation. Castration was said to be the most serious of maims. Self-castration by a man is hard to imagine, but not impossible. A more likely scenario would

50 Ibid.
51 J F Stephen *Digest of the Criminal Law* (FH Thomas, 1878) 145–146.

have been a man persuading a surgeon to castrate him. The reasons for categorising castration as maim are unclear. Blackstone emphasised the effect of maim as weakening a man's courage.[52] Stephen included any part the loss of which 'permanently weakened' the man.[53] Yet, just because a man was a eunuch did not mean he became unfit to fight.

In her article on the history of the law and contraceptive sterilisation, Penney Lewis considered the legality of voluntary sterilisation of both men and women.[54] She examined debates in the early twentieth century on the legality of non-therapeutic sterilisation, citing Lord Riddell who, in an address in 1925 to the Medico-Legal Society, argued that although vasectomy differed from castration and would not have the same effect of weakening the patient as castration, that was not the point. The man was 'deprived of his powers of procreation'.[55] The non-therapeutic sterilisation of women was 'just as objectionable'. In 1934, a committee on sterilisation set up by the Ministry of Health, chaired by Lord Brock, said in its report that there were 'military objections to allowing a man to do or undergo anything which disabled him from begetting sons'.[56] As Lewis notes, such a 'conception of the law of maim would not be limited to men'.[57] In the absence of case law, no definitive answer can be given. There appears to be no insuperable obstacle to suggesting that women could have been guilty of maim if they sought to damage their reproductive capacities.

The legality of male sterilisation was addressed in 1954 in *Bravery v Bravery*.[58] Dissenting, Lord Justice Denning held that non-therapeutic sterilisation was contrary to public policy and thus illegal.[59] Denning acknowledged that a surgical operation done for a person's health is lawful because there is just cause for the intervention. If there is no such just cause then, regardless of the patient's consent, it is unlawful. A vasectomy performed for no good reason was:

> plainly injurious to the public interest. It is degrading to the man himself and to any women he might marry, to say nothing of the way it opens to licentiousness: and, unlike contraceptives, it allows no room for a change of mind on either side.[60]

52 Blackstone *Commentaries* (n 20) Book IV 206.
53 Stephen (n 51) ibid.
54 P Lewis 'Legal Change and Contraceptive Sterilisation' (2011) 32 *Journal of Legal History* 295.
55 Lord Riddell 'The Legal Responsibility of the Surgeon'; see Lewis ibid 298.
56 Ministry of Health *Report of the Departmental Committee on Sterilisation* (1934).
57 Lewis 'Sterilisation' (n 54) 299.
58 [1954] 1 WLR 1169.
59 Ibid at 1180.
60 Ibid.

Denning did not refer to maim by name. Citing Coke's case of *Wright* and quoting the passage from Stephen stating that a soldier who had his front teeth pulled to avoid a controversial military drill, biting cartridges, committed a crime. Denning endorsed the existence and rationale of maim. The other two judges disagreed, saying bluntly that they 'felt bound to disassociate ourselves from the more general observations of Denning'. Denning's sentiments about voluntary sterilisation injuring the public interest would command little support today. The very words maim or mayhem married to the notion that the state can limit our choices about our bodies is redolent of antiquated notions of feudalism; that a 'subject' holds his body by gift of the monarch. Denning's stance in *Bravery* will incline liberally minded readers to hope that Lord Mustill's assertion in *R v Brown* that maim was obsolete was correct.

The death of maim?

Although in *R v Brown* in 1994, Lord Mustill declared that common law maim was obsolete,[61] it has never been expressly abolished,[62] and even if Mustill is technically correct its ghost lives on. In *Brown*, the House of Lords addressed the question of whether consent sufficed to render an assault occasioning actual bodily harm lawful. A group of men had engaged in a series of bizarre sado-masochistic practices. The 'assaults' were wholly consensual; none of the men had needed medical attention. All the men were convicted of assaults occasioning actual bodily harm on each other and their convictions were upheld by a majority of 3 : 2. Sexual pleasure, at any rate of the kind sought by the accused, did not constitute good reason for the 'harms' inflicted. Eschewing or ignoring maim, the majority held that while consent was necessary to defend a charge of assault occasioning actual bodily harm contrary to Section 47 of the Offences Against the Person Act 1861, consent alone was not sufficient. Public policy required that there must be good reason for the harm. Lord Mustill and Lord Slynn dissented. They agreed that a certain level of harm would render any consent ineffective, but held that such harm must amount to grievous bodily harm.

Only Lord Mustill considered maim, which he described as an antique crime which no longer existed. No one had been charged with maim in modern times.[63] Not only was the offence obsolete, Lord Mustill further opined that the rationale of maiming as a distinct offence was quite out of

61 [1994] 1 AC 212, 262.
62 P D G Skegg *Ethics and Medicine* (Oxford University Press, 1984) 43.
63 Stephen (n 51).

date, describing the offence as based on the permanent disablement of an adult male from serving the King as a soldier. He judged it impossible to rest the case before the court on such a claim. He made no mention of any other grounds for maim. His was a lone voice and the death of maim cannot be conclusively assumed. Ironically, had the men in *Brown* been charged with maim they would probably have been acquitted on the grounds that their injuries did not meet the requisite level of disabling harm. The convicted men in *Brown* suffered no loss of body part or permanent disability; they remained fit to fight.

Brown endorsed the medical exception confirming that proper medical treatment, including reasonable surgical interference, justified acts which would otherwise be crimes. Maim remains relevant to law and healing in setting the limits (if any) on what we can do or have done to our bodies, what kinds of surgical treatment a person can agree to, defining the 'medical exception'.[64] Most surgery will meet the test. Removing an inflamed appendix is justified by the greater risks of a burst appendix and peritonitis. Amputating a limb was highly dangerous in the sixteenth century. The alternative death by gangrene was worse. It remains unclear whether there are surgical interventions falling short of the bar, for example is elective amputation lawful?[65] Are there limits to extreme cosmetic surgeries,[66] including cosmetic vaginal surgery,[67] to which a person may consent? Lewis highlights how uncertainty about the boundaries of the exception can be shown to have caused concerns about the legality of developments in medicine such as living organ donation.[68]

Maim dead or alive

In the wake of *Brown*, the criminal law still constrains what we can do with our bodies. If the crime of maim is indeed deceased its ghost haunts us still. The fundamental principle once articulated in maim that we are not wholly free to choose to do whatever we choose to our bodies survives.

64 P Lewis 'The Medical Exception' (2012) 65 *Current Legal Problems* 355.
65 T Elliott 'Body Dysmorphic Disorder, Radical Surgery and the Limits of Consent' (2009) 17 *Medical Law Review* 149; R Smith 'Body Integrity Disorder: A Problem of Perception' in A Alghrani, R Bennett and S Ost (eds) *The Criminal Law and Bioethical Conflict: Walking the Tightrope* (Cambridge University Press, 2012) 71.
66 D Griffiths and A Mullock 'The Medical Exception and Cosmetic Surgery: Culpable Doctors and Harmful Enhancement?' in Fovargue and Mullock (eds) (n 6) 105.
67 S Sheldon and S Wilkinson 'Female Genital Mutilation and Cosmetic Surgery: Regulating Non-Therapeutic Body Modification' (1998) 12 *Bioethics* 263.
68 Lewis 'Medical Exception' (n 64).

An eclectic and disputed list of public goods are said to suffice to justify bodily harm, including participation in 'manly' sports or dangerous exhibitions, ritual circumcision and, of course, the 'medical exception'. The latter is in principle uncontroversial. As Lord Mustill put it in *Airedale NHS Trust v Bland* 'bodily invasions in the course of proper medical treatment stand *completely outside the criminal law* (my emphasis)'.[69] Echoing Stephen, he added that if medical treatment and particularly surgery were not excepted, most surgery would be criminal for 'much of the bodily invasion involved in surgery lies well above the point at which consent could even arguably be regarded as defence'. Procedures which would be criminal become lawful once medicalised. Should a twenty-first-century Shylock carve out his pound of flesh from Antonio, even with the latter's agreement, he would commit a crime. A surgeon removing exactly the same flesh to cut out a cancer acts lawfully in providing proper medical treatment.

A relatively recent case, *R v BM*, provokes some final thoughts on maim.[70] The Court of Appeal addressed 'body modification'. While maim is not expressly mentioned in the judgment, its influence endures. BM was a tattooist and body piercer,[71] who extended his trade to more radical body modifications. He removed the ear of one customer, excised the nipple of another, and slit the tongue of a third to create the look of a reptile. The prosecution conceded that all three customers gave consent. The Court of Appeal was asked to rule whether BM's actions constituted wounding with intent to do grievous bodily harm contrary to Section 18 of the Offences Against the Person Act 1861. The Court held that body modification provided no exemption from the general rule that consent alone does not justify the infliction of serious harm. Lord Chief Justice Burnett acknowledged that the decision in *Brown* failed to offer an 'easily articulated principle by which any novel situations may be judged'. He found a general interest in society for 'limiting the approbation of the law for significant violence', stressing that there was some need to protect people against themselves, especially the vulnerable or mentally ill. In examining public interest, the Chief Justice noted that serious harm, even if fully consented to, carries with it risk of 'unwanted injury, disease or even death and *may impose on society as a whole substantial cost* (my emphasis)'.[72] In assessing whether an exception to the rule was justified he asked: was the activity in question regarded as productive of 'discernible social benefit'?[73] Was the intervention such that

---

69 *Airedale NHS Trust v Bland* [1993] AC 789, 891.
70 [2018] EWCA Crim 560.
71 He was registered to conduct such a business with his local authority.
72 *BM* (n 70) [39].
73 Ibid [40].

it would be seen as simply unreasonable to criminalise the activity even if consented to by a competent adult? In the case of body modification, there was no sufficient analogy with tattooing and piercing nor could BM claim that his interventions fell within the established 'medical exception'. He had carried out surgical procedures for reward, for no good reason, without any medical qualifications, and outwith the regulatory superstructure which protects the public. Lord Burnett indicated that the medical exception would probably only apply to interventions by qualified doctors. Addressing self-harm, he said:

> The personal autonomy of his customers does not provide the appellant with a justification for removing body modification from the ambit of the law of assault. It is true that Mr Lott could have cut off his own left ear and in doing so would have committed no offence.[74]

Should maim have survived the 1861 Act, the simple fact that an individual harmed himself, cut off his own ear, would not have prevented his prosecution, though evidence that the injury inflicted was only disfiguring and not disabling might have resulted in his acquittal. If such grisly but non-disabling procedures were carried out by another (whether 'qualified' or not), the level of harm would fall below the threshold of maim.

In its inclusion of self-harm, maim expressed a principle that competent adults were entitled to determine what was done to their bodies *until and unless* their choices had an adverse effect on the community. Subjects of the Crown in the seventeenth century and before owed responsibilities as well as enjoying rights. The judgment in *BM*, if unconsciously, echoes that approach in its emphasis on the cost that might be imposed on society if body modifications resulted in infection or other complications.

Ruling that body modification was not within the scope of the medical exception, the appeal court did not address the boundaries of that exception in any detail, save to suggest that only someone qualified to perform the surgery in question should be able to invoke the exception. It is unclear whether such a person must be a registered medical practitioner, or if some other qualification will suffice. Barry Lyons notes that with the increasing diversity of 'medical' services on offer, for example, chiropractic and osteopathy, we have returned to something akin to the medical marketplace.[75] Limiting the medical exception to medical practitioners registered by the GMC would, after several centuries, achieve in part the aims of the orthodox professionals to drive out 'quacks' and 'irregulars'. The converse question

---

74 Ibid [44].
75 Barry Lyons 'Papist Potions and Electric Sex: A Historical Perspective on "Proper Medical Treatment" ' in Fovargue and Mullock (eds) (n 6) 51, 67.

also arises. Is *any* procedure carried out by a properly qualified practitioner within the medical exception? That cannot be so. A maverick surgeon who, copying BM, carried out the splitting of a tongue would be unlikely to be able to rely on their GMC registration to defend their action, although he might be able to make a case for the psychological benefit to the patient rendering the procedure in their best interests.

The uncertain boundaries of the medical exception have generated significant problems for medical progress in what Lewis described as new and controversial medical procedures (NCMP).[76] These have included the legality of voluntary non-therapeutic sterilisation,[77] organ donation by living donors,[78] cosmetic surgery and voluntary participation in non-therapeutic research. In retrospect, all have, after some years and concerns, either been shown to have benefit to the individual, even if not an immediate health benefit, and not to be injurious to society. The basis of the extension of the medical exception to such NCMP has been said to be that they have been accepted by the medical profession.[79] Glanville Williams argued that the decision whether a novel intervention constituted proper medical treatment should be a matter for the medical profession itself saying 'Controls exercised by the medical profession itself shoauld [*sic*] be accepted as sufficient'.[80] If Williams is right, *Bolam* returns to limit the boundaries of proper medical treatment. Holt CJ's view that physicians not judges were best placed to determine 'wholesome medicine',[81] trumps Coke's forthright assertion of the role of judicial scrutiny.[82]

Antiquated laws depriving married women of sovereignty over their own bodies and rendering wives' bodies marital 'property' have been formally consigned to history. We should not forget that remnants of married women's subjugation survived until less than half a century ago, nor overlook the lessons of treating any persons as property. As the next chapter will illustrate, pronouncements by theologians and 'learned medical men' that women were weak and dangerous buttressed such laws. Attitudes to women, especially in the context of reproduction, bear traces of that past. Another 'antique', the crime of maim, offers evidence that none of our ancestors enjoyed unfettered choices about what could be

---

76 Lewis 'Medical Exception' (n 64) 355.
77 Lewis 'Sterilisation' (n 54).
78 Law Commission Consultation Paper No 139 *Consent in the Criminal Law* (HMSO, 1995) paras 8.32.
79 J Montgomery *Health Care Law* (2nd edn) (Oxford University Press, 2003) 232.
80 G Williams *Textbook of Criminal Law* (Sweet & Maxwell, 1983) 590.
81 *Dr Groenvelt versus Dr Burwell & Al* (1698) 90 English Reports 883, 885.
82 *Dr Bonham's Case* (1609) 77 English Reports 646, 650.

done to 'their' body. 'My body, my choice' could not suffice to legitimate suicide, abortion or bizarre 'medical interventions'. Nor are 'our' bodies exclusively ours even now. Individual preferences can still be subordinated to public good and, in relation to health care, the fuzzy boundaries of the 'medical exception' open the door to deference to medical judgement of what constitutes such good.[83]

---

83 S Fovargue and M Brazier 'Transforming Wrong into Rights: What is "Proper Medical Treatment"?' in Fovargue and Mullock (eds) (n 6) 16–25.

8

Reproductive bodies: mothers, midwives and morals

Mothers not men

[W]omen are made and meant to be not men, but mothers of men.[1]

This quotation from Dr Withers Moore, President of the British Medical Association, speaking in 1889, summed up attitudes to women which persisted into recent times and which have not been wholly abandoned even now. Articulated within his efforts to continue to exclude women from medical practice, Withers Moore exemplifies the confinement of women to their reproductive function. Viewed as principally a vehicle for procreation, the incapacities English law imposed on women appear explicable, if unpalatable. The emphasis on women as mothers in combination with changing theories about human reproduction advanced by philosophers, anatomists and learned medical men may have influenced the way English law treated all women. The marriage of law and medicine defined most women in terms of their reproductive organs. The 'medical' belief that women were physiologically and psychologically inferior buttressed laws depriving women of rights over their bodies and own fates. They were not 'fit' to practise medicine or any learned profession.

Human reproduction has generated a plethora of legal and bioethical problems from 'time immemorial.' Henry VIII's need for a male heir changed history. In less exalted ranks of society, sons were the means of security in old age. The State had an interest in maintaining a healthy population. Reproductive behaviour was not a private domain. Laws regulating reproductive behaviour have largely focused on female behaviour. While sexual morality was initially a matter for the ecclesiastical jurisdiction rather than the secular courts, enforcing moral standards crept into secular law and

1 W Moore 'The Higher Education of Women' *British Medical Journal* 14 August 1889 295 at 299 as cited by M Thomson *Reproducing Narrative: Gender, Reproduction and Law* (Routledge, 1998) 37.

the regulation of reproduction. The link between sexual activity and pro-creation muddied the waters, making it hard to disentangle judgements on sexual morals from measures designed to safeguard the welfare of birthing women and their children, or the more pragmatic interests of the State.

At first sight it may seem that there is little to link antiquated laws and scientific theories disproportionately disadvantaging women and questions posed today by human reproduction. Remnants of 'old' law and attitudes endure. The Assisted Reproductive Technologies (ARTS) have enabled many infertile women and men to found families, and assisted others, including single people and same-sex couples, to found a family of their choice, in the manner of their choice. The very nature of what constitutes a family, who is in law mother or father, is challenged.[2] Both the science of reproductive medicine, and the predominantly liberal social attitudes with which new developments have been greeted in this country, would be alien to most of the population of the United Kingdom in the middle of the twentieth century, never mind the fifteenth to nineteenth centuries.

Technologies may be novel. Engagement between law, medicine and human reproduction is not. The role of the state and the legitimacy or other-wise of limitations on individuals' reproductive choices is a theme persisting across the centuries. The previous chapter identified how the common law limited a subject's sovereignty over their own body. Laws regulating repro-duction sought to achieve the birth of the 'right sort' of children, healthy children who would not place a financial burden on the community, or disturb public order, historically children born within marriage. Health workers were deployed to implement those laws. In attempting to regu-late reproductive behaviour, regulation of the health workers providing care for women giving birth was a key feature in the intervention of the Church and Crown. Insofar as the regulatory effort focused on access to, and the quality of care for, women and their infants, it is not controversial. Intervention to safeguard the well-being of the woman and her child is to be distinguished from interventions grounded in moral judgements about reproductive choices and sexual behaviour. The original Section 13(5) of the Human Fertilisation Act 1990 requiring that fertility clinics take account of the welfare of the child *including the need for a father* predominantly repre-sented a moral judgement on single motherhood, and in particular, access to fertility treatment by gay women. In their antipathy to single motherhood and concerns about sexual behaviour, legislators in 1990 followed a long tradition in English law of seeking to regulate morality and, in particular, women's sexual morality.

2 *R (McConnell) (AIRE Centre intervening) v Registrar General for England and Wales* [2020] EWCA Civ 559.

From circa 1500 until the mid-eighteenth century, female midwives played a dual role providing care to birthing women and 'policing' morals. For over 200 years, midwifery offered women social status and authority. The next sections of this chapter look back at aspects of the history of law and midwifery to complete an account of law regulating healing and examine a number of ethical questions relating to 'reproductive bodies'. Later sections of the chapter focus on how theories of 'medical science' may have influenced the law predominantly to the disadvantage of women. What were perceived at the time to be 'scientific' findings reinforced perceptions of women as weak yet dangerous, supporting a common goal of medicine and law to exclude women from any of the learned professions, and influencing the development of laws apparently distant from law and healing. In weird theories of embryology and 'scientific' myths about female biology, examples of 'science making law' can be espied, theories explaining the common law's attitude to laws of succession. Finally, the premium which English law placed on bloodlines and lineage, what we now would describe as genetic identity, is assessed.

The status of the unborn child and abortion is not dealt with in this chapter. So huge is the tangled history of this seemingly eternal conflict that it requires a chapter of its own, the next chapter, Chapter 9.

Female midwives: a profession for women?[3]

Pelling and Webster describe midwives in the sixteenth century as being 'at the fringe of official medicine' and coming 'only under a system of ecclesiastical jurisdiction'.[4] The importance of female midwives until the eighteenth century as the key providers of maternity care has often been forgotten and should not be underestimated. Childbirth was a woman's world. Men, male surgeons, only entered the birth chamber when summoned by the midwife to use their instruments to remove a dead or dying fetus blocking the birth canal.

Rather than being at the fringe of official medicine, midwives were detached from the tussles between the orthodox medical men (discussed in Chapters 3 and 4). Not until the nineteenth century did medical men

---

3 This section draws heavily on research conducted into the regulation of midwives undertaken jointly with Dr Sarah Fox as part of the author's Leverhulme Emeritus Fellowship. See in particular, S Fox and M Brazier 'Regulating English Midwives c 1500–1900' (2020) 20 *Medical Law International* 308.

4 M Pelling and C Webster 'Medical Practitioners' in C Webster (ed) *Health, Medicine and Mortality in the Sixteenth Century* (Cambridge University Press, 1979) 179.

defame women midwives as 'quacks' to be dominated or suppressed. In the sixteenth and seventeenth centuries a midwife was a respected member of her parish who undertook a number of 'public' functions over and above her role as the provider of hands-on care. Midwives caring for a woman in labour did not act alone. Until the advent of the man-midwife in the eighteenth century,[5] childbirth was a social as much as a medical event.[6] Labouring women would be tended by female relatives and neighbours as well as the local midwife.[7]

Midwifery offered women an occupation, arguably a profession, generating income and status. Recognition of the social importance of midwives' role as health practitioners coupled with the need for regulation to monitor fitness to practise is evidenced by the system for episcopal licensing of midwives. Ecclesiastical regulation of midwives resembled episcopal licensing of male physicians and surgeons. Episcopal licensing of physicians and surgeons fell into disuse and gradually migrated into the secular domain in the sixteenth to seventeenth centuries.[8] Episcopal licensing of female midwives continued well into the eighteenth century when it decayed, not to be replaced by any scheme of formal regulation until the Midwives Act 1902. During the 200 years or so that episcopal licensing endured, despite its flaws, English midwives were respected and valued as independent practitioners. Midwives in this era were not so much on the fringe of medicine as separate from the world of both the orthodox practitioners and traditional healers, in an exclusive space within which they were recognised as independent skilled practitioners.

Midwives and myths

Describing midwives as respected practitioners contradicts the picture of the midwife prevalent in the nineteenth century. The image of Sairey Gamp in Charles Dickens's *Martin Chuzzlewit* (published in 1844) depicted midwives as dirty, avaricious and unskilled.[9] That depiction of midwives as incompetent sluts dominated parliamentary debates about statutory regulation of midwives in the nineteenth century. It is a myth. In *The Midwives*

---

5 A Wilson *The Making of Man-midwifery: Childbirth in England, 1660–1770* (Harvard University Press, 1995).
6 Fox and Brazier (n 3) 315–316.
7 S Fox ' "The Woman was a Stranger": Childbirth and Community in Eighteenth-Century England' (2019) 28 *Women's History Review* 421.
8 See above Chapters 3 and 4.
9 A Summers 'Sairey Gamp: Generating Fact from Fiction' (1997) 14 *Nursing Inquiry* 14.

of Seventeenth-Century London,[10] Doreen Evenden provides abundant evidence of a very different reality to that portrayed by Dickens. Evenden notes the stereotype of the midwife 'portrayed as ignorant, incompetent and poor'.[11] She rehearses the unflattering accounts of female midwifery[12] to be found in early writing on English midwives in the nineteenth century: accounts attacking the women's lack of education, poor skills and manifest inferiority to the medically qualified men (man-midwives later to become obstetricians) who sought to break into the formerly all-female preserve of childbirth.[13] She notes that the authors are men,[14] often medical practitioners who were themselves man-midwives. Evenden meticulously and critically analyses primary sources and the literature relating to the training, practice and licensing of midwives in the seventeenth century. She demonstrates that allegations of the inadequacy of female midwives were not supported by evidence.[15]

In 1900 when Parliament debated a Midwives Bill to introduce a statutory framework for regulating midwives, a framework similar to, but separate from, the Medical Acts regulating medical professionals, the Dickensian myth prevailed. Anecdotal claims were made about the poor practice and superficial education of female midwives in comparison to medical men. The MP for Liverpool, T P O'Connor, countered that 'the picture drawn of the drunken, incompetent nurse [midwife] is entirely the result of an imagination inflamed by philanthropic feeling'.[16] Two years later, in the House of Lords, the Duke of Northumberland opined that 'any drunken old hag' could declare herself to be a midwife.[17] The Lord Bishop of Winchester asked if their Lordships were aware that 'for many centuries no woman could practise as a midwife without the direct sanction of the Bishop of the Diocese'.[18]

10 D Evenden *The Midwives of Seventeenth-Century London* (Cambridge University Press, 2000).
11 Ibid 1.
12 P Willughby *Observations in Midwifery* (H Blenkinsop, 1863: reprint edn, SR Publishers, 1972).
13 Evenden (n 10) 6–13.
14 Willughby (n 12): and see J H Aveling *English Midwives, Their History and Prospects* (1872; reprint edn: Hugh K Elliott Ltd, 1967) .
15 And see I Loudon *Death in Childbirth: An International Study of Maternal Care and Maternal Mortality* (Oxford University Press, 1992).
16 Midwives Bill, House of Commons, Second Reading, 9 March 1900 Vol 80 Column 538.
17 Midwives Bill, House of Lords, Second Reading, 20 June 1902 Vol 109 Column 1936.
18 Ibid Column 1937.

Episcopal licensing

From about 1500, an aspiring midwife had in theory to obtain a licence from her bishop. Historians are unsure exactly when the Church began formally licensing midwives in England. Evenden and Guy suggest the early 1500s,[19] enduring (with a break during the Interregnum) until its decay in the eighteenth century.

The extraordinary feature of episcopal licensing of midwives in England is that there appears to have been no statutory basis in secular or canon law for the system.[20] Henry VIII's Act of 1511 endorsing episcopal licensing of physic and surgery makes no mention of midwives. Nor is there evidence of any relevant formal canon law promulgated either by the Roman Church before the Reformation, or the Church of England later.[21] Guy argues that express provisions of canon law were unnecessary. The Church's interest derived from the fact that any midwife might be called on to baptise a dying infant. Roman Catholic doctrine of the time taught that the unbaptised or improperly baptised infant could not enter Heaven but was condemned to limbo. After the Reformation, the newly established Church of England retained an interest in correct baptism to ensure that no liturgical error permitted the devil to seize the child's soul and that any baptism was in strict conformity with the rites of the Anglican Church, not contaminated by any Roman Catholic practices. Guy concludes:

> The authority vested in the midwife by ecclesiastical law to baptise in case of necessity thus placed her in a sense in the 'front line' of the church's ministry. And if so vital a function had been conceded to her by the church, inevitably the church required a central role in her regulation.[22]

Concern about correct baptism and the infant's soul undoubtedly played a significant role in initiating the Church's assumption of responsibility for regulating midwives. Its importance is highlighted in the oath sworn by midwife Eleanor Pead in 1567 on being granted her licence by her bishop:

> In the ministration of baptism in the time of necessity I will use apt and the accustomed words of the same sacrament ... I christen thee in the name of the Father, the Son and the Holy Ghost and none other profane words ...pouring

---

19 Evenden (n 10) 25; J Guy 'The Episcopal Licensing of Physicians, Surgeons and Midwives' (1982) 56 *Bulletin of the History of Medicine* 538. Forbes noted clerical interest in midwifery possibly dating back to the early fourteenth century; T Forbes 'The Regulation of English Midwives in the Sixteenth and Seventeenth Centuries' (1964) 8 *Medical History* 236.
20 Guy (n 19) 538; Evenden (n 10) 25.
21 Guy (n 19) ibid.
22 Guy (n 19) 338–339.

water upon the head of the infant I will use pure and clean water ... and I will notify the curate of the parish church of every such baptizing.[23]

If liturgically correct baptism was the only basis for episcopal interest, an account of ecclesiastical regulation of midwifery would have little place in a consideration of law and healing. It is misguided, however, to conclude that the spiritual welfare of the dying infant was the only objective of ecclesiastical regulation and thus episcopal licensing had nothing to do with regulating health care. Evenden acknowledges the importance of the midwife's role in the rite of baptism to the Church and adds four further factors pertinent to the ecclesiastical regulation of midwifery: (1) pre-occupation with sorcery; (2) concerns about bastardy; (3) the association of midwifery with medical practice in which since 1511 local licensing had played a major part; (4) the professional competence of the midwives.[24]

Undue emphasis on baptism, a sacrament in both the Roman Church and the Church of England, gives credence to the argument that the Church was primarily concerned to ensure that the midwife was of good character, and thus fit to be entrusted with the sacred duty of baptism, and that there was no risk that she might engage in sorcery or witchcraft.

What of competence? Even Forbes, who contended that licensing was primarily concerned with moral character and religious observance, conceded that candidate midwives had to show that they were 'respected in their parish for their morality, discretion, sobriety and *for their experience in their craft* (my emphasis)'.[25] Evenden notes: 'Indeed there is evidence that competence was more important than moral rectitude in the minds of many, including at least some church officials.'[26]

And later: 'Contemporaries did not make a clear distinction between character and professional competence. For them the two were obviously and intimately associated.'[27]

The relationship between a health professional's character and professional fitness to practise endures. Midwives, nurses and doctors still face disciplinary proceedings in respect of conduct not directly related to their skills. Today, character may not entail the same focus on sexual morality, but respecting sexual boundaries within professional/patient relationships is still enforced. And disciplinary proceedings against midwives or doctors can still follow the professional's conviction for a serious crime even though

23 Evenden (n 10) Appendix A 'Eleanor Pead's Oath'.
24 Ibid 26.
25 Forbes (n 19) 242.
26 Evenden (n 10) 16.
27 Ibid 69.

the crime is unrelated to professional competence. The concept that a health professional must be of good character endures.

The case that licensing was part of a regulatory framework designed to protect the safety of birthing women and monitor the competence and practice of the midwives is well illustrated by examination of what was required of a woman seeking a licence. She had to serve a lengthy apprenticeship, as a deputy to a licensed and experienced midwife. When she applied for her licence, the midwife was required to produce testimonials from clergy, neighbours, fellow midwives, local physicians and surgeons. Unlike the medical men, the 'apprentice' midwife had also to provide testimonials from women whom she had delivered. These women were normally obliged to attend the bishop's court with the aspiring midwife and give evidence on oath.

The final stage of the long road to qualification involved attendance before the bishop's chancellor and if successful paying a substantial fee for her licence estimated at £1–£2.[28] (£1 in 1600 equates to approximately £307 in today's money.) The new midwife would then swear a solemn oath and receive a certificate to display at visitations of the bishop or his nominees to the parish. Midwives' oaths can be seen as the prototype of a Code of Ethics reflecting ethical concerns that persist today. Swearing her oath was not the end of oversight of the midwife by the bishop and his officers. They would make visitations, hear complaints of poor practice, and seek to identify women practising without a licence. Fines and other penalties were imposed. The ultimate sanction was the excommunication of the offending midwife, be she practising without a licence or found guilty of malpractice.

Episcopal licensing of midwives shared many characteristics of modern regulation of health professionals. It embodied a system of external regulation markedly different from the extensive powers of self-regulation conferred on the College of Physicians in London in 1522. In theory, an external authority, the diocesan bishop, controlled entry to the profession with powers to discipline errant licensees and prohibit unlicensed practice. Three problems prevent too close an analogy between ecclesiastical regulation of midwives and current professional regulation. First, there is substantial evidence that many women practised without a licence. Some midwives spent their whole career as a deputy; others never sought a licence, possibly because of the cost. The extent to which local bishops enforced the licensing system and exercised oversight of practice varied considerably from diocese to diocese. Second, episcopal licensing of midwives lacked statutory authority from Church or State. That absence of formal status did not seem to have been problematic until close to the end of the era of ecclesiastical

28 Ibid 38–40.

regulation. Once challenged, the Church lacked effective powers to enforce its discipline on women who refused to apply for a licence. Wilson reports that in 1634 an unlicensed midwife challenged the Church in an ecclesiastical court and it was held that 'The Church could not punish a woman for unlicensed practice.'[29] Or rather it could not impose secular penalties such as a fine or gaol, only penance and, in extreme cases, excommunication. Until the Toleration Act 1689, communion with the Established Church was mandatory. The Act allowed Protestant dissenters to set up their own churches and schools. Women who were not members of the Anglican Church were unperturbed by any threat to excommunicate them from a church they did not belong to. In sum the Church proved to be relatively impotent in imposing its will on 'intransigent midwives who refused to apply for a midwifery licence'.[30] The Church appears to fail in two of the normal incidents of professional regulation, protecting a monopoly for the licensed professional, and possessing effective means of enforcing its rules. However, similar problems arose in relation to the licensing of surgeons and physicians outside London.

A third and enduring difficulty for the Church in seeking to drive unlicensed women out of business was defining midwifery: a problem shared with the College of Physicians defining the practice of physic (discussed in Chapter 3). At what point did a neighbour attending a woman in labour, having experience of childbirth herself, and having helped with other deliveries, cross the line from being a good neighbour to become an unlicensed midwife? Is the crucial question one of payment?

Yet despite drawbacks in the regulatory framework, the system appears to have worked and birthing women had access to such care as was available at that point in time. A mix of external formal regulation and informal local regulation in and by the community where the midwife practised contributed to its success. Births took place in the woman's home attended by her married female relatives and neighbours, all of whom would have extensive experience of childbirth and who would keep a close eye on the midwife, be she licensed or not. Becoming an independent midwife involved a period of working under the supervision and mentorship of an experienced and well-regarded midwife, whose practice the mentee might ultimately 'inherit'.[31] Evenden describes the regulation of midwives in the

29 A Wilson 'Childbirth in Seventeenth and Eighteenth-century England' PhD thesis, University of Sussex, 1983, 41, cited in Evenden (n 10) 47.
30 Evenden (n 10) 7.
31 F Badger 'Illuminating Nineteenth-Century Urban Midwifery: The Register of a Coventry Midwife' (2014) 23 *Women's History Review* 683.

seventeenth century as 'fundamentally a self-regulatory system of train-ing and apprenticeship'.[32] She argues that licensing was 'not central to the expertise or competence' of the profession. Sarah Fox and I have argued that external ecclesiastical and informal community regulation were sym-biotic and mutually dependent. Episcopal licensing formalised practice embedded in the community. And community practice informed the more formal procedures of the Church.[33] Licensing lent status to practitioners even if not all midwives sought an individual licence. Examining the effects of the decay of ecclesiastical regulation, Evenden concedes that licensing was *'important for the societal respect and credit of the traditional profes-sion* (my emphasis)'.[34]

Old oaths and modern ethics

The content of oaths sworn by a midwife on the grant of her licence from the bishop is instructive in exploring how far licensing of midwives was pre-dominantly concerned with religion rather than fitness to practise.[35] In the oath sworn by Eleanor Pead in 1567 her duty to baptise a child who might not live constituted over a third of her oath.[36] But even in 1567 Eleanor undertook other obligations, in particular to be 'ready to help and aid poor as well as rich women being in labour and travail of child'.[37]

Eighty years later an oath of 1649 continued to address baptism. The emphasis had changed to require that the midwife did not collude in a Roman Catholic rite:

> You shall not be privie, or consent that any priest or other partie shall in your absence, or in your companie or of your knowledge or sufferance baptise any child by any Masse, Latin Service or Prayers than such as are appointed by the laws of the Church of England.[38]

By 1649, the established Church's concern about baptism focused less on care for the soul of the infant and more on the battle with the Church of

---

32 Evenden (n 10) 175.
33 Fox and Brazier (n 3).
34 Evenden (n 10) 175.
35 See S Fox and M Brazier 'Midwives' Oaths: Ethical Promises in Early Modern Midwifery' (forthcoming).
36 Evenden (n 10) Appendix A.
37 Ibid.
38 Ibid Appendix B Anon. Additionally the midwife in 1649 was required to ensure that the child was taken to be baptised in the parish church save for cases of necessity when the midwife could still perform a private baptism using the rite prescribed in the Book of Common Prayer and reporting her action to the bishop or his officers.

Rome. By 1713 when Mary Cooke swore her oath express mention of baptism had disappeared.[39]

Other promises made by the midwife were directly related to matters of ethical practice and are surprisingly forward-looking. The 'rather remarkable change in the oath argues for an increased interest in the practical rather than the spiritual qualifications of the midwife'.[40] The midwife had to swear to be diligent and faithful – to be beneficent. She undertook to be ready to treat every woman in labour be she rich or poor, and not in 'times of nessitie to forsake the poore woman to go unto the riche'. She must not use any 'ungodly wayes' to coerce the vulnerable woman to pay any extortionate fee. If the woman or child was in peril, she must summon aid from other midwives and those who were experts in the profession. If the midwife became aware of a colleague not executing her profession properly, she should report to the bishop, as she should any evidence of unlicensed practice. In appointing any deputy (apprentice), the midwife must be assured of the woman's skill, suitability and character. The oaths were central to the regulatory framework of episcopal licensing and granted women in labour a right to expert assistance, and protection from undue influence. The midwife was required to understand limitations in her own skill and be ready to call for help. In the requirement to report poor practice the oath of 1649 mandated whistle-blowing, something not achieved in modern medical law until 2014 when Section 81 of the Care Act 2014 introduced the statutory duty of candour.

Other provisions of the oaths are less palatable to modern thinking.[41] In both 1567 and 1649 the midwife was injuncted to ensure that no woman named a man father to her child who was not the true father, nor claimed a child to be hers who was not her own, nor should the midwife participate in any way in a concealed birth. The obligation to 'grass' on their clients and obsession with bastardy is alien and uncomfortable, but conferred on the midwife a role in secular law maintaining the integrity of blood lines and inheritance of property.

Midwives in the legal process and local government

The social status enjoyed by midwives as 'experts' in pregnancy and childbirth was reinforced by public duties in local government and the

39 Evenden (n 10) Appendix C.
40 Ibid 29.
41 Sections of the oaths relating to sorcery have little resonance now. Prohibition of any involvement with aborting a child reflects the secular criminal law of the times. Nor can the dangers of abortion to the mother at the time be overlooked.

legal process, duties which fell to the midwife because of that expertise. Establishing whether a woman was, or had been, pregnant was required in several circumstances. A woman sentenced to death could 'plead the belly'. If that claim was substantiated her execution would be postponed until she had given birth. The court would summon a jury of matrons to determine the veracity of her claim.[42] The task and knowledge demanded of a matron-juror makes it distinctly possible that midwives would have been selected for this role. In 1792, it was held that a jury of matrons must always be a jury of midwives.[43]

If a child's legitimacy or questions of proof of pregnancy were in issue the response was 'call the midwife'. Until circa 1800, midwives were often expert witnesses in bastardy hearings. They would be called to testify as to the length of gestation, for example if a widow gave birth many months after her husband's death. In bastardy hearings, the parish sought to identify the biological father of a child born to an unmarried woman in order to obtain an order to require the father to recompense the parish for the cost of the care of the mother in childbirth and the subsequent cost of maintaining the infant. Midwives were expected to use their access to the unfortunate woman and their authority to persuade her to disclose the name of the father.

The driving force in many cases was practical. Relatives argued about inheritance, reflecting the huge value placed by the common law on lineage and parishes sought to shift responsibility for children born out of wedlock to the father, so avoiding a call on the public purse. In 1623, English law adopted a more overtly moral stance in relation to illegitimacy. An *Act to prevent the destroying and murthering of Bastard Children*, commonly referred to as the Infanticide Act, introduced draconian measures targeted at the 'many lewd Women that have been delivered of Bastard Children, [who] to avoyde their shame and to escape punishment, doe secretlie bury, or conceale the Death, of their children'. If a woman gave birth to a child who if born alive would be a bastard and then attempted to conceal the death of the child:

> that it may not come to light, whether it is borne alive or not but be concealed, in every such Case the Mother so offending shall suffer Death as in case of Murther, *except such Mother can make pffe by one Witness at the least, that the Child (whose Death was by her soe intended to be concealed) was borne dead* [my emphasis].

42 J Baker *An Introduction to English Legal History* (5th edn) (Oxford University Press, 2019) 559.

43 *In the Matter of Martha Brown ex p Newton Wallop* (1792) 29 English Reports 794.

Women accused of infanticide had to prove *either* that the infant had been born dead, *or* that they had not been pregnant.[44] Once again midwives acted as 'expert witnesses' in such matters of proof. Midwives had access to women's bodies during birth and pregnancy, illness or death. By custom, they could 'search' the body of a woman suspected of having given birth to an illegitimate child, inspecting her stomach and squeezing her breasts for signs of lactation.[45] And where they suspected a child had been born, the midwife led the search for the body of the child,[46] and gave evidence in court.

The public functions as a guardian of blood lines and sexual morality consolidated the midwife's position in society as a respected and independent practitioner. The demise of the public face of midwifery was roughly contemporaneous with the decay of episcopal interest in regulating midwives and contributed to the demise of the respect for midwives as health-care workers and the gradual medicalisation of childbirth. By the end of the eighteenth century in legal disputes about inheritance and paternity, expert testimony was more likely to be sought from a male medical practitioner than a female midwife.[47]

The Infanticide Act was repealed by Lord Ellenborough's Act in 1803, the Act introducing the first statutory prohibition on abortion. In 1834, the Poor Law Amendment Act repealed legislation by which a single woman could 'charge any Person with having gotten her with any child of which she shall be pregnant' or allow 'the Mother of any Bastard Child' to seek maintenance from the putative father. The midwife's role in local government advising on paternity claims became redundant.

The demise of licensing and medical men

Episcopal licensing of midwives and medical men ceased temporarily from about 1641 during the English Civil Wars resuming in 1661 after the Restoration of the Monarchy.[48] In the birth chamber little changed in those twenty years. Within forty years or so episcopal licensing began to decay.

---

44 W Blackstone *Commentaries on the Laws of England* (Oxford University Press, 2016) Book IV 198.

45 M Jackson *New-born Child Murder: Women, Illegitimacy and the Courts in Eighteenth-Century England* (Manchester University Press, 1996) 65.

46 Ibid particularly Chapter 3 'Examining Suspects: Conflicting Accounts of Pregnancy, Birth and Death', 60–78.

47 D M Dwyer 'Expert Evidence in the English Civil Courts 1550–1800' (2007) 28 *Journal of Legal History* 93.

48 Fox and Brazier (n 3) 322–323.

Its demise was relatively sudden.[49] Medical historians suggest a number of explanations for the demise of midwifery licensing.[50] The declining power of the Church and the growing popularity of the (male) proto-obstetricians are often advanced as key causes. Greater religious tolerance of non-conformist dissenters played a role.[51] It seems that the Church gradually withdrew from its secular role at the same time that more and more man-midwives sought to enter the market.

Evenden summed up:

> [O]nce the role of the Church diminished, and with it the status attached to licensing, the seeds of decay were sown. By the 1750's the midwives' traditional, practical skill proved no match for the claims of the man midwife, waiting in the wings with his shiny instruments and promises of 'scientific expertise'.[52]

At this point the absence of a secure legal foundation for what had been a successful framework for regulation became relevant. There was no Act of Parliament or Royal Charter which could be relied on to counter either the encroachment of the man-midwives on the traditional midwives' regulatory space, or the decline of interest on the part of the ecclesiastical authorities. Licensing had nonetheless had a value of its own. The Church may not have actively monitored every midwife in the realm. In undertaking the regulatory role, the Church bestowed respectability on midwifery, distinguishing midwives from unregulated healers. In the heyday of episcopal licensing, that status was reinforced by the public role of midwives in the parish and the legal system.

The cessation of licensing did not have much immediate impact on midwifery on the ground. The informal framework of oversight in the community continued to operate and the majority of women continued to be delivered by local female midwives. The memory of female midwives as ecclesiastically licensed practitioners faded from view. The loss of status opened the door for medical men to reduce midwives to the role of handmaiden or decry them as dangerous sluts. While the Medical Act 1858 which effected partial unification of the three orthodox medical professions made no reference to female midwives, before and after 1858 there were many calls for regulation of midwives principally focused on the declared need for 'medical' supervision of such women. Discussed more fully in

---

49 Evenden (n 10) 174 indicates that the midwifery licensing system in London had begun to break down by 1720.
50 Fox and Brazier (n 3) 324–325.
51 Toleration Act 1689.
52 Evenden (n 10) 175.

Chapter 4, the College of Physicians unsuccessfully sought powers in 1806 to regulate all health-care practitioners in England and Wales. Anyone (male or female) practising midwifery without a licence from the College would be acting unlawfully. In effect the College would regulate midwifery even though physicians had little to do with childbirth. In 1806, the group calling themselves the 'Associated Faculty' argued for a system of regulation extending to 'the whole field of medical care throughout the kingdom'[53] including man-midwives and female midwives. Male midwives would be required to prove that they had attended lectures in anatomy and received instruction from an experienced *accoucheur* for one year. Man-midwives sought to enhance their status, adopting a new title obstetrician, or the French style of *accoucheur*. Female midwives could obtain a certificate of proficiency from an obstetrician. In 1825 the Obstetric Society was established, to be succeeded in 1858 by the London Obstetrical Society. The Society offered training to female midwives and certificates to women who passed its examinations. Lying-in hospitals which had gradually been established in most cities and major towns also offered training and certification to women.[54] The certificated midwife unlike her licensed ancestress was subject to male supervision. Her practice and training and, in some cases, employment would be prescribed by the emergent obstetricians. In 1875, the General Medical Council (GMC) unsuccessfully put forward proposals to establish a centralised system for the registration of female midwives by the GMC itself.

Many women continued to practise without any sort of certification, leading to the derogatory attacks by medical men about ignorant and unqualified midwives, allegations that were rarely backed by evidence. In the course of the nineteenth century, however, medical men acquired an increasingly influential voice in the legislative process, exemplified, as the next chapter will show, by their success in shaping abortion laws. The medical men sought to dominate women whom they perceived as female 'workers' and in no sense fellow professionals. From 1883 to 1902, six Bills designed to regulate midwives were introduced in Parliament. A Select Committee on Midwives' Registration reported in 1893. Medical practitioners found themselves in a quandary, or rather two quandaries.

(1) Limiting the practice of midwifery to women who had undergone training and certification had one significant drawback for male practitioners who focused their practice on obstetrics. These gentlemen had little interest in natural births or post-natal care: such care was unprofitable.

53 Ibid 116.
54 Fox and Brazier (n 3) 325–327.

Nor was there likely to be a sufficient number of qualified (certificated) midwives to meet demand. The obstetricians did not want to abolish midwives, just confine the women to a subordinate role. They graciously conceded that experienced if unqualified midwives of good character could deal with natural labour. Establishing a distinction in legislation whereby a midwife might lawfully only attend a natural labour was greeted with contempt in Parliament. One noble Lord enquired how the midwife was to 'know whether a case was abnormal or not'.[55]

(2) A pressing concern for many male practitioners was a fear that granting legal status to female midwives to practise as independent professionals would open the door to allowing women to practise medicine. In 1865, Elizabeth Garrett Anderson took advantage of legal loopholes to obtain the diploma of the Society of Apothecaries, forcing the GMC to register her as a medical practitioner. In heated debates about midwives the broader controversy about women's suitability to practise healing in any capacity found a strong voice. Eventually, in 1902, Parliament passed the Midwives Act establishing a framework for the certification of female midwives analogous to the provision for the registration of medical practitioners by the 1858 Medical Act.[56]

Science 'making law'? Weak and dangerous women

In 1879, Walter Rivington wrote of the opponents of medical education for women:

> Many of the most estimable members of our profession perceive in the medical education and destination of women a horrible and vicious attempt deliberately to unsex themselves ... the gratification of prurient and morbid curiosity and thirst for forbidden information ... the assumption of offices which Nature intended for the sterner sex.[57]

Medical men, campaigning against women practising medicine, often opposed all female higher education arguing that the female brain was inferior and that intellectual activity damaged women's health, especially in rendering women vulnerable to gynaecological disorder.[58] The latter might

---

55 Lord Thring Midwives Bill, Vol 109 Column 1238, 20 June 1902.

56 Men were unable to qualify as certified midwives until 1983; see the Sex Discrimination Act 1975 (Amendment of section 20) Order SI 1202 (1983).

57 W Rivington *The Medical Profession* (Bailliere, Tindall and Cox, 1879) 135.

58 J N Burstyn 'Education and Sex: The Medical Case against Higher Education for Women in England 1870–1900' (1973) 171 *Proceedings of the American Philosophical Society* 79.

unfit women from their prime duty to be 'mothers of men'. Opponents of women doctors (and female lawyers) upheld enduring perceptions of women as weak and dangerous, substantiated in their view by scientific evidence. Such sentiments, expressed less than 200 years ago, represent much older judgements on female flaws to which I now turn.

The disempowerment of women offers an illustration of the relationship between law and healing as a two-way process. Judges and Parliament made laws regulating healing and healers. 'Medical knowledge' in turn influenced the law, in some cases effectively 'making law'.[59] 'Scientific' theories about women's physiological and psychological deficits buttressed laws adverse to women. Laws imposing significant incapacities on married women and granting husbands patriarchal control of their 'marital property' were rooted in theories about female weakness and (mis)understandings of human reproduction. Developments in 'medical science' could of course contribute positively to better law-making and law enforcement.[60] For the most part 'scientific contributions' to the evolution of the English law relating to women remained profoundly retrogressive well into the twentieth century. The marriage of law and medicine entrenched attitudes affecting every aspect of a woman's life for centuries, especially her reproductive life.

It will swiftly become apparent that much of the so-called science has been proven to be myth. That does not matter; just as legal fictions permeated the growth of the common law, so medical myths resulted in popular understandings or often misunderstandings of evolving biomedical 'science'.

Imagery of woman

The portrayal of women advanced by an unholy alliance of medicine and religion depicted a 'creature' both weak and dangerous.[61] Woman's principal function was to bear children. The Book of Genesis proclaimed 'I will greatly multiply your pain in childbirth, in pain shall you bring forth children yet your desire shall be for your husband' (Genesis 3:7).

---

59 D L Faigman *Legal Alchemy: The Use and Misuse of Science in the Law* (New York: W H Freeman, 2000) 9–11.
60 K D Watson *Medicine and Justice: Medico-Legal Practice in England and Wales 1700–1914* (Routledge, 2020).
61 This section draws from E C Romanis, D Begovic, M Brazier and A Mullock 'Reviewing the Womb' (2021) 47 *Journal of Medical Ethics* 820.

Infertility might have appeared to be a preferable option. Barren women were, however, at best pitied and at worst despised. John McKeown quotes Martin Luther:

> [W]e see how weak and sickly barren women are. And those who are fruitful are healthier cleanlier and happier, and even if they bear themselves weary – or ultimately bear themselves out-that does not hurt *let them bear themselves out this is the purpose for which they exist* [my emphasis].[62]

Infertility spared a woman the perils of childbirth. Remaining unwed permitted her to control her own property as a *feme sole*. In practice, for richer or poorer women spinsterhood was not a desirable state. Laws relating to inheritance meant daughters rarely inherited substantial property. The vast majority of women needed a husband to support them and so avoid the cold charity of a brother or the parish. Declared 'weak and sickly' by Luther, other theologians and physicians were less kind describing barren women as monstrous.[63]

Medical practitioners thought that barren women were particularly susceptible to the 'wandering womb', a condition attributed to many female ills. The 'wandering womb' was not fixed in its proper place. It wandered around the female body pressing on heart and lungs.[64] It was described as 'a migratory uterus prowling about the body like a wild animal pressing on the chest'[65] threatening the woman's life via 'suffocation of the mother' and emitting noxious fumes. The depiction of women as unclean and smelly became even less attractive once menstruation was considered. The womb preparing for its purpose in bearing children via menstruation attracted further odium. For example, menstruating women were described as 'venomous during the time of their flowers and so very dangerous that they poison beasts with their glance and little children in their cots'. A child conceived during menstruation might be born 'leprous, or epileptic or hunchback, or blind or malformed ... all would bear some badge of ignominy if only red hair'.[66] Wombs and the women who possessed them evoked disgust and fear.[67]

---

62 J McKeown *God's Babies: Natalism and Bible Interpretation in Modern America* (Open Book Publishers, 2014) 201.

63 M Thomson *Reproducing Narrative: Gender, Reproduction and Law* (Routledge Revivals, 2018) 171–196.

64 H Merskey and F J Merskey 'Hysteria, or "Suffocation of the Mother"' (1993) 148 *Canadian Medical Association Journal* 395.

65 C Rawcliffe *Medicine and Society in Later Medieval England* (Sandpiper Books, 1995) 197.

66 Ibid 175.

67 J Sawday *The Body Emblazoned: Dissection and the Human Body in Renaissance Culture* (Routledge, 1996) 9–15.

Not all medical practitioners believed in the migratory uterus.[68] By the sixteenth century, human dissection enabled anatomists to examine the interior of female corpses and it was clear that wombs did not literally wander. The anatomists then declared that female reproductive organs could be seen as inversion of the male, pronouncing that the 'neck of uterus is like the penis, and its receptacle with testicles and vessels is like the scrotum'.[69] Women were defective versions of the male. And for good measure, learned men also warned of the libidinous nature of women. Even after anatomists had displayed the interior of female bodies with the womb fixed in its place, wandering wombs continued to be part of popular folklore. Popular misunderstandings of science influenced society even when contradicted by evidence. Edward Shorter commented 'through popular culture as well rode a visceral male fear of women's magical powers'.[70]

When eventually no respectable medical man could adhere to the view that our wombs could literally suffocate us, Victorian doctors latched on to the womb as the cause of hysteria.[71] The womb disordered the female brain. Given how both the Church and medicine portrayed women's bodies and minds as defective it is scarcely surprising that the law should consider that having a female body unfitted a woman for most forms of public office. Nor is it strange that one of the few women to hold such office, Queen Elizabeth I, when she was encouraging her troops as the Spanish Armada approached the coast, should proclaim that while she had the body of a weak and feeble woman, she had the 'heart and stomach of a king'.

Generation and primogeniture[72]

The imperfection of women as perceived by medicine and theology might of itself be seen as grounds for laws to ensure that most property rested in male hands and in particular the great estates of the realm were not as a general rule held by women.[73] While women were not judged fit to hold most public

---

68 *The Trotula*, a medieval compendium on women's medicine, rejected the notion of 'suffocation of the mother': M Green (ed) *The Trotula: An English Compendium* (University of Philadelphia Press, 2002).

69 *De Vesalius De Corpora Fabrica* (1543) in S De Renzi 'Women and Medicine, 1500–1800' in P Elmer (ed) *The Healing Arts: Health Medicine and Society in Europe 1500–1800* (Manchester University Press, 2004) 198.

70 E Shorter *A History of Women's Bodies* (Penguin, 1984) 286.

71 E C Abbott 'The Wicked Womb' (1993) 148 *Canadian Medical Association Journal* 381.

72 M Brazier 'The Body in Time' (2015) 7 *Law Innovation and Technology* 161.

73 Baker (n 42) 287.

offices, or inherit a peerage, women were essential to reproduction. Luther's belief that bearing her husband's children was a woman's principal duty was widely shared. It ought to follow that wives and mothers should have been accorded a high value, not treated less favourably than their unwed sisters and subject to the legal incapacities described in Chapter 7.

Reaching back to antiquity, theories (myths) about the generation of children often cast the mother in a limited role in terms of her contribution to the creation of children she bore.[74] Contested theories about human reproduction help to explain primogeniture and laws which made married women to a great extent the property of the husband; placed such a strong emphasis on wifely fidelity; and regarded the offspring of the couple as the 'property' of the father. The changing views of women's contribution to reproduction, as well as the then scientific debates about female biology, can be seen to have had the same kind of impact on societal attitudes and law as the development of the advanced reproductive technologies do today. Science, and popular understandings of science, interacted with philosophical (and theological) debates in framing legal principles.[75]

What were mothers thought to contribute to the formation of the child?[76] The woman's womb was a necessary medium in which the father's seed could grow.[77] Theories of embryology abounded. I address only a few in little detail to give a flavour of how people thought about procreation across the ages. Aristotle argued that the embryo was formed when the male seed interacted with menstrual blood. The woman nourished the seed.[78] Galen contended that women too produced seeds, 'weaker in nature' than the male seed.[79] The womb itself was seen as playing a minor role in the formation of the child. McLaren describes such views of the generation of the fetus as epigenetic: that is to say that the environment of the womb contributed to the characteristics of the child to be, and those characteristics are not wholly the outcome of the genetic make-up of the child.[80]

By the seventeenth century, anatomists offered a more accurate picture of female reproductive organs. It became clear that women did produce eggs. Examining semen under the microscope the scientists discovered

---

74 A McLaren 'The Pleasures of Procreation: Traditional and Biomedical Theories of Conception' in W F Bynum and R Porter (eds) *William Hunter and the Eighteenth-Century Medical World* (Cambridge University Press, 1985) 332.

75 Ibid.

76 De Renzi (n 69) 205–215.

77 L Birke, S Himmelweit and G Vines *Tomorrow's Child: Reproductive Technologies in the 90s* (Virago Press, 1990) 67–70.

78 De Renzi (n 69) 207–208.

79 Ibid.

80 McLaren (n 74) 332–340.

sperm, originally described as 'animalcules'.[81] A more scientific analysis of reproduction beckoned, which could have been expected to have concluded that it was the fusion of sperm and egg which created a child, a child to whom both parents made an equal genetic contribution. Instead, a new myth was born, *pre-formationism*, which held that the fully formed child was present *either* in the male sperm *or* the female egg. *Ovism* maintained that the tiny child was contained in the mother's egg. *Animalculism* contended that it was in sperm that the tiny person was to be found. The latter triumphed.[82] *Ovism* was rejected by many doctors, philosophers, theologians and popular opinion.[83] The 'male sperm formed the embryo, and the only contribution the mother made was to receive the animalcule and nourish it'.[84] Science appeared to re-enforce ancient thinking. While proponents of *animalculism* accepted that the uterine environment could have some effect on the fetus, *animalculism* placed women firmly in the role of gestators.[85]

We know now that Aristotle and the *animalculists* were wrong. But if you believed that the child carried in her womb had no genetic link to its mother, a wife was in effect a 'gestational carrier', looking after the man's child as it developed in the womb. Nor could she refuse to conceive his child because a wife could not refuse consent to marital intercourse.[86] Husbands enjoyed a right to procreate, and wives a duty to provide the means by which they might do so. In return for her services, the husband was obliged to provide for the needs of his wife: the woman whose womb was essential to his reproductive enterprise. The child was 'his'. Husbands had the strongest of interests in ensuring that no other man's *animalcule* was carried in his wife's womb and passed off as his. Infidelity resulting in pregnancy by another man lost the husband not fifty per cent but a hundred per cent of his investment. Michael Thomson quotes the Greek playwright, Aeschylus:[87]

The mother is no parent of that which is called
Her child, but only nurse of the new planted seed
That grows. The parent is he who mounts. A stranger she
Preserves a stranger's seed.[88]

81 De Renzi (n 69) 210–215.
82 Birke et al (n 77) 69.
83 De Renzi (n 69) 213.
84 Anton van Leeuwenhock quoted in De Renzi ibid 213.
85 M Fissell 'Gender and Generation; Representing Reproduction in Early Modern England' (1995) 7 *Gender and History* 433.
86 *R v R* [1991] 1 AC 591.
87 Thomson 'Reproducing Narrative' (n 63) 19, 165.
88 Aeschylus *The Eumenides, Oresteia* Vol II trans R Latimore (Chicago University Press, 1953) 565–570.

If women were not thought to make any genetic contribution to a child, primogeniture begins to make sense. When a son reproduced, a grandson who shared your genes was born. A daughter's child would according to *animalculism* derive from her husband's *animalcule*, with no 'genetic' contribution from its mother and thus none from her father. The physical resemblance of children to their mothers and maternal family might be expected to have given rise to doubts about the child being generated wholly by the father's sperm. *Animalculism* however, as we have seen, allowed for environmental influences on the developing fetus. Failure to succeed in procreation or failure to produce a male heir was ascribed to a defective uterus, a barren wife whose womb failed in its duty.

If no substantive contribution was made by the female, and a daughter passed on none of her father's genes, logically women should have been barred from succession to his property altogether. Yet under common law, while a younger son succeeded in preference to his elder sisters, in the absence of an entail, if a man died intestate with no sons, his daughters shared the estate as co-parceners.[89] English women were not wholly excluded from inheriting paternal property and thus transmitting that property to their husbands' sons. Most titles of honour (save for the Crown) and estates with substantial land and assets were, however, entailed to ensure patrilineal descent. Preference was given to collateral males over direct female descendants. Should Lord X die leaving only daughters, his entailed estate and title passed to his nearest male relative – even second or third male cousins, excluding daughters. Hence Mr Collins acquired the home and estate of the Bennett sisters in *Pride and Prejudice*. The exclusion of daughters from most titles of honour persists to the time of writing. A Bill to challenge this antiquated rule, the Succession to the Peerages Bill, was first introduced in Parliament in 2013. A later version 2017–19 lapsed on the prorogation of Parliament. There was and is one major exception to male primogeniture. In both England and Scotland while prior to the Succession to the Crown Act 2013 a younger brother still took precedence over an elder sister, a daughter could inherit the Crown in the absence of a son. No Salic laws placed an absolute bar on women inheriting the Crown.

Bloodlines and genes

Primogeniture exemplifies the importance attached to genes.[90] Emphasis on genes and the genetic family has an ancient history in the common law

---

89 Baker (n 42) 286–288.
90 And still does; see *In re the Baronetcy of Pringle of Stichill* [2016] UKPC 60.

which placed the highest of values on bloodlines.[91] Even if the word was unknown, genetics mattered. 'The English had an inordinately high regard for blood lineage.'[92] As a consequence of this reverence for blood, the common law made no provision for adoption, nor did it permit the legitimation of an illegitimate child if his parents subsequently married. Not until the Adoption of Children Act 1926 and the Legitimacy Act of the same year did English law recognise either adoption or legitimation. Exclusion of adoption was in marked contrast to most civil law jurisdictions which followed Roman law in recognising two forms of adoption, *adrogatio* and *adoptio*. The former allowed the adoption of an adult as an heir. The latter more closely resembled adoption of a child in England today. English common law only recognised as heir legitimate children born in wedlock who were heirs of the blood:[93] 'he is only heire which succeedeth by right of blood.'[94] This archaic rule of common law lives on, given new force by Sections 29 (4) and 48 of the Human Fertilisation and Embryology Acts 1990 and 2008 which respectively provide (inter alia) that succession to titles of honour are not subject to the statutory provisions on parenthood relating to children born using donor gametes. The general rule effected by the two statutes that if a woman is treated with donor sperm with her husband's consent, the husband is the legal father of the child is displaced. Patrilineal descent is retained, thus on the death of the Earl of Lonsdale in June 2021, his title passed to his younger son, an elder brother having been conceived by donor insemination.[95]

91 C Agnew and G Black 'Significance of Status and Genetics: Succession to Titles, Honours, Dignities and Coats of Arms' (2018) 77 *Cambridge Law Journal* 321.
92 L A Huard 'The Law of Adoption: Ancient and Modern' (1955–1956) 9 *Vanderbilt Law Review* 743.
93 Ibid 745–746.
94 E Coke *Institutes of the Laws of England* Pt II, 237b.
95 *The Times* 2 July 2021, 50.

9

The not (yet) born child

The intractable question

Ronald Dworkin described debates about abortion as 'so intractable, so stuck in venom and hate' because of obsession about whether the fetus is a person. No argument could be decisive, and the warring parties brooked no compromise.[1] The history of fetal status and abortion law has attracted more attention from medical lawyers than virtually any other area in medico-legal history, and alas supports Dworkin's pessimistic diagnosis. Any account of abortion law from medieval times to the Offences Against the Person Act 1861 reveals that a number of factors, other than fetal status, also influenced the development of English law. They included the dangers to women of crude abortion techniques, social attitudes to women, safe-guarding sexual morals and deterring promiscuity, so limiting illegitimate births. Nonetheless, arguments about the value to be accorded to fetal life persisted. In part that persistence derived from disputes within the medical professions concerning the value of fetal life. Influential doctors such as Thomas Percival made patent their belief that fetal life was 'sacred', a belief which in turn coloured their professional opinion on the evolution of the law.[2] Before the late eighteenth century, orthodox medical practitioners had low visibility either in performing abortions or participating in public debate. Abortion was not seen as significantly a 'medical' problem. The growing powers and voice of the medical professions, effectively laying the foundations for medicalising abortion, became highly influential in framing legislation through the nineteenth century.

Abortion is only one of many questions requiring consideration of fetal status. Some questions are age-old – for example, did a child born

---

1 R Dworkin *Life's Dominion: An Argument About Abortion and Euthanasia* (Harper Collins, 1983) 238.
2 T Percival *Medical Ethics* (J Johnson, 1803).

posthumously have a claim on his father's estate? Biomedical science gave rise to new questions. While much of this chapter considers the history of English law relating to abortion, I begin by exploring the oft-cited principle of the common law that a fetus does not enjoy any legal personality until born alive.

No legal personality: but not a 'nothing'

Despite Blackstone's claim that life begins 'in contemplation of the law as soon as the infant is able to stir in his mother's womb',[3] the contrary opinion seems to have prevailed. The mantra that a 'foetus enjoys, while still a foetus no independent legal personality – a foetus cannot, while still a foetus, sue and cannot be made a ward of court'[4] has been recited in a host of judgments in the past fifty years. It has been invoked to prevent a husband claiming to act as the 'guardian' of the fetus to stop his pregnant wife from having an abortion,[5] to reject attempts to make the fetus a ward of court,[6] and to endorse a woman's right to refuse a Caesarean section.[7] In 2014, in *CP v Criminal Injuries Compensation Authority*,[8] the Court of Appeal held that a woman whose alcohol consumption during pregnancy resulted in her child being born with Fetal Alcohol Spectrum Disorder (FASD) was not guilty of a crime of violence contrary to Section 23 of the Offences Against the Person Act 1861 (poisoning the child) because at the time when the harm occurred the fetus was not a legal person.

The 'no fetal personality' rule is rather like French regular and irregular verbs; a principle subject to exceptions to the rule. Read literally, denying the fetus any status would create a paradox in relation to laws criminalising abortion, a paradox which helps explain why Dworkin's 'intractable' problem will never be resolved. If an entity has no legal status, how can its destruction be a matter for the criminal law? If the fetus is a legal person it follows that its unjustifiable destruction constitutes homicide. But even if a fetus were to be regarded as a legal person, s/he resides in another's body; access to the fetus and the continued existence of the fetus inevitably

---

3 W Blackstone *Commentaries on the Laws of England* (Oxford University Press, 2016) Book I 129.
4 *Burton v Islington Health Authority* and *De Martell v Merton and Sutton Health Authority* [1992] 3 All ER 833 CA.
5 *Paton v British Pregnancy Advisory Services* [1979] QB 276.
6 *In Re F (in utero)* [1989] 2 All ER 193.
7 *St George's Healthcare NHS Trust v S* [1998] 3 All ER 673.
8 [2014] EWCA Civ 1554.

engages the bodily integrity of the pregnant woman. Lord Justice Judge sought to resolve the contradiction, stating that while a child in utero was not, and is not, a legal person able to be a party to legal proceedings or assert any legal rights while still unborn, even by proxy,[9] it did not follow that the fetus qua fetus was ever an entity in relationship to which the law had no concern, 'a nothing'.[10]

Pleading her belly

In the centuries when the death penalty applied to countless numbers of crimes a woman convicted of a capital offence could 'plead her belly', claiming that she was pregnant. If a jury of matrons confirmed that she was quick with child, her execution would be delayed until she was delivered or she proved not to be pregnant.[11] Should the woman become pregnant again during her temporary stay of execution, she could not seek a second stay of execution. Blackstone commented that in such a case the woman 'may now be executed before the child is quick in the womb; and, shall not, by her own incontinence, evade the sentence of justice'.[12] The law acknowledged that the fetus had some claim to protection of its life, a claim which trumped the administration of justice, but only once. In prioritising fetal life once, the law accorded value to the unborn child. In denying its mother a second chance, the common law diluted that value.

Nonetheless, the fetus carried in a convict's womb enjoyed a degree of value qua fetus. Other departures from the no-personality 'rule' afforded value to the child yet to be born, granting rights to the child only if and when 'born alive'. Later in the chapter, we shall see that Coke argued that while aborting a fetus was a 'great misprision', destroying the fetus in the womb was not homicide.

Posthumous children

An apparent departure from the 'no legal personality rule' is found in the law of succession where the common law partially adopted a maxim of the civil law, that an unborn child was deemed to be born 'whenever its interests required it'.[13] A child in utero (*en ventre sa mere*) at the time of his father's death, if born alive, enjoyed the same rights of succession to their

---

9 *Paton* (n 5).
10 *St George's Healthcare NHS Trust* (n 7) 688.
11 The rule remained in force until the Sentence of Death (Expectant Mothers) Act 1931.
12 Blackstone *Commentaries* (n 3) Book IV 388.
13 *Blasson v Blasson* (1864) 46 English Reports 534, 536.

late father's, or other relatives', estates as if they had been born before the death. A practical reason was suggested. Once born, the posthumous child needed maintaining. '[T]he debt of nature which a father owes to provide for all his children will extend to posthumous ones.'[14] In *Wallis v Hodson*, Lord Hardwicke LC made a more radical ruling in a claim by a posthumous sister for a share of her deceased brother's estate:

> [T]he plaintiff was en ventre sa mere at the time of her brother's death, and consequently a person in rerum natura, [in being] so that by the rules of the common and civil law, she was, to all intents and purposes a child.[15]

Lord Hardwicke seemed to grant the fetus legal personality.[16] The House of Lords in *Villar v Gilbey*[17] criticised the breadth of his assertion insofar as he referred to the common law. Lord Atkinson, explaining the application of the principle to bequests by other relatives, described the principle as a fiction or legal indulgence 'which treats the unborn child as actually born applies *only* for the purpose of enabling the unborn child to take a benefit which if born alive they would be entitled to.' Deeming the posthumous child to be treated as living at the date of the death applied 'whenever its interests require it'.[18] If a brother left his estate to 'the children of my sister' dying when she was pregnant with her third child, once born that child was entitled to a share in the estate.

In *The George and Richard*[19] a child *en ventre* at the time of her father's death in a shipwreck but subsequently born alive was held to be entitled to claim damages for loss of dependency under the Fatal Accidents Act 1846. Not until 1992 was the question of liability at common law for prenatal injuries directly addressed by an English court.[20] The thalidomide scandal which resulted in thousands of children being born with multiple impairments after their mothers took the drug in pregnancy led to the passing of the Congenital Disabilities (Civil Liability) Act 1976. The Act applied to all births after the passing of the Act. The plaintiffs in *Burton v Islington Health Authority*[21] were born before 1976 and the Court of Appeal was called on to rule on liability at common law for prenatal injuries. The Court held that although a fetus in utero was not a legal person, when

---

14 *Wallis v Hodson* (1740) 26 English Reports 642, 643.
15 Ibid 643.
16 See also *Millar v Turner* (1747) 28 English Reports 457.
17 [1907] AC 139, 149.
18 *Blasson* (n 13) 534, 536.
19 (1871) LR 3 A & E 466.
20 P J Pace 'Civil Liability for Pre-Natal Injuries' (1977) 40 *Modern Law Review* 141.
21 [1992] 3 All ER 833.

the child acquired legal personality at birth, they became entitled to claim damages for injuries inflicted before birth. The apparent paradox whereby the fetus is protected against injury but not destruction[22] may be rationalised in part. Outwith the criminal law on abortion, the common law generally provided no rights to the fetus, the unborn child. The not yet born child would be protected against injury or disadvantage occasioned prior to birth.

Abortion and the criminal law

The history of the criminal law prohibiting abortion and protecting the unborn child has generated a huge literature. Appeals to history play a prominent role in disputes about abortion laws today. Arguments that 'old' law has lessons for modern judges and legislators have been deployed in the courts, most dramatically in the decisions of the US Supreme Court in *Roe v Wade*[23] and *Dobbs v Jackson Women's Health Organization*.[24] Those who, like Charles Clarke, the former Education Secretary, demand that a study of history should have practical relevance may applaud. The drawback is that versions of history are often made to fit the philosophical and/or political case espoused by the author. Contested accounts of past abortion laws are conscripted into service by both proponents of stricter regulation, even prohibition, of abortion and campaigners for de-criminalisation.

In looking at the history of abortion law in England, I distinguish between two eras, the 'common law era' until Lord Ellenborough's Act of 1803, the first statute regulating abortion, and the 'statutory era' from 1803 to 1861 and the Offences Against the Person Act 1861. Examining abortion law in England from the Middle Ages to 1861, it will be seen that rather than prohibitions on abortion becoming more liberal over time, in England in the nineteenth century abortion legislation became less liberal and penalties more draconian. It might be assumed that the protection of the fetus, the 'defence of unborn life', was a principal purpose of abortion laws. Any such assumption has been vigorously challenged, and alternative objectives advanced. It has been argued that nineteenth-century legislation in England and many American states had less to do with protecting unborn children, and more to do with the endeavours of the orthodox medical professionals to assert control of pregnancy and childbirth.

22 Pace (n 20) 141.
23 410 US 702 (1973).
24 572 US (2022).

Much of the literature hails from the USA. Insofar as it addresses the common law era before the legislatures in England or any US state enacted statutory prohibitions, the law in England and the then American colonies may be taken to be the same. Moving to the statutory era, while nineteenth-century legislation on both sides of the Atlantic reveals similarities in legislative policy between England and the American states, exploring the political and social influences on legislators reveals significant differences.

Before delving further into the disputed histories of abortion laws, the 'doctrine of quickening' needs to be noted. At common law, and in the first two Acts of Parliament addressing the criminal law and abortion, 'quickening' was seen as a key milestone in fetal development, playing a pivotal role in defining criminality in cases of abortion. Jurists disagreed about the meaning and impact of 'quickening.' In general, 'quickening' was deemed to occur when the fetus was perceived by its mother to move in the womb. That point in pregnancy was regarded as of physiological importance in marking a developmental step indicating that the fetus was now a living creature, and of theological importance as the point in gestation when the fetus became ensouled.[25] Whether the abortion was pre- or post-quickening determined the nature and degree of any crime committed. By the end of the eighteenth century some doctors were arguing that the popular belief had no scientific basis. 'Quickening' remained central to English law until 1837. Feeling the child move in the womb for the first time is an emotionally moving experience for pregnant women. Maternal perception of fetal movement will occur sometime after the fetus actually begins to move in the womb. The timing of maternal sensation of movement depends on a variety of factors including the woman's weight and previous experience of gestation. That experience signifies nothing about any physical or spiritual change in the entity in the womb.

Contested and partial opinions

US historian Cyril Means offered a radical interpretation of abortion history to support a pro-choice stance in modern law. In 1968, he argued that nineteenth-century legislation in New York imposing strict prohibitions on abortion was motivated by the risk and danger that crude methods posed to women undergoing abortions, and had nothing to do with protecting the fetus.[26] He contended that the 'sole historically demonstrable purpose'

25 Thomas Aquinas *Summa Theologica* I, Q.76, art 1.
26 C C Means Jr 'The Law of New York Concerning Abortion and the Status of the Foetus 1664–1968: A Case of Cessation of Constitutionality' (1968) 14 *New York Law Forum* 411.

behind nineteenth-century legislation in England and America criminalising and placing restrictions on abortion was 'the protection of pregnant women from the danger to their lives imposed by surgical or potional [medical] abortion, under medical conditions then obtaining'.[27] Means asserted 'concern for the life of the conceptus was foreign to the secular thinking of the Protestant legislators who passed these laws'.

In 1971 Means went further, claiming that until the passage of the restrictive statutes in the nineteenth century (Lord Ellenborough's Act 1803 in England) 'English and American women enjoyed a common law liberty to terminate at will any unwanted pregnancy'.[28] From 1327 to 1803 in England, and from 1607 to 1830 in America, pregnant women and their abortionists were free to terminate the pregnancy at any stage in gestation, or at least faced no secular penalties. Until 1803, abortion, Means maintained, 'was and always had been, in England, a crime at canon law of purely ecclesiastical cognizance'. Once abortions could be performed safely, Means concluded that all that *should* be required for a lawful abortion was the consent of the pregnant woman. Means had a profound influence on the Opinion of the US Supreme Court in *Roe v Wade*.[29] Justice Blackmun said:

> [W]e feel it is desirable briefly to survey, in several aspects, the history of abortion, for such insight as that history may afford us, and then to examine the state purposes and interest behind the criminal abortion laws.[30]

Blackmun accepted virtually all the claims made by Means, stating that:

(1) 'It is undisputed that at common law, abortion performed before "quickening" .... was not an indictable offense.'
(2) It now appears doubtful that abortion was ever firmly established as a common law crime even with respect to the destruction of a quick fetus.
(3) Nineteenth-century legislation imposing restrictions on abortion backed by criminal sanctions were motivated by the State's concern to 'protect the pregnant woman, that is, to restrain her from submitting to a procedure that placed her life in serious jeopardy'.[31]

---

27 C C Means Jr 'The Phoenix of Abortional Freedom: Is a Penumbral or Ninth-Amendment Right About to Arise from the Nineteenth-Century Legislative Ashes of a Fourteenth-Century Common-Law Liberty?' (1971) 17 *New York Law Forum* 335, 336.
28 Ibid.
29 *Roe v Wade* 410 US 113 (1973).
30 Ibid 130.
31 Ibid 133–136.

Means' claims that abortion was never a crime at common law received support from other US historians. James Mohr joined Means in contending that abortion was not a crime before quickening: 'The common law did not formally recognize the existence of a fetus in criminal cases until it had quickened.'[32] Mohr said of Means that despite caveats about some of his arguments, Means' basic insight seems 'undeniably on the mark'. When in 1989, in *Webster v Reproductive Health Services*,[33] the Supreme Court was asked to adjudicate on the constitutionality of a Missouri statute declaring that human life begins at conception and imposing significant restrictions on access to abortion, 282 historians prepared an amicus curiae brief ('The Historians' Brief') largely endorsing Means, Mohr and Blackmun. In 1971 Means had congratulated himself suggesting that his novel thesis was 'no longer seriously challenged'.[34] Were that so, *Roe v Wade* might have been seen as an exemplar of history having a practical effect in the making of modern law. The trouble is that Means' thesis was flawed.[35] As I will demonstrate later in this chapter, the jurisprudence of the great common law jurists, such as Bracton, Coke, Hale and Blackstone, predominantly supported the case that abortion was a crime, albeit differing on the nature of the crime. More importantly, reported cases before 1803 show that contrary to Means' thesis and Blackmun's Opinion in *Roe*, abortion, certainly post-quickening, and probably before was a common law crime. Inconvenient 'evidence' was interpreted to fit the thesis, or explained in a manner designed to discredit the force of that evidence, for example Means' claim that Coke's hatred of abortion led him to create a new crime. The fragility of Means' 'evidence' rendered *Roe* itself vulnerable to attack, opening the door to the controversial decision of the Supreme Court nearly fifty years later in *Dobbs v Jackson Women's Health Organization*[36] overruling *Roe v Wade* itself. The majority in *Dobbs* were scathing in their criticism of *Roe*'s reliance on Means, described by Justice Alito as 'reliance on two discredited articles by an abortion advocate', which resulted in an 'erroneous understanding' of the common law and in turn played an important part in the Court's

---

32 J C Mohr *Abortion in America: The Origins and Evolution of National Policy 1800–1900* (Oxford University Press, 1978) 3. Much of Mohr's book is devoted to his analysis of abortion policy driving restrictive legislation enacted in the states of the USA, and in particular the crusade by the orthodox medical practitioners (styled 'regulars' by Mohr) to drive out 'irregulars'.

33 492 US 490 (1989).

34 Means (1971) (n 27) 336.

35 J Keown *Abortion, Doctors and the Law* (Cambridge University Press, 1988) 3–4 and J Keown *The Law and Ethics of Medicine* (Oxford University Press, 2012) 112–120.

36 572 US 2022.

thinking.[37] Show that Means was wrong and part of the foundations for *Roe* collapsed. It must be noted, however, that the majority in *Dobbs* was equally selective in their choice of authorities to castigate Means.

Debate on the history of abortion laws continues to be bedevilled by claims and counter-claims that your 'opponent's' analysis of the cases and literature is driven by a desire to use history to bolster the pro-choice or pro-life lobby to which the author adheres. The debates between Joseph Dellapenna and Carla Spivack illustrate the issue. In *Dispelling the Myths of Abortion History*,[38] Dellapenna 'set about to set the record straight regarding the history of abortion', counter-claiming that abortion, at any stage in gestation, had always been treated as a crime 'focused on protecting the life of the unborn child'.[39] Means' claims were not facts but myths.[40] Dellapenna charged that pro-choice historians had distorted history.[41] In turn, Dellapenna was accused of distorting the evidence 'to press an absolutist position about the legal history'.[42] Spivack contended that at common law 'a fetus in its early stages was not accorded full human status'. She challenges Dellapenna's interpretation of the case law even suggesting that within marriage self-abortion pre-quickening was an acceptable and common form of birth control.[43] Examining the policy underpinning abortion law in the common law era, she says:

> [T]o whatever extent the law – secular and ecclesiastical – did frown on abortion, it subsumed this concern within the much greater concern with illicit sex and illegitimacy and imposed counter-measures to punish abortion in a context in which it served to hide, and enable, sex outside marriage.[44]

Spivack stresses 'the importance of intellectual and social history to an understanding of the law'.[45] Few would disagree. But the question 'Was

---

37 Ibid 48.
38 J W Dellapenna *Dispelling the Myths of Abortion History* (Carolina Academic Press, 2006).
39 Ibid xii.
40 Ibid 13.
41 Dellapenna notes that in 1968 Means was General Counsel for the National Association for the Repeal of Abortion Laws, and research for the second paper was funded by another pro-choice organisation, the Association for the Study of Abortion. And see Keown (2012) (n 35) decrying 'advocacy scholarship'.
42 C Spivack 'To "Bring Down the Flowers": The Cultural Context of Abortion Law in Early Modern England' (2007–2008) 14 *William and Mary Journal of Women and the Law* 107 at 108.
43 Spivack ibid 110–111.
44 Ibid 110 and see S Gavigan 'The Criminal Sanction as it Relates to Human Reproduction: The Genesis of the Statutory Prohibition of Abortion' (1984) 5 *Journal of Legal History* 20.
45 Spivack (n 42) 107.

abortion a common law crime?' is not asking why abortion was or was not a secular crime or should the criminal law punish abortion. It simply asks whether abortion was a crime in the common law era. In thrall to a passionate commitment to pro-choice or pro-life lobbies, it is tempting to distort the evidence to fit your stance in Dworkin's intractable debate.

The common law era

I begin by attempting to assess claims that before Lord Ellenborough's Act abortion was not a crime at common law, or at least was not a crime in the early stages of pregnancy, before quickening. There is no concrete evidence as to the incidence of prosecutions for abortions before 1803. Estimates of the number of abortions performed vary widely. Advocates of the case that abortion was not a common law crime, or at least not pre-quickening, contend that before 1803 early abortions were common, carried out for the most part by women helping other women.[46] They argue that the frequency of abortion with little evidence of consequent prosecutions indicates that abortion was not a crime.[47] References to abortions in contemporary literature and correspondence are used to support the case that abortion was almost commonplace. Spivack notes that until later in the eighteenth-century childbirth was a female preserve. 'The female private world was not one on which the common law trained its sights.'[48]

Dellapenna suggests that the lack of evidence of prosecutions indicates that abortions were rare. Abortions were dangerous for the woman and/or largely ineffective. Attempts to abort via an attack and injury to the pregnant woman (injurious abortions) involved a degree of violence to dislodge a fetus which risked killing the woman. Abortifacients (potions) to drink or administered via a pessary in the vagina or a clyster (enema) were in the main ineffective, and, if effective, had to be taken in such large doses that the woman often died too. Crude surgery (instrumental abortion) was likely to result in serious and often fatal infection. Infanticide was a ghastly but physically safer option for women.[49]

Like every aspect of abortion history, accounts of the risk and success of abortion techniques are themselves vigorously contested.[50] The absence of

---

46 A McLaren *Reproductive Rituals: The Perception of Fertility in England from the Sixteenth Century to the Nineteenth Century* (Methuen, 1984).
47 Ibid.
48 Spivack (n 42) 142.
49 Dellapenna (n 38) 36–56.
50 McLaren (n 46) 30–31.

hard evidence of the frequency of prosecution tells us little about the central issue of whether abortion was a crime at common law. Practical and procedural problems rendered prosecution difficult. Given the rudimentary nature of understanding of the body, particularly of female bodies, the absence of X rays or ultrasound scans proving that an attack, a potion or an attempted surgical abortion caused the death of the child in utero would, to say the least, be difficult.

The jurists

The 'fathers' of the common law disagreed about fetal status as vehemently as their descendants in the twenty-first century. The contested opinions of the 'ancients' are often manipulated in current battles over abortion. Put somewhat frivolously, cherry pick the jurist of your choice to support the stance you take on modern abortion law.

In support of the case that the child in utero is as much a person as I am, the medieval lawyer, Henry de Bracton, declared in about 1250:

> If one strikes a pregnant woman or gives her a potion in order to procure an abortion, if the foetus is already formed or animated, especially if it is animated, he commits homicide.[51]

Much turns on what Bracton meant by 'formed or animated'.[52] Are either of these terms to be equated with 'quickening'?[53] Animated, translated from the Latin *animates*, has been taken to mean quickening, but both 'ensouled' or simply alive are also reasonable translations. Bracton, in stating that it sufficed to amount to homicide to destroy a fetus formed or animated, seems to envisage two stages of fetal development, the formation of the fetus (perhaps at conception) and a later stage which might be quickening or the stage in gestation at which Thomas Aquinas taught marked ensoulment (forty days for a male and eighty for a female).[54]

Dellapenna interprets Bracton to contend that abortion at any point in gestation was homicide at common law, either on a test of formation or because quick with child/animation meant simply that the fetus was alive in

---

51 Bracton *De Legibus et Consuetudiinibus Anglise* as cited in Keown (1988) (n 35) 5, 172.
52 Keown also discusses Fleta who expressly condemned self-abortion adding 'A woman also commits a homicide, if by potion or the like, she destroys a quickened child in her womb'. *Fleta* Vol 2 Book 1 Ch 23 (reprinted in 53 Selden Society 88–89 (H G Richardson & G O Sayles (eds) (1953)) as cited in Keown (1988) (n 35) 5.
53 Dellapenna (n 38) 139.
54 Thomas Aquinas *Summa Theologica* I, Q.76, art 1.

the womb. He concedes that it may be that the case for prenatal homicide is stronger after some second stage of gestation, 'especially if it is animated, with animation to be interpreted as ensoulment' or quickening.[55]

Means' champion is William Staunford who nearly 300 years after Bracton in *Les Plees del Coron* (Pleas of the Crown) (1557) rejected Bracton's equation of abortion with homicide, contending that 'the contrary of this seems to be the law'.[56] Means presents Staunford as 'proof' that abortion 'simply was not an offense of any kind, no matter at what stage of gestation it was performed'.[57] Staunford's own words (as set out by Means) contradict any assertion that there was 'no offense of any kind'. Staunford wrote that to kill a 'child in the womb of its mother: this is not a felony neither shall he forfeit anything'. He offers two reasons (1) 'the thing killed has no baptismal name' and (2) 'because it is difficult to judge whether the accused caused the child's death whether the child died of the battery of its mother, or through another cause'. Suggesting that abortion was no felony due to lack of a baptismal name, is swiftly contradicted by Staunford himself citing a case of infanticide in which a mother had killed her unbaptised child at birth. The second point, the difficulty of proving that the child died in the womb be it from the attack on its mother or the administration of an abortifacient or some crude surgical abortion is instructive, highlighting the procedural difficulty which might have discouraged prosecution but does not prove that abortion was no crime.

Moreover, all Staunford claimed was that abortion was no felony. Means takes the words 'neither shall he forfeit anything' as meaning that no criminal offence was entailed in abortion. At the time Staunford was writing, criminal offences were divided into felonies and misdemeanours.[58] In theory, the distinction between the two was that felonies comprised the most serious offences. Convicted felons faced the death penalty and forfeiture of all their property. Misdemeanours were punished by lesser penalties and the convicted person was not subject to forfeiture. The line between the two was blurred and made yet more complex by a shadowy third category, 'misprision'. Misprision of felony was strictly speaking an offence relating to concealment of a felony and could be punished by some more limited forfeiture of chattels. Confusingly, misprision later came to be used to denote very serious misdemeanours.[59] The claim by Staunford that 'neither shall he

---

55 Ibid.
56 Means (1971) (n 27) 340–341.
57 Ibid 342.
58 Abolished by Criminal Justice Act 1967, s 1.
59 J Baker *An Introduction to English Legal History* (5th edn) (Oxford University Press, 2019) 542.

[the abortionist] forfeit anything' excluded procuring an abortion from the categories of felony and within its strict meaning misprision, but does not establish that abortion was not a misdemeanour.

It is the opinion of Sir Edward Coke in his third *Institutes* published post-humously in 1641 which has most often been cited and analysed in relation to the common law on abortion:

> If a woman be quick with childe, and by a Potion or otherwise killeth it in her womb or if a man beat her whereby the childe dieth in her body, and she is delivered of a dead childe, this is a great misprision, and no murder; but if the childe be born alive, and dieth of the Potion, battery or other cause, this is murder: for in law it is accounted a reasonable creature, in rerum natura, when it is born alive.[60]

Holding that killing the fetus in the womb was 'no murder' but a 'great misprision' classifies the destruction of a not yet born child as a lesser wrong than killing the infant after birth, or causing the born child to die after delivery. His 'compromise' has been attacked from all quarters. Means charged that a combination of Coke's visceral hatred of abortion, and his battle to curb the jurisdiction of the ecclesiastical courts, led him to 'create' a crime when no such crime existed.[61] Dellapenna counter-charged that Coke did change the law, not by 'inventing' a new crime but by downgrading the crime from homicide to very grave misdemeanour. As was the case with Staunford, Coke in using the term misprision should be taken to mean a 'great misdemeanour'. In slightly differing formulations Coke's opinion has been adopted by later jurists, notably Hale, Hawkins and Blackstone.[62]

Disagreements notwithstanding, Coke (and his successors) confirmed that abortion was a crime at common law. A common law liberty to abort never existed. The boundaries of the crime are less clear. Whether Coke regarded abortion at any stage in gestation depends on how to interpret 'quick with childe'. Did he mean that there was no crime before quickening as Mohr argued?[63] Or did 'quick' simply mean alive in the womb? The concept of 'born alive', the Rubicon separating the 'great misprision' of abortion from homicide, troubles medical law till this day, and is revisited at the end of this chapter.

---

60 E Coke *Institutes of the Laws of England* Pt III 50.
61 Means (1971) (n 27) 345–349.
62 Keown (1988) (n 35) 10–11.
63 Mohr (n 32) 3.

Case law

What of the case law, the judgments which informed the opinions of the jurists and some of which were decided by those same jurists sitting as judges in the Royal Courts? Writing in 1984, Shelley Gavigan commented that common law sources on abortion were 'close to non-existent'.[64] Research undertaken by amongst others Keown, Rafferty, Dellapenna and Spivack have identified more reported cases.

Discovering more reports provides further glimpses into the picture of the past. They do not offer a conclusive account of the common law. The same problems which beset analysis of medieval and early modern cases of medical litigation (discussed in Chapter 5) affect study of extant reports of prosecutions for abortion. The choice of cases to report was random. Reports are often fragmentary, difficult to interpret. Multiple or partial copies may survive. Latin and Norman French impede the task for those lacking the requisite linguistic skill, and the accuracy of translations is sometimes disputed. The outcome of the trial rested heavily on procedure rather than substantive law, in particular questions of proof. Modern commentators generally address the same cases but offer sharply different interpretations, interpretations which corroborate the author's stance on abortion law today. The likelihood of uncovering a case which provides incontrovertible evidence of the common law is slim. Criminal trials took place across the realm. No system of precedent provided for a definitive ruling by a higher court. I cannot attempt to address all the cases identified by medical and legal historians, nor do I deal with Anglo-Saxon law, or appeal of felony in the very early common law.[65]

Means' contention that women enjoyed a common law liberty to abort is founded on what he describes as 'the primary case which establishes this liberty', a case he names *The Twinslayer's Case* (1327).[66] Other reports of Means' primary case have since been unearthed. Means relied on a report in a Year Book (essentially notes made by lawyers attending the Court). The accused was indicted for a brutal attack on Alice Carles who was 'greatly pregnant' with twins. It was alleged that as a result of the violent attack on the woman, one of the twins died in the womb. The second twin was delivered and baptised by the name John. He died of his injuries two days after birth. Means relied on the following extract from the report 'D (the

---

64 Gavigan (n 44) 12.
65 Spivack (n 42) 129–132.
66 Y.B. Mich 1 Edw 3. f. 23, pl 18 (1327).

defendant) came, and pled not guilty, and for the reason that the justices were unwilling to adjudge this thing a felony, the accused was released to mainpernors (on bail), and then the argument was adjourned sine die'. From this extract Means asserted:

> The singular importance of this case is obvious. It establishes beyond all cavil that an abortion, whether resulting in the intrauterine death of the twin who died at once or the death after birth alive was not a felony at all at common law.[67]

If Means' interpretation of *The Twinslayer's Case* were correct, it would support the argument that in 1327 a fetus enjoyed no legal status and killing it was not a secular crime. Giving *The Twinslayer's Case* its proper attribution, *Rex v de Bourton*, Dellapenna highlighted problems undermining the 'singular importance' of *The Twinslayer's Case*. First, the proceedings were interim only; the accused was bailed to appear at a later hearing.[68] The accused apparently made no challenge to 'the legal sufficiency of the charge'.[69] Second, Dellapenna had the advantage of research by Sir John Baker in accessing a manuscript version of the Year Book and later researching and translating the original court records. Baker discovered original records of *de Bourton*. The older and fuller reports set out a complex account of a series of proceedings primarily focused on bringing the accused to trial and ensuring the presence of recalcitrant jurors. It is hard to disagree with Dellapenna that at best *de Bourton* is 'an inconclusive report on whether abortion under the circumstances was a crime'.[70] Dellapenna's own assertion that the original records of the case 'indicate clearly that the matter was undoubtedly a felony' lacks force. *De Bourton* highlights the procedural problems of medieval criminal law, poses questions about abortion, but gives no conclusive guidance.

The second case cited by Means is *Rex v Anonymous 1* (1348) which he names *The Abortionist's Case*. The case is not reported in the Year Books. Means assign its origins to the *Graunde Abridgement* compiled by Sir Anthony Fitzherbert. Only a very short report exists. The substantive accuracy of the report is not to my knowledge disputed. What follows is taken from a translation by Baker cited by Dellapenna.

> One was indicted for that he killed a child in its mother's belly, and the opinion [was] that he shall not be arraigned on this since no name of baptism was in the indictment, and also is hard to know whether he killed it or not.[71]

---

67 Means (1968) (n 26) 338.
68 Dellapenna (n 38) 145–146.
69 Nor is any distinction suggested between the case of the twin who died in the womb and his sister who survived to be born alive but died soon thereafter.
70 Dellapenna (n 38) 146.
71 Ibid 130.

Lack of a baptismal name could not preclude prosecution or many cases of infanticide could not be prosecuted.[72] *The Abortionist's Case* does no more than highlight the problem of proof. In 1348 and for centuries thereafter, evidential means of establishing that assault on the woman, or the potion given to her, or the attempt at surgical abortion was the cause of the death in utero were simply not available. Such an interpretation of the fourteenth-century cases was confirmed at the start of the seventeenth century in *R v Sims*.[73]

> The child born living and bruised trespass and assault brought against one Sims by husband and wife for beating the woman.
>
> Cook [*sic*] Coke the case is such as appears by examination.
>
> A man beats a woman who is great with child and after the child is born living, but hath signs and bruises on his body received by the said batterie, and after dyed thereof I say that it this is murder.
>
> Fenner and Popham absentibus caeteris, clearly of the same opinion, and the difference is whether the child is born dead, and where it was born living, for if it be dead born, it is no murder for non constat whether the child were living at the time of the batterie or not or if the battery was the cause of its death but when it is born living and the wounds appear on his body and then he dye, the Batterror shall be arraigned for murder for now it may be proved whether these wounds were the cause of the death or not, and for that, if it be found he may be condemned.

Again, the outcome of the case turned on proof. *De Bourton*, *The Abortionist's Case*, and *Sims* are all examples of injurious abortions committed against the will of the woman in the course of a criminal assault on her. As such they shed little light on the question whether a woman was free to choose to abort, the common law liberty advocated by Means, save to demonstrate that in principle killing a fetus was a crime.

Spivack, however, argued that such involuntary abortions were not abortion as we understand the term today. *The Twinslayer's Case* et al 'resemble modern torts and are based on recognition of the injury to the mother'.[74] Whether Spivack is right or wrong, she identifies a recurring problem. Medieval women who miscarried as a result of violent assault suffered two 'wrongs', injury to their body and the loss of the expected child. They, like Madame Vo in 2004,[75] may have perceived the wanted child as deserving

---

72 Means (1971) (n 27) 342.
73 (1601) 75 English Reports 1075.
74 Spivack (n 42) 110.
75 *Vo v France* [2004] ECHR 326.

protection in its own right, but such protection brings us once more to the 'intractable' problem of fetal personality. Spivack suggested that cases of injurious abortion cannot be used to establish that the fetus had any legal personality. She also argues that case law does not establish that self-induced abortion prior to quickening was a secular crime. Spivack declares that abortion within marriage pre-quickening was outwith the concern of the common law courts.[76]

The early cases do not demonstrate that abortion was not a common law crime. Nor do they conclusively establish that it was. Relatively more recent case law, cases before 1803, strongly indicates that abortion was a common law crime. In 1602, Margaret Webb was charged with drinking ratsbane with the intention of 'spoiling[77] and destroying the child in the womb'.[78] The very brief record of the case ends that she was 'Pardoned by the general pardon'. There is no indication in the accounts of the reports in Keown[79] or Dellapenna[80] whether Webb was charged with felony or misdemeanour nor any conclusive statement whether or not she was found guilty. A pardon pre-supposes guilt and thus that a crime had been committed. Webb is of particular interest in that it is a case of self-abortion. There appears to be no indication at what stage in pregnancy Margaret drank poison, before or after quickening.

In 1732, Eleanor Beare faced three charges of 'Misdemeanor'. Fuller coverage of Beare survives than does of Webb and other cases though only in a popular journal, not an official Law Report.[81] Eleanor was charged that (1) she provided a poison to Nich. Wilson to give to his wife to destroy the child in her womb; (2) she inserted an 'iron instrument' into the body of Grace Belfort causing her to miscarry; (3) she similarly used an instrument and/or gave an abortifacient to a woman 'unknown to the jury'. Beare pleaded not guilty to all charges. She was found guilty on the first two indictments and the judge ruled that it was not necessary to proceed with the third charge. She was sentenced to stand in the pillory and to three years' imprisonment. *Beare* confirms that abortion was a misdemeanour. Dellapenna surmises that the abortion took place at less than fourteen weeks gestation 'before quickening was likely'.[82]

---

76 Spivack (n 42) 136–138.
77 Baker translates the original Latin as 'getting rid of'.
78 *R v Webb*. Calendar of Assize Records, Surrey Indictments, Elizabeth I (London, 1980, ed J S Cockburn) 512 case 3146: as discussed in Keown (1988) (n 35) 7–8; and Dellapenna (n 38) 193–194.
79 Keown (1988) (n 35) 7–8.
80 Dellapenna (n 38) 193–194.
81 *Gentlemen's Magazine* August 1732, 931.
82 Dellapenna (n 38) 236.

In *R v Lichefeld* (1505),[83] Thomas Lichefeld was charged with 'feloniously harbouring' Jane Wynspere who it was alleged being 'inspired by the devil' drank several 'impure' potions to destroy her unborn child. The potions ultimately killed her as well as the child. Lichefeld had offered her shelter after she had aborted the child and before she died. Providing such aid to a felon was itself a crime. Dellapenna argues that the felony in question was the self-abortion. While suicide and attempted suicide were crimes considered to be self-murder, when Jane killed herself, attempted suicide required proof of intent to commit suicide. Once Jane was dead, harbouring a corpse was not a crime. The charge against him necessarily presumed that the abortion was a crime and a felony at that. The charges were dismissed on procedural grounds. An accessory to crime could not be prosecuted when the principal could not be brought before the court. *Lichefeld* is one of the many inconclusive proceedings but important for two reasons. It indicated that abortion was not solely a matter for the ecclesiastical courts, and that self-abortion was a common law crime.[84]

In 1781 Margaret Tinckler was convicted of the murder of Jane Parkinson 'by inserting pieces of wood into her womb'.[85] Jane was pregnant 'five or six months gone' by a married man who feared his wife would find out about his infidelity. The accused also shook the unfortunate Jane violently. The child was born alive but died immediately after delivery. Jane herself died eleven days after she gave birth having declared several times that 'Peggy Tinckler has killed me and the "dear child".' Much of the law report is devoted to the question of whether Jane's *cri de coeur* that Tinckler had killed her and other statements she had made to neighbours could be used in evidence as dying declarations. The defence argued unsuccessfully that as Jane was herself a participant in the primary crime her evidence was inadmissible. Tinckler's conviction is further evidence that abortion was a crime and that a woman who consented to abortion was equally guilty of a crime.

Where were the healers? 'Therapeutic' abortions

There is little evidence of orthodox medical practitioners being involved in early abortions in the common law era. Medical men only became visible

---

83 *R v Lichefeld* K.B.27//974, Rex m 4 (1505) as cited in Dellapenna ibid 177–178; and see the report of the coroner's inquest in R F Hunnisett (ed. and transl.) 'Calendar of Nottinghamshire coroners' inquests 1485–1558' in *Record Series of the Thornton Society* (Nottingham, 1966) Vol 25, 8, inquest 10, as discussed in Keown (1988) (n 35) 6–7.

84 Keown (1988) (n 35) 6–7; and see *Rex v Wodlake* (1530) discussed in Dellapenna (n 38) 178–180.

85 E H East *A Treatise on the Pleas of the Crown* (Butterworth and Cooke, 1803) 354–356.

later in gestation. When the fetus was stuck in the birth canal, threatening the life of the woman, a surgeon would be summoned to employ instruments to remove the fetus. Surgical interventions were not limited to removing dead fetuses. Craniotomy and dismemberment were used to remove and destroy a living fetus, when the mother's life was at risk. Therapeutic abortions were not considered unlawful. Writing in 1803 before Lord Ellenborough's Act came into force and thus addressing common law, Thomas Percival (who as we shall see took a stern view of the evils of abortion in general), stated that abortion was not always unlawful. 'For the configuration of the pelvis in some females is such as to render the birth of a full-grown child impossible or inevitably fatal.'[86] The salutary purpose of preserving the life of the mother justified the otherwise unlawful intervention.

In 1830, Willcock wrote:

[T]here is one case and one case only where the accoucheur or medical practitioner is not only excused but justified in the attempt and that is for the purpose of saving the mother when from a knowledge of her constitution, or the circumstances attending the conception, pregnancy, or approaching parturition in the exercise of due discretion and scientific judgment he is satisfied that the attempt to save the child will place the mother in the utmost danger.[87]

As obstetric surgery developed, craniotomy was no longer the only option to save mothers. Induction of labour and the development of the Caesarean section offered the possibility of saving both mother and child. Nor was pelvic disproportion the only condition which might result in interventions to protect the mother's life or health. Keown provides an account of therapeutic abortion in medical practice in the nineteenth century, making the case that the oft-voiced view that medical practitioners did not perform therapeutic abortions at all is a myth.[88] Well before the end of the common law era, a tacit assumption of the legality of therapeutic abortions reflected that (1) the life and welfare of the woman was paramount; (2) most, though not all, medical professionals, attributed high value to fetal life, but not as great a value as to maternal life; (3) the justification for the destruction of the fetus required that a balance be struck between the danger to the woman and the life of the fetus. Determining the outcome of that exercise was regarded as a *medical* judgement. The medicalisation of abortion had begun to gain pace before 1803.

---

86 Percival (n 2) 78.
87 J Willcock *Laws Relating to the Medical Profession with an Account of the Rise and Progress of the Various Orders* (J & W T Clarke, 1830) 87.
88 Keown (1988) (n 35) 5–83.

The statutory era

Contestants in debates about abortion as a common law crime agree on one matter. The common law lacked clarity: a lack of clarity which created the space in which arguments continue to rage about the existence of any common law crime. Legislation on abortion enacted in the nineteenth century culminated in Sections 58 and 59 of the Offences Against the Person Act 1861.

The history of abortion legislation in the nineteenth century reveals themes still present in current debates on de-criminalisation, including some real, if patriarchal, concerns about risks to women, deep divisions in attitudes to the value to be attached to fetal life, questions of sexual morality and misunderstandings of biology by both legislators and laypeople. Means' contention that the 'sole demonstrable purpose' of nineteenth-century laws in England and America was the protection of pregnant women and that Protestant legislators in the nineteenth century had no concern for fetal life is contradicted by the evidence in England. Anglican legislators,[89] jurists[90] and physicians[91] expressed strongly held views in support of protection of the fetus.

The succession of Acts of Parliament leading up to the 1861 Act incrementally tightened the prohibition of abortion, exhibiting stronger condemnation of induced termination of pregnancy than is evident in the common law era. A crucial element in the emergent law relating to the criminalisation of abortion was that as legislation imposed more draconian prohibitions of abortion, abortion law became one of the battlegrounds on which the orthodox medical practitioners sought to dominate the provision of medical care (driving out other competing healers). And medical practitioners intervened to 'prescribe' medical ethics, medicalising moral and social matters.

Parliament first intervened in 1803 enacting the Malicious Shooting and Stabbing Act, commonly known as Lord Ellenborough's Act, named after the Lord Chief Justice who introduced the Bill. Reforming the law relating to abortion was part of a statute designed to clarify and to an extent codify offences against the person. Abortion was just one such offence addressed in Section 1. The Preamble declared that the Act addressed crimes for which the common law provided inadequate means of prevention and punishment

---

89 Notably the peer who introduced the first Act of Parliament relating to abortion, Lord Ellenborough himself (Keown ibid 20).
90 Blackstone *Commentaries* (n 3) Book IV 199.
91 Percival (n 2) 78–80.

lending support to the case that abortion was a common law offence, if an ineffectual offence.

Post-quickening abortions became felonies. After several amendments during its passage through Parliament, Section 1 provided that if any person or persons:

> shall wilfully, maliciously and unlawfully administer to, or cause to be administered to or taken by any of His Majesty's subjects any deadly poison or other noxious or destructive substance or thing with intent such of His Majesty's subjects thereby to murder or thereby to cause and procure the miscarriage of any woman then being quick with child …

they would be guilty of a felony punishable by death. Prior to the Act, abortion had been a misdemeanour. Section 2 made pre-quickening abortion a felony too, but not punishable by death. Section 2 provided that it was a felony for any person or persons:

> wilfully and maliciously to administer or cause to be administered or taken by any woman any medicine, drugs or other substance or thing whatsoever or shall use or employ or cause or procure to be used or employed any instrument or means whatsoever with intent thereby to cause or procure the miscarriage of any woman not being or not being proven to be quick with child at the time of administering such thing or using such means.

Section 3 repealed the Infanticide Act 1623 (which reversed the burden of proof when a woman was charged with murdering her illegitimate child). She would be guilty of murder unless she could prove her infant was born dead.

There is, surprisingly, little evidence of any particular trigger for introducing legislation on abortion in 1803. Alannah Tomkins comments that in relation to abortion, the Act 'was passed in the notable absence of popular demand'.[92] Keown notes that there was no evidence of widespread alarm, 'either among public or clergy'.[93] Clarification of the chaotic state of the common law seems to have been the objective of this first foray into statutory regulation of abortion. The imposition of the death penalty was influenced by Lord Ellenborough's philosophy of punishment that the ultimate penalty should be imposed for the maximum number of offences. Making post-quickening abortion a capital crime indicates that the legislators assented to the view that abortion was, as the Preamble to the Act declared, a 'heinous offence'.

---

92 A Tomkins *Medical Misadventure in an Age of Professionalisation 1780–1890* (Manchester University Press, 2017) 139.
93 Keown (1988) (n 35) 21.

If designed to clarify the law, the 1803 Act created anomalies of its own. I highlight just some of them. Keown sets out the whole picture of the failures of the 1803 statute.[94] While Section 2 made it clear beyond question that abortion at any stage in pregnancy was a criminal offence, a distinction was still made between pre- and post-quickening, a crucial distinction as procuring a miscarriage post-quickening carried the death penalty. Extraordinarily, Section 1 addressed only abortions procured by ingesting some poisonous or noxious substance. The non-capital offence in Section 2 covered all forms of abortion embracing both procuring a miscarriage by way of any medicine, drugs or other substance or thing whatsoever, or employing any instrument or means whatsoever with intent to procure such a miscarriage. The omission of instrumental abortion from the capital offence was on the face of it anomalous given the growing body of evidence that abortifacients administered orally or anally were largely ineffective in destroying the fetus while instruments properly deployed were likely to succeed in achieving the end of killing the fetus. The omission might be explained by a variety of factors including the following. Parliament was ill-informed about medical and scientific evidence. Legislators and medical practitioners were particularly concerned about 'fraudulent' sales by quacks of potions and other abortifacients dangerous to the woman and unlikely to achieve the desired end. Later in the century, orthodox medical practitioners made stringent efforts to drive out the druggists from the practice of medicine and focused in particular on the sale and advertising of pills and potions discreetly claimed to terminate a pregnancy, to cure 'suppression of the menses' or 'female irregularities'.[95] It is less clear that such attitudes were common in 1803. Keown notes, however, that even at the start of the 1800s, some medical practitioners were expressing serious concerns about the number of abortions being performed and the evidence that on many occasions the woman lost her life along with her child. He cites John Burns' warning in 1799 of the danger of purgatives used to procure miscarriages which were usually ineffective and if the potions were taken in high enough doses to procure an abortion often killed the mother too.[96]

Overall, the tenor of Lord Ellenborough's Act, both in its content and what can be discerned from parliamentary debates, testifies to the strong influence of Christian thinking coming close to taking the law back to Bracton's contention that abortion of a quickened fetus was homicide. Note, however, the inclusion in Section 1 of the word 'unlawfully', signalling that

94 Ibid 26–27.
95 P Knight 'Women and Abortion in Victorian and Edwardian England' (1977) 4 *History Workshop* 57.
96 Keown (1988) (n 35) 35–36.

there might be circumstances making the procedure justifiable, the question which was to become the *casus belli* of debates on abortion for more than two centuries to come.

Section 13 of the Offences Against the Person Act 1828 (Lord Lansdowne's Act) repealed sections 1 and 2 of Lord Ellenborough's Act. The 1828 Act rectified the anomaly relating to instrumental abortions, providing that prohibition of post-quickening abortions extended to abortions procured by the use of 'any instrument or means whatsoever with intent thereby to cause or procure the miscarriage of any woman'. Quickening remained relevant. Post-quickening abortions still attracted the death penalty, despite evidence that the justification for the death sentence for post-quickening abortions rested on a supposed distinction in terms of fetal development increasingly condemned as fictional.[97] As in 1803, Lord Lansdowne's Act in 1828 addressed criminal abortion in the context of the whole range of offences against the person, laws which the then Home Secretary, Sir Robert Peel, declared to be 'obscure and intricate'. The objective of the Act was to 'simplify and clarify' the law.

Nine years later, the Offences Against the Person Act 1837 abolished the death penalty for abortion in line with the general philosophy of the Criminal Law Commissioners to reduce the number of capital offences, replacing execution with a maximum sentence of transportation for life. Section 6 at long last abolished any distinction based on quickening. Several questions relating to the definition of criminal abortion remained unanswered. Further amendments relating directly to the criminal law and abortion were to be made in Sections 58 and 59 of the Offences Against the Person Act 1861.

The 1861 Act sought to re-enforce prohibition of abortion, plugging loopholes in the existing law. Section 58 made it a felony for any third party *unlawfully* to procure or attempt to procure the miscarriage of any woman by any means, whether or not she was with child. The woman herself committed a felony if she carried out or attempted self-abortion but only if she was proven to be, or to have been, with child. Section 59 made it a misdemeanour *unlawfully* to supply any means with intent to procure such a miscarriage. That single word 'unlawfully' left the door open to continue 'lawful' therapeutic abortions, with the medical professionals acting as the door-keepers. Keown, tracing the 'increasingly restrictive development of the law against abortion between 1803 and 1861', concludes that Parliament was 'influenced to a significant degree by the emerging medical profession's condemnation of abortion and its proposals for reform'.[98]

97 Ibid.
98 Ibid 48.

The 'medical voice' and abortion law in nineteenth-century England

It cannot be disputed that over the nineteenth century doctors acquired a strong voice in relation to the law regulating abortion. Keown marshals the evidence carefully from contemporary literature and evidence to Parliament.[99] Questions remain concerning *why* the medical profession gained such an influential voice by 1861, and what drove their condemnation of abortion and motivated the profession's determination to criminalise abortion more effectively. No single factor appears to explain the evolution of the medical 'voice' in the debates leading up to the 1861 Act. Contemporaneous changes in the nature of the profession and medical practice more generally played a part.

First, the regulation of medical professionals generally underwent significant reforms within the same time period. Three years before the 1861 Act, Parliament passed the Medical Act 1858. Discussed in Chapter 4, the Act effected a partial unification of the orthodox medical professions, the physicians, surgeons and apothecaries, and established the Medical Register. Only a person who met the qualifications set out in the Act could be entered on the Register and it became a criminal offence for a person to 'wilfully and falsely' pretend to be registered under the Act or use any name or title implying that he was so registered. The desire of many orthodox doctors that 'quackery' be made a crime was not fulfilled. The Act did, however, enhance the social status of the medical professional, granted them protection of title by the State and increasingly seen as having a role in the development of medical ethics, and thus making medical law.[100] In the next chapter, I examine the parallel influence of the medical profession on the passing of the Anatomy Act 1832.

Second, from the late 1700s medical men had become more involved in the care of pregnant and labouring women. By the end of the century, man-midwives (usually surgeons or surgeon-apothecaries, and sometimes styled *accoucheurs*) attended an increasing number of deliveries. In 1825 the first Obstetric Society was founded with limited success,[101] and was succeeded in 1858 by the London Obstetrical Society. A new specialism, obstetrics, developed and the obstetricians fought to control pregnancy and childbirth.

Third, in many cases the 'expert' advice offered by the medical men testified to the dangers to women of any form of abortion. In 1814, John Burns repeated his warning that purgatives rarely worked, and might kill the mother.[102] Similar claims about the dangers of instrumental abortions were

---

99 Ibid 26–48.
100 J Miola *Medical Ethics and Medical Law: A Symbiotic Relationship* (Hart Publishing, 2007).
101 D I Williams 'The Obstetric Society of 1825' 42 *Medical History* (1998) 235.
102 J Burns *The Principles of Midwifery* (1814) cited in Keown (1988) (n 35) 45.

voiced again and again. Insofar as medical pressure to legislate to restrict abortions was based on evidence of maternal mortality and morbidity, and assuming that that evidence was sound, ensuring that legislators were aware of such evidence was a role properly undertaken by doctors with expertise in matters of female reproduction. The risks to women of procedures designed to end a pregnancy were real, not just simply anti-abortion rhetoric. The protection of women looks at first sight to fit with Means' thesis that safety was the sole purpose of legislation. Nineteenth-century medical men might have been paternalist but were they beneficent? Or were they seeking a monopoly in the business of obstetric care? Orthodox doctors who testified to the innate risks to women added an additional warning, claiming that risk of maternal mortality and morbidity was vastly increased when the abortionist was unskilled and ignorant, by which the doctor meant s/he was a non-orthodox healer.[103] The Medical Act had failed to deliver the exclusion of 'quacks' from the medical market place; at least the orthodox could try and exile them from abortion provision.

Safety was not the only driver of medical opposition to liberal access to abortion. Thomas Percival's views exemplify the stance of many of the thoughtful and gentlemanly physicians of the time, the 'virtuous physician'. Percival identifies a range of matters which he regarded as pertinent to framing the law on abortion and casts light on medical opinion at the beginning of the 'statutory era'. Percival condemned as false what he describes as opinion from 'ancient times' that the fetus be regarded as a 'portion of the womb of the mother'[104] and thus 'she was supposed to have an equal and full right over both'. He is right insofar as the opinion is based on physiology; the fetus is not in any biological sense part of the pregnant woman.[105] Percival also rejected the correlative 'ancient' claim, one that sounds rather modern today, that the mother has the right to determine the fate of the fetus she carries.

> [N]o female can be privileged to injure her own bowels much less the *foetus* which is now well known to constitute no part of them. To extinguish the first spark of life is a crime of the same nature both against our Maker and society as to destroy an infant, a child or man these regular and successive stages of existence being the Ordinances of God, subject alone to his Divine Will, and appointed by sovereign wisdom and goodness as the exclusive means of preserving the race and multiplying the enjoyment of mankind.[106]

103　Mohr (n 32) 32–40.
104　Percival (n 2) 79.
105　*Attorney General's Reference (No 3 of 1994)* [1997] 3 All E R 936, HL.
106　Percival (n 2) 79.

Percival appeals to Christian doctrine in categorising abortion as a crime against our Maker, proclaiming that the fetus is to be accorded the same value as infant, child or man. Abortion, he states, is a crime against society as well as 'our Maker'. In stating that '[n]o female can be privileged to injure her own bowels', it should be remembered that at the time Percival was writing, self-harm and self-killing fell within the purview of the criminal law. 'Your body' was not incontrovertibly yours: abortion threatened the preservation of the race. Only in the most desperate case was a therapeutic abortion permissible. Many other orthodox practitioners shared Percival's views equating abortion at any stage of pregnancy with a 'detestable species of murder',[107] the 'destruction of a human being'.[108] Not all medical practitioners agreed. Dr Blundell, rejecting argument that craniotomy was only permissible when the child was dead, said tersely:

> [W]ith the dogmas of the divine, it is not my province to interfere, and I am glad of it; without therefore babbling about theology and syringes, I may be permitted to remark that in British midwifery the life, nay, the preservation of the patient from the grave lesions to her person is to be looked upon as paramount to every consideration relating to the foetus and when these require the sacrifice, craniotomy is justifiable.[109]

Danger to women and dangerous women

The danger to women of primitive abortion methods is largely accepted though some commentators have argued that the risk to the woman has been exaggerated.[110] The danger posed by women has been advanced as a further explanation of secular law's condemnation of abortion.[111] Prevention of fornication, not protection of fetuses, was the purpose of restrictive legislation. Spivack argued that the 'new' laws were driven by the opportunity abortion offered to indulge in and conceal extra-marital sex. Illicit sex threatened public order. The cost to the community of illegitimate children added an economic ground to any moral case to enforce sexual morals. In particular, Spivack links illegitimacy with rising levels of vagrancy in early modern England.[112] She notes the emphasis in *R v Lichefeld*[113] that Jane Wynspere,

107 C Severn *First Lines of the Practice of Midwifery* (London, 1831).
108 J G Smith *The Principles of Forensic Medicine* (London, 1821) 290.
109 J Blundell 'Lectures on the Theory and Practice of Midwifery' (1827–1828) 2 *Lancet* 129, 134.
110 Mohr (n 32) 30–32.
111 Gavigan (n 44) 28–30.
112 Spivack (n 42).
113 *R v Lichefeld* (n 83).

whom Lichefeld was accused of harbouring, was a 'single woman'. Simplistic stereotypes of women as the tender sex prevailed. Opening the prosecution of Eleanor Beare, counsel for the Crown proclaimed that 'to destroy the Fruit in the Womb carries in it something so contrary to the natural Tenderness of the Female Sex that I am amazed how ever any woman should arrive at such a degree of Impiety and Cruelty'.[114]

Forceful rejection of any claim that abortion laws might have been influenced by a desire to deter extra-marital sex and limit illegitimate births is about the only matter on which Dellapenna[115] and Means agree. Means devotes just one page to dismiss any contention that nineteenth-century laws were passed to discourage sexual promiscuity, arguing that neither the common law nor any statute overtly discriminated between married and single women.[116] He took no account of the evidence from the case law and the legislature signalling intent to punish 'loose women'. Recall the Preamble to the Infanticide Act aimed at the 'many lewd Women that have been delivered of Bastard Children, [who] to avoyde their shame and to escape punishment, doe secretlie bury, or conceale the Death, of their children'. Abortion as a means of birth control practised by 'some vile women' was condemned.[117] A commentator writing in 1832 regarded abortion as likely to corrupt sexual morals allowing sexual pleasures to be indulged in with impunity, and tellingly declared that even if abortion 'were feasible without any physical injury [it would] be an act from which a delicate mind will shrink with disgust'.[118] Given the several ways (discussed in the previous chapter) in which well into the twentieth century English law reduced women to a subordinate status, and the fear of the female, with her predatory womb apparent in the imagery of women, it would be surprising if matters of sexual morals and female 'frailty' did not feature in the development of law in both the common law and statute.

'Science' and certainty

Through all the changes and disputes about abortion law from Bracton to today, one factor was immutable. Once a child was 'born alive' not only did killing them constitute homicide, but should the born infant die of injuries

114 *Beare* (n 81).
115 Dellapenna (n 38) 267–268.
116 Means (1971) (n 27) 381–382.
117 McLaren (n 46) 111–112.
118 As cited by Gavigan (n 44) 29.

deliberately inflicted in utero that too was murder.[119] The difficult question was what 'born alive' meant. In 1832, the judge in *R v Poulton*[120] directed the jury that 'being born must mean that the whole body is brought into the world'. Evidence that the child breathed was not sufficient as a child might breathe in the course of delivery, yet die before delivery was complete. The judge concluded: 'Whether this child was born alive or not depends mainly on the evidence of medical men.' In 1833 in *R v Enoch*,[121] Parke J reiterated that signs of breathing were not enough to make the killing murder; the child must have had an independent circulation. A year later in *R v Brain*,[122] Park held that, just as breathing was not sufficient to find a child was born alive, so it was not essential to show the child had breathed. Children might be born alive 'yet do not breathe for some time after their birth'. A child who was wholly delivered from the mother's body was born alive, even if the child was still attached to the umbilical cord.[123]

Nineteenth-century judges struggled to identify criteria which could determine at what stage in delivery a fetus became a legal person.[124] Medical experts offered some guidance relating to fetal development, for example examining the lungs to establish whether a child had breathed. No scientific test could conclusively answer the question. A lacuna in the law exacerbated the conundrum. English law made no provision to prevent the killing of the fetus in the course of labour, before it had an existence independent of the mother. The fetus in the course of delivery was unprotected. Once labour commenced, Sections 58 and 59 of the 1861 Act prohibiting procuring miscarriage became irrelevant. Not until over half a century later did the Infant Life Preservation Act 1929 close the gap in the law. The Act introduced a new offence of child destruction, unlawfully destroying the life of child 'capable of being born alive', a phrase which proved as troubling for twentieth-century judges as 'born alive' was for their predecessors.[125]

---

119 *R v West* (1848) English Reports 329. And if a child born alive subsequently died of injury caused by gross negligence, a charge of manslaughter would lie: *R v Senior* (1832) 168 English Reports 1298.
120 (1832) 172 English Reports 997.
121 (1833) 172 English Reports 1089.
122 (1834) 172 English Reports 1272; *R v Sellis* (1837) 173 English Reports 370.
123 *R v Crutchley* (1837) 173 English Reports 355; *R v Reeves* (1839) 173 English Reports 724.
124 See E C Romanis 'Challenging the "Born Alive" Threshold: Fetal Surgery, Artificial Wombs and the English Approach to Personhood' (2019) 28 *Medical Law Review* 93.
125 *C v S* [1988] 1 QB 135; *Rance v Mid-Downs Health Authority* [1991] 1 QB 587. Mason notes that the Act introduced a version of the concept of viability into English law, J K Mason *The Troubled Pregnancy: Legal Rights and Wrongs in Reproduction* (Cambridge University Press, 2007) 20.

An examination of the history of abortion law reveals the law strug-
gling with uncertainty. There is an entity which counts for something, an
entity which like a chameleon changes 'shape' as it develops into a legal
person. Law turned to 'science' to attempt to find that missing certainty.
'Quickening' was once the litmus test, only to be discredited as understanding of gestation developed. Live birth looks like a more stable marker but
the cases noted earlier show its complexities. 'Let the medical men decide'
may have seemed a viable way out of the problem. Yet the very scientific
developments which were called on to answer what was and is meant by
born alive create new uncertainty. Advances in neonatal medicine, fetal surgery and maybe soon Artificial Womb Technology force re-consideration of
born alive.[126] At a practical level 'old' case law fails to provide a satisfactory
definition for the needs of modern medicine.[127]

'Old' cases highlight two persistent themes. 'Science', be it the understanding of medieval scholars of the importance of quickening, or modern
biomedical science, cannot cure the uncertainty. No empirical test will define
the moment the fetus becomes a legal person endowed with human rights.
The question is not a scientific question.[128] The 'old' cases also highlight
the fundamental dilemma which arises in any consideration of the 'not yet
born child'. Regardless of Dworkin's 'intractable' problem, whether or not
the fetus is a person, the body of the fetus resides in the body of a woman.
Victorian judges in emphasising the need for an existence independent of the
mother before the fetus became a child recognised the exceptional nature of
the maternal/fetal relationship. Perhaps the hour has come to heed Judith
Jarvis Thomson, cease to attempt to resolve the irresoluble question of personhood and focus on the obligations of a woman, if any, to continue to
maintain the body of the entity within her even if it may be a person.[129]

126 Romanis (n 124) 102–103, 109–113.
127 Nuffield Council on Bioethics, *Critical Care Decisions in Fetal and Neonatal
    Medicine: Ethical Issues* (2006).
128 D L Faigman *Legal Alchemy: The Use and Misuse of Science in the Law* (W H
    Freeman and Co, 2000) 39–45.
129 J J Thomson 'A Defense of Abortion' (1971) 1 *Philosophy and Public Affairs* 47.

10

Honouring the dead: commodifying the corpse

Rest in peace?

The treatment of the dead body has generated controversy from antiquity, reflecting persistent themes in medico-legal history, the importance of physical bodies and the gulf between popular sentiment and the educated elite. The availability of cadaver organs and other body parts for transplant is of incalculable value to the people whose lives are saved or enhanced by organ donation. Medical research and education rely heavily on access to tissue. Although the first successful transplant did not take place until 1905, demand for dead bodies for research and education stretches back many centuries. At much the same time as the literary and artistic Renaissance flowered in Western Europe so did a parallel 'anatomical Renaissance'.[1] Human corpses for dissection were needed both to educate medical students about the human body and for research as medicine gradually developed as a rational science.

Where were the bodies to come from? Many people fiercely opposed interference with the bodies of their dead and dreaded the possibility of ending up on the dissecting table. Ensuring an adequate supply of corpses for medical students and research was as thorny a problem in the sixteenth to nineteenth centuries as it is to match supply and demand of organs for transplant now.

Passionate feelings aroused in relation to uses of human remains has provoked vitriolic debate and public disorder. So angry were opponents of the first Anatomy Act 1832 that a mob burned down the anatomy school in Sheffield. Prior to 1832, when the principal lawful source of bodies for dissection were the bodies of executed criminals, riots at public executions

---

1 J Sawday *The Body Emblazoned: Dissection and the Human Body in Renaissance Culture* (Routledge, 1996).

were not uncommon. The exploits of the bodysnatchers are still part of folk memory.

In her marvellous book *Death, Dissection and the Destitute*,[2] Ruth Richardson addressed the passage of the Anatomy Act 1832 through Parliament, and the earlier history of dissection. In the 'Afterword' to her second edition, Richardson wrote that she had expected her readership to come from academic historians like herself, interested in 'the Victorian celebration of death and its negative archetype, the pauper funeral'.[3] As the date for publication of her second edition approached, evidence emerged that at hospitals throughout the United Kingdom organs and tissue had been routinely retained after post-mortem examinations 'for a variety of purposes, including audit, medical education and research, or had simply been stored'.[4] The retention of organs and tissue had for the most part been undertaken without consent or knowledge of the deceased or their families, or with wholly inadequate consent. The retention of organs from children in Bristol and Liverpool attracted the greatest media attention but the practice was not limited to children. Families discovered that organs had been retained from adult relatives. The organ retention 'scandal' was born.[5] Richardson found that she had a broader audience embracing 'most recently, parents wronged by professional and institutional secrecy surrounding the purloining of body parts after autopsies on their children'.[6] Understanding the history of law and medicine's turbulent relationship with the corpse might have avoided the bitter disputes that arose. The 'scandals' at the start of the twenty-first century mirrored the battles of the past. Richardson quotes William Faulkner: 'The past is not dead yet. It is not even past yet.'[7] Public disquiet about desecration of their dead is deeply rooted. The corpse has often been very differently regarded by the family and community in which the deceased lived their life, and medical practitioners who seek to utilise the body to advance biomedical science, as well as 'industries' who stand to profit from the dead. A stark conflict emerged between popular opinion and biomedical science, which was often exacerbated by conflict between rich and poor.

---

2 R Richardson *Death, Dissection and the Destitute* (2nd edn) (University of Chicago Press, 2000).
3 Ibid 409.
4 Bristol Inquiry Interim Report *Removal and Retention of Human Material* (HMSO, 2000) para 4.
5 M Brazier 'Retained Organs: Ethics and Humanity' (2002) *Legal Studies* 551.
6 Richardson (n 2) 409.
7 Ibid.

Canon law and the integrity of the body[8]

Before examining that conflict and the fraught history of the regulation of human dissection, the core reasons for objection to interference with dead bodies and the role of canon law need to be addressed. In Western Europe, the teaching of the medieval Church about the integrity of the physical body forms a starting point for any analysis of the development of later secular laws addressing the particular question of anatomical dissection.

Elaborate customs relating to the disposal of the dead and a commitment to honour the dead long pre-dates Christianity. In some, though not all traditions, maintaining the physical integrity of the dead body was a driving force in formulating rules governing how human corpses should be treated. Classic examples are the pyramids of Ancient Egypt. The pharaohs built monuments to their power and status in this earthly life. Rigorous precautions were taken to safeguard the corpse; dreadful penalties were threatened against those who disturbed the dead. Such precautions proved no more successful against the depredations of the tomb-robbers than were attempts to foil the bodysnatchers in England and Scotland.

In Christian Europe through the Middle Ages, into and after the Renaissance, beliefs that the dead must remain intact derived from Church doctrine about the Resurrection. If the body was not intact when laid in the grave how could the dead person rise again on the day of judgement?[9] Assertions that it was only the soul which would be resurrected constituted heresy.[10] Literal belief that one's physical body would rise again as it had been when laid in the grave would make it eminently reasonable to object strongly to any removal of parts from your own body or the bodies of those you love. The teaching of the medieval Church and canon law was less straightforward and forged in disputes about 'bodily division', a practice whereby the corpse was divided and different parts of the body interred in different places. Such a practice became common for Royal dead. King Henry I of England died in Rouen having wished to be buried in Reading Abbey. His entrails, brain and eyes were buried at Rouen to prevent putrefaction and the remainder of his corpse then taken to Reading.[11] The heart of his great-grandson, Richard the Lionheart, was buried at Rouen where his grandfather had been interred. The rest of his body was laid to rest at Fontevrault Abbey at the feet of his

---

8 M Brazier 'The Body in Time' (2015) 7 *Law, Innovation and Technology* 161.

9 C W Bynum *The Resurrection of the Body in Western Christianity 200–1336* (Columbia University Press, 1995).

10 Ibid 217.

11 P Binski *Medieval Death* (British Museum Press, 1996) 63.

father and sister.[12] The reasons for 'bodily division' were diverse. Some were ceremonial, granting different sites the honour of being a resting place for a deceased prince. Others were said to be by way of multiplying the prayers for the dead to shorten time in purgatory.[13] Many were simply practical. The bodies of the wealthy who had died far from home, perhaps in the Crusades, were eviscerated, boiled and divided so that some at least of the remains could be transported home.[14] As to poorer people who stayed at home and were buried in the local churchyard, their bodies too might be disturbed if pressure on space meant graves had to be reused and bones removed to a charnel house or ossuary.[15]

In the face of evidence that Christian corpses were in practice being divided and 'mutilated', what did the Church, the canon law provide? Canon 1 of the Fourth Lateran Council 1215 seemed to endorse a doctrine that the dead body must remain intact. The Profession of Faith declared that when at the end of time Christ comes again to 'judge the living and the dead' then 'All of them shall rise with their own bodies, which they now wear.'

In a Papal Bull *Detestande Feritatis* (Of Unspeakable Cruelty) (1299) Pope Boniface VIII prohibited 'bodily division' requiring that the body must be immediately interred at the requested burial place or near the place of death. If the place of death was not the chosen burial site, the body could later be exhumed and reburied but only when the corpse was fully decayed. Evisceration and boiling were expressly banned. Brown argues that Boniface was equally opposed to any form of severing the body and cremation.[16] The Bull was largely ignored. Brown suggests the Bull may have been triggered by a dispute about the burial of King Philip III of France whose wishes to be buried at St Denis in Paris were ignored by his son, who had his father's body divided, and buried his remains in three places.[17]

The view that *Detestande Feritatis* banned autopsies or anatomical dissection is now rejected by most historians.[18] Evidence of autopsies performed in Christian Europe dates back to about 1250 in Bologna. Initially the autopsy was performed as part of the judicial process to ascertain the cause of death in cases of suspected homicide.[19] Techniques of dissection learned in

---

12 E A R Brown 'Death and the Human Body in the Late Middle Ages: The Legislation of Boniface VIII on the Division of the Corpse' (1981) 12 *Viator* 221.
13 Ibid 239–242.
14 Ibid 227.
15 Bynum (n 9) 203.
16 Brown (n 12) 221–223.
17 Ibid 236–237.
18 C Rawcliffe *Medicine and Society in Later Medieval England* (Sandpiper, 1995) 128.
19 R Porter *The Greatest Benefit to Mankind: A Medical History of Humanity from Antiquity to the Present* (Fontana Press, 1997) 131–133.

the performance of judicial autopsies soon extended to more widespread use of dissection in education and research. In fourteenth-century Bologna public dissections of executed criminals which were initially intended to 'prove' earlier theories of medicine met with public opposition, as was to be the case in England later.[20]

How far if at all did the Church teach that interference with the corpse affected the physical resurrection of the body? Opinion among the Fathers of the Church was divided. Boniface VIII's Bull notwithstanding, the practice of bodily division, on occasion with papal dispensation, the veneration of parts of the deceased saints, 'sacred relics'[21] and permission for dispersed burials of such relics contradict any absolute dogma of the integrity of the corpse. Far back in the fifth century St Augustine preached that 'the fate of the body was of no real consequence to its eventual resurrection'.[22] St Augustine emphasised that care of the dead and honouring the physical remains of the person was a duty to be embraced, but that man could trust in God to accomplish the miracle of resurrection.[23]

It would seem then that the Church did not ban *all* interferences with the physical integrity of the corpse. Nearly two centuries after *Detestande Feritatis*, Pope Sixtus IV declared that dissection of the corpse was not absolutely prohibited if the body came from an executed criminal and was ultimately afforded Christian burial.[24] Church doctrine was more nuanced than an outright ban on interference with the corpse. Post-dissection the remains must be reverently buried. In the context of reverence to relics the Church acknowledged contradictions in revering mortal remains and sought to prevent trafficking in relics and the growth of superstitious cults.[25] Put rather roughly the Roman Church in the Renaissance did not prohibit the use of dead bodies in the cause of science or religious practice but did require respectful treatment and attempted to ban 'markets'. Christian (and Muslim)[26] sensibilities of the time were nonetheless offended by dissection. Just as Richardson shows was the case for their descendants

---

20 D G Jones 'The Dead Human Body: Reflections of an Anatomist' in V T Chuan, R Huxtable, N Peart (eds) *Healthcare Ethics, Law and Professionalism* (Routledge, 2019) 225–241 at 228–229.

21 Brown (n 12) 228.

22 Sawday (n 1) 218.

23 St Augustine of Hippo 'Of the Care to be Taken of the Dead' as discussed in Sawday (n 1) 218–219.

24 L I Conrad, M Neve, V Nutton, R Porter and A Wear *The Western Medical Tradition 800 BC to AD 1800* (Cambridge University Press, 1996) 147–148.

25 Rawcliffe (n 18) 21–24.

26 Conrad et al (n 24) 131.

in the seventeenth to nineteenth centuries,[27] and later in the retained organs controversy at the turn of the millennium, many laypeople living in the Renaissance regarded dissection as contrary to their faith and respect for the deceased, whatever the princes of the Church might say. There was and continued to be a gap between orthodox Christian teaching and popular culture. Medieval debates about the conflict between the need for bodies for dissection to advance the development of scientific medicine and mistaken beliefs about religious proscriptions against interfering with dead bodies are mirrored today in the beliefs of many Muslims and Orthodox Jews and a number of Christians that their religion bans any violation of the physical integrity of the dead, including organ donation.[28] An orthodox Jewish scholar, Maurice Lamm, puts the argument thus:

> [M]an was created in the image of God and in death his body still retains the unity of that image. One may not do violence to the human form even when the breath of life has expired.[29]

'Bring up the bodies'

In the sixteenth century, interest in human anatomy grew rapidly among both medical practitioners and the educated elite. The publication of Vesalius's classic work *De humani corporis fabrica* in 1543 was followed by many other works exploring human anatomy.[30] Understanding anatomy, of what the body is comprised and how the human body functions, was a necessary pre-condition of developments in medical science.[31] In Europe, anatomy theatres became places of entertainment. Sawday commented 'the anatomy theatre rivalled the stage for the hold it exerted on those who flocked to these Vitruvian structures'.[32] The development of interest in anatomy in England was slower than across the Channel; the College of Physicians was 'ambivalent about science in medicine'.[33] It is clear, however, that English surgeons were carrying out dissections from the early 1500s,

---

27 Richardson (n 2) 76–77.
28 S McGuinness and M Brazier 'Respecting the Living Means Respecting the Dead Too' (2008) 28 *Oxford Journal of Legal Studies* 297, 306–309.
29 M Lamm *The Jewish Way in Death and Mourning* (Jonathan David, 1998) 10.
30 Jones (n 20) 228–231.
31 Sawday (n 1) 65.
32 Ibid 75–76.
33 B Woolley *The Herbalist: Nicholas Culpeper and the Fight for Medical Freedom* (Harper Perennial, 2004) 349–350.

and in 1636 Inigo Jones designed an anatomy theatre based on the famous anatomy theatre in Padua.

Anatomists needed bodies. There is little evidence that the public who came to watch the spectacle, or the anatomists themselves, volunteered to donate their own remains. Corpses needed to be conscripted. Echoing Pope Sixtus IV that dissection of a corpse was permissible if the body came from an executed criminal and was ultimately afforded Christian burial,[34] in 1506, King James IV of Scotland granted the Edinburgh Guild of Surgeons the right to dissect a number of the bodies of executed criminals. In 1540, Henry VIII of England 'donated' the bodies of four hanged felons annually to the Company of Barber-Surgeons in London. Elizabeth I made a similar donation to the College of Physicians in 1565. Further royal gifts were to follow.[35]

The measly number of felons' corpses granted by the Crown[36] to the anatomists came nowhere near meeting demand as English doctors caught up with their Continental peers in the pursuit of medical research. The source of those bodies, executed criminals, added further fuel to popular disquiet and growing anger. Dissection became tainted with criminality. To be left to the mercy of the surgeons to be chopped up after death was seen as the ultimate punishment, depicted by Hogarth in his iconic cartoon of a public dissection at the Surgeons' Hall in London, a cartoon accompanied by the following verse:

> *Behold the Villain's dire Disgrace*
> *Not Death itself can end*
> *He Finds no peaceful Burial-place*
> *His breathless Corpse – no Friend* [37]

The association of dissection with criminality was reinforced in 1752 when Parliament passed an Act 'for better preventing the Horrid Crime of Murder' – popularly known as the 'Murder Act'. The Act empowered judges to add to a sentence of death an additional punishment that, after execution, the body of the convicted murderer be handed over to the anatomists for dissection, as 'a Further Terror and Mark of Infamy'.[38] Exceptionally evil

---

34 Conrad et al (n 24).

35 M Brazier and S Ost *Medicine and Bioethics in the Theatre of the Criminal Process* (Cambridge University Press, 2013) 22.

36 Richardson (n 2) 52–53. She notes that the anatomists in England and Scotland often unlawfully exceeded their 'quota' of corpses.

37 Hogarth *Fourth Stage of Cruelty* (1751); reproduced in Richardson (n 2) at 33.

38 E T Hurren *Dissecting the Criminal Corpse; Staging Post Execution Punishment in Early Modern England* (Palgrave Macmillan, 2016).

murderers were denied a grave. In the public mind, the dissected man or woman was deprived of their hope of the Resurrection. Belief in the necessity of the corpse remaining intact in readiness for the Resurrection persisted regardless of the teachings of the clerics. Despite the disdain of some of the educated classes, the very people most at risk of ending up on the anatomists' table regarded the additional penalty imposed by the 'Murder Act' as robbing them of immortal life as well as this earthly existence. For the penalty to be worse than death, worse than hanging, it must go further than simply ending this life. Such was the horror generated by the prospect of dissection that crowds witnessing public executions made attempts to rescue the corpse for decent burial.[39] The 'Murder Act' failed to provide the number of corpses needed by anatomists and failed to stem the practice of bodysnatching which had begun to emerge before 1752, and inflamed opposition to interference with the human dead.

The reign of the bodysnatchers

Unmet demand before and after the 'Murder Act' set the scene for the infamous practice of bodysnatching, that is stealing fresh (or relatively fresh) corpses from the grave. By the eighteenth century, demand for bodies to dissect was huge. Surgeons engaged in research required a steady supply of bodies of both sexes and all ages. The anatomy schools, which provided much of such medical education as was available, needed cadavers so that students could practise and learn from anatomical dissection. Anatomy schools were in effect private businesses competing for fee-paying students. The most eminent surgeons of their day, the Hunter brothers,[40] William and John, were both heavily involved in running such schools. Schools advertised for business, i.e. students, and traded in bodies and body parts.

Bodysnatching was perceived as answering the 'need'. Across Great Britain, a new trade emerged. Gangs of men lurked in graveyards ready to creep back at night and exhume new corpses for sale to the anatomists. Nicknamed the Resurrectionists and satirised as the Corporation of Corpse Stealers, Richardson notes that 'a comfortable living' could be made from the practice.[41] Bodysnatching was not confined to ill-educated men who made it their livelihood. There is evidence that some surgeons (including John Hunter), their students and apprentices not only purchased corpses

---

39 Sawday (n 1) 59–60.
40 See generally W Moore *The Knife Man: Blood, Body-Snatching and the Birth of Modern Surgery* (Bantam Books, 2005).
41 Richardson (n 2) 57.

from the Resurrectionist but 'robbed' graves themselves.[42] Hunter's ruthlessness in obtaining bodies at 'any price' is illustrated by the lengths he went to acquire the body of Charles Byrne, known as the 'Irish Giant'.[43] The 'Giant' had spent his unhappy life being exhibited at freak shows, poked and prodded by surgeons. He dreaded the prospect that his body would end up in the clutches of those same surgeons, fearing that if his body was dissected, he would be denied Resurrection.[44] Byrne made arrangements for his body to be sealed in an iron coffin and buried at sea 'in order that his bones might be placed far out of the reach of the chirurgical fraternity'.[45] News of Byrne's death started a bidding war among London's anatomists. A huge coffin was taken to Margate, loaded on a boat and once well out at sea the coffin was cast into the waters as Byrne had wished. The coffin did not contain Byrne's corpse. Hunter had bribed the undertakers to sell him the body and set up an elaborate fraud to swop the body for heavy stones while the Giant's friends got drunk holding a wake at a tavern. The body was conveyed back to London and the custody of John Hunter. The skeleton was later exhibited at the Entrance to the Royal College of Surgeon's pathology museum named the Hunterian Museum in honour of John Hunter.

While the drama of the 'Giant' played out in London, bodysnatching across the realm was routine. The prospect of relatives and friends being dragged from the grave was bad enough; more radical enterprises to make profit from the dead further inflamed popular opposition to dissection. Fears that bodysnatchers might graduate to murder, killing their chosen victims and selling the corpse thus cutting out the tedious business of grave robbing were not confined to the populace who detested the very notion of dissection. Sir Henry Halford, President of the College of Physicians, gave evidence to the Select Committee of the House of Commons established early in 1828 to investigate obtaining subjects for dissection in anatomy schools and 'into the state of the Law affecting the persons employed in obtaining or dissecting bodies'. He warned that when there was 'difficulty in obtaining bodies and the value of corpses was so great', the Resurrectionists could be tempted 'to commit murder for the purpose of selling the bodies of their victims'.[46] His warning proved apt when later in that year the homicidal activities of Burke and Hare in Edinburgh came to light. Contrary to myth, Burke and Hare were never bodysnatchers. They skipped that preliminary step and murdered at least sixteen poor and indigent victims and sold their corpses

---

42 Moore (n 40); Richardson (n 2) 37–39.
43 Richardson gives his name as O'Brien.
44 Moore (n 40) 417.
45 Ibid 422.
46 Richardson (n 2) 132.

to the anatomy school of Dr Robert Knox. Burke and his wife stood trial for the murder of the final victim, Mary Docherty. Hare turned King's Evidence and was granted immunity from prosecution. The case against Mrs Burke was found not proven and Burke alone found guilty. He was hanged and publicly dissected in January 1829. No charges were brought against Dr Knox. His involvement in the murderous business of Burke and Hare illustrated the complicity of some of the medical profession in the darkest end of the business of obtaining subjects to dissect. Richardson offers a full account and analysis of Knox's complicity in murder.[47]

Two years later, a less well-known couple, Bishop and Williams, were charged in London with murdering three 'poor street folk'[48] with the purpose of selling the bodies. Unlike Burke and Hare, Bishop and Williams were seasoned Resurrectionists who had supplied London anatomy schools with up to a thousand bodies before diversifying to murder.[49] Both men were hanged on 5 December 1831.

Inadequate laws

Even an abbreviated account of the business of bodysnatching and its gory offspring, murder to order, begs questions about the role of the law in preventing such practices. How did bodysnatching flourish – 'surely', any reasonable lay person might say 'robbing graves, stealing corpses must have been illegal'? The problem was that simply stealing a dead body was not of itself said to be a crime. Dicta in cases from the seventeenth century were cited as authority that there could be 'no property in a corpse' and so corpses could not be stolen. Two judgments relied on to support this 'rule' have been shown to rest on shaky ground. In *Haynes' Case*[50] (1614), William Haynes was convicted of stealing the winding sheets (shrouds) from four bodies which he had disinterred. The judge(s) found that 'the property of the sheets remain in the owners... when the body was wrapped therewith; for the dead body is not capable of it.' As Quigley notes, the correct interpretation of *Haynes' Case* is not that the corpse could not be property but rather that the dead could not own property.[51] A second case called in aid to support claims that the corpse could not be property is *Dr Handyside's Case*. This was said to concern an action for trover (claim for unlawful

---

47 Ibid 132–143.
48 Ibid 196–197.
49 Ibid.
50 *Haynes' Case* (1614) 77 English Reports 1389.
51 M Quigley *Self-Ownership, Property Rights and the Human Body: A Legal and Philosophical Analysis* (Cambridge University Press, 2018) 56–57.

interference with property), the property in question being the bodies of conjoined twins. The judgment is cited as holding that the claim failed because 'no person had any property in corpses'.[52] The very provenance of *Handyside's Case* is dubious. Peter Skegg[53] explains that there appears to be no mention of *Handyside's Case* before the early nineteenth century when it is noted by East in 1803.[54] There is no definite recorded date for the case. As it is supposed to have been heard by Sir John Wiles, Chief Justice of the Court of Common Pleas from 1732 to 1761, it must have been within that time span, which means, as Skegg points out, that East himself could not have had any personal knowledge of the case.[55]

Property in the human body, living or dead, whole, or in separated parts, has generated voluminous literature, as biomedical science discovers ever more uses for human material. Case law from the era of bodysnatching is meticulously unpicked. The modern scholar, like those who sought to suppress bodysnatching in the eighteenth and nineteenth centuries, is faced with several obstacles to any clear and definitive account of the common law governing the uses and abuses of corpses.

Whether right or wrong, judges accepted the mantra 'no property in a corpse', and thus the bodysnatchers could not be convicted of larceny (theft) of the corpse. An Act of Parliament passed in the reign of James I made it a felony to 'take up any dead man, woman or child out of his her or their grave' to be employed in 'witchcrafte', to steal dead bodies for the purpose of witchcraft.[56] The Act was held to have no application to the taking of corpses for other purposes such as dissection.[57] Blackstone wrote in his *Commentaries* that 'stealing the corpse itself which has no owner (though a matter of great indecency) is no felony unless some of the grave clothes be stolen with it'.[58] The judges, though bound by the no property 'rule', concurred with Blackstone as to the indecency of the practice and sought to find circuitous means to avoid the 'rule'. Charging the accused with stealing the clothes or sheets in which the body was wrapped was one such means. Digging up the soil to recover the corpse constituted trespass. Defacement of

52 E H East *A Treatise on the Pleas of the Crown* Vol 2 (Butterworth and Cooke, 1803) 652.
53 P D G Skegg 'Human Corpses, Medical Specimens and the Law of Property' (1976) 4 *Anglo-American Law Review* 412.
54 East (n 52) 652.
55 Skegg (n 53) 421.
56 'An Act against Conjuration, Witchcrafte and dealing with evil and wicked Spirits' (1603–4).
57 *R v Lynn* (1788) 100 English Reports 394.
58 W Blackstone *Commentaries on the Laws of England* (Oxford University Press, 2016) Book IV 236.

the monument or gravestone amounted to malicious damage. Judges were innovative in finding offences for which bodysnatchers could be punished. At times, judicial language used in condemning the bodysnatchers and their medical 'clients' is closer to the views and feelings of the populace, than to the anatomists and medical men who scorned superstitious beliefs about the resurrection of the body and emotional attachments to the carcase.

In *R v Lynn*[59] (1788) the defendant was convicted of entering a burial ground, taking a coffin out of the earth and removing the corpse for the purposes of dissection. Seeking to set aside the conviction, counsel argued that no crime was committed, or if there was a crime, it was subject to ecclesiastical jurisdiction and not the common law. Citing Sir Edward Coke, it was argued that 'the burial of the cadaver is *nullius in bonis*, and belongs to ecclesiastical cognizance; but as to the monument, action is given at the common law for defacing thereof'. It was taken for granted that stealing the corpse was not of itself criminal. Taking the shroud or digging up the soil was an offence against the executors of the deceased's estate. Argument that the court should regard the taking of a body for dissection differently from the taking of a corpse for some sort of indecent exhibition was countered by reference to an apparently unreported case *R v Young*. The master of a workhouse, a surgeon and a third man were convicted of conspiracy to prevent the lawful burial of an inmate who had died in the workhouse.

The judges ruled:

> [T]hat common decency required that the practice should be put a stop to. That the offence was cognizable in a Criminal Court, as being highly indecent, and contra bonos mores; at the bare idea alone of which nature revolted. That the purpose of taking up the body for dissection did not make it any less an indictable offence.[60]

Dismissing the attempt to overturn the conviction, the court referred to the regular practice of the Old Bailey in trying such cases and declared that in refusing even to hear the case in full, they did so 'lest that alone should convey to the public that they entertained a doubt respecting the crime alleged'.[61]

In *R v Cundick*[62] (1822) it was held that to sell the body of a convict executed for a capital offence for dissection where dissection was not part of the sentence was a misdemeanour at common law. Edward Lee had been publicly executed in September 1821. The keeper of the gaol where Lee

---

59 *Lynn* (n 57).
60 Ibid 395.
61 Ibid.
62 *R v Cundick* (1822) 171 English Reports 900.

had been confined engaged George Cundick, an undertaker, to bury Lee's body. Cundick did not bury the corpse. It was alleged he sold the body to a surgeon for the purpose of dissection. The body was eventually found at the surgeon's house partially dissected. No charge was brought against the surgeon nor was he called to testify. Cundick engaged in an elaborate deception to cover his tracks. He assured the keeper of the gaol that he had buried Lee and lied to Lee's relatives. He clandestinely went through a mock funeral, burying a coffin full of rubbish, and was later seen conveying a heavy package in a hackney coach. In blistering language, the indictment charged that Cundick:

> [B]eing an evil-disposed person, and of a most wicked and depraved dispos-
> ition, and having no regard to his said duty, nor to religion, decency, morality
> or the laws of this realm, did not nor would bury the said body so delivered to
> him but ...unlawfully and wickedly and *for the sake of filthy lucre and gain*,
> did take and carry away the said body, and did sell and dispose of the same,
> for the purpose of being dissected, cut to pieces, mangled and destroyed to
> the *great scandal of religion, decency and morality, in contempt of our said
> Lord the King and his laws, to the evil example of all other persons in like case
> offending and against the peace* [my emphases].

The defence challenged the indictment arguing inter alia that it was unsup-ported by the evidence. The only evidence was that the body was not buried. There was no proof of sale, lucre or gain, nor, in the absence of testimony from the surgeon, was there evidence that he had bought the body or acquired it for the purpose of dissection. The judge rejected the challenges and put the matter to the jury saying that if the accused was convicted these objections could be raised in 'another place' by way of a move to quash the judgment. The jury found Cundick guilty. *Cundick* has been taken to estab-lish that any treatment of a dead body other than respectful funeral rites constituted a misdemeanour, an offence *contra bonos mores*.[63]

In *Cundick* only the undertaker faced prosecution. The surgeon who bought Lee's corpse seems to have walked free. The prosecution of the Resurrectionists, working class men of dubious reputation, was not a cause for great concern to anatomists who 'bought' the bodies. The unfortunate men convicted could easily be replaced. The risk that one of their own number might face trial was a much greater fear.

Cases where medical men faced prosecution were of the utmost concern. Were an anatomist to be actively involved in digging up bodies, his con-duct would be no less criminal than that of the Resurrectionists. The key issue was: did receiving a body unlawfully disinterred make the surgeon

---

63 Report from the Select Committee on Anatomy 22 July 1828 6–7.

a party to the crime? As we have seen in *Young* a surgeon was tried for conspiring with the master of Shoreditch workhouse and a third man to prevent the lawful burial of a deceased inmate. In *R v Gill* a 'respectable teacher of anatomy' was convicted in Liverpool of possession of a dead body with intent to dissect and knowing that the body had been unlawfully disinterred.[64] *R v Davies*[65] triggered panic in the anatomy schools. Five men, John Davies (a medical student at the Warrington Dispensary), William Blundell (apprentice to a stationer), Edward Hall (a surgeon-apothecary at the Dispensary), Richard Box and Thomas Ashton (occupations unknown) were charged with (1) conspiracy to unlawfully procure and receive the body of Jane Fairclough and (2) having possession of a dead body knowing it had been unlawfully procured. The conspiracy charges against all the men were dismissed. Davies and Blundell were convicted of unlawful possession. *Davies* placed any medical man or student at risk of criminal liability simply by receiving corpses to dissect.

Two other points need making about *Davies*. First, in his directions to the jury Baron Hullock indicated some sympathy with the accused saying:

> The only bodies legally liable for dissection in this country, were those executed for murder. *However necessary it might be, for the purposes of humanity and science, that these things [exhumation and dissection] should be done,* yet, as long as the law remained as it was at present, the disinterment of bodies for dissection was an offence liable to punishment [my emphasis].[66]

Second, the sentences imposed on the convicted men, fines of £20 for Davies and £5 for Blundell, were relatively mild and the sentencing judge commented that 'there were degrees of guilt and in this case the defendants were not the most criminal parties'.[67]

Reforming the law

Laypeople and anatomists sought reform of the law. Early in 1828 the House of Commons established a Select Committee on Anatomy to review existing law and make proposals for legislation.[68] The appointment of the Committee has wrongly been attributed to the outcry generated by Burke

64 Ibid 6.
65 See J B Bailey *Diary of a Resurrectionist* (Swan Sonnenschein & Co, 1896) 95–97.
66 Richardson (n 2) 107.
67 Bailey (n 65) 98.
68 An earlier attempt to criminalise the theft of bodies from churchyards can be seen in an unsuccessful Bill of 1795: 'A Bill More effectually to prevent the Stealing of Dead Bodies from Church Yards, Burying Grounds or other Places of Interment.'

and Hare. Richardson demonstrates that such claims are incorrect given the Committee published its report before the murders were discovered.[69] The Committee was, rather, a response to the concerns of the medical professions about the inadequate supply of bodies, and their unease about connections with the Resurrectionists. The prosecutions in *Gill* and *Davies* were the clarion call for law reform. Commenting on *Davies*, the Committee stated that a 'most intelligent magistrate' had testified to the Committee that

> very slight evidence would connect the receiver with the disinterment; and that purchase from the exhumator would suffice to send the case to a jury, the knowledge of the fact of disinterment being to be collected from the circumstances, if strong enough to justify the inference. It is stated that there is scarcely a student or teacher of Anatomy in England, who under the law, if truly thus interpreted, is not indictable for a misdemeanor.[70]

The Committee's Terms of Reference indicate that the primary objective of the 'reformers' was to facilitate the practice of anatomy. The Committee was appointed

> to inquire into the manner of obtaining Subjects for dissection in the Schools of Anatomy, and into the State of the Law affecting the Persons employed on obtaining or dissecting Bodies; and to whom several PETITIONS for the removal of Impediments to the cultivation of the Science of ANATOMY were referred.[71]

The Committee saw its function as inquiring into the difficulties facing the anatomists 'whether arising out of the state of the law, or an adverse feeling on the part of the people; and into the evil consequences thence ensuing, as well as to the sciences of Medicine and Surgery, as to all who teach and practise them, and eventually to the public at large'.

Openly and forcefully on the side of 'Science', the Committee's report never questioned the importance of anatomy in medical education. The nub of their inquiry was how to obtain enough corpses for dissection. The inadequacy of existing laws was briefly outlined. Public outrage at proposals in 1796 to extend the 'Murder Act' to felons executed for burglary or robbery was noted. What of bodysnatching?[72] Ritual statements of disapproval and public concern are made. The Committee seems to have been less concerned with the evil of stealing bodies and more worried about the adverse consequences of criminalising the activity. The grave robbers are at one stage

---

69 Richardson (n 2) 101.
70 Select Committee (n 63) 6.
71 Select Committee (n 63).
72 The Committee refers to bodysnatchers as 'exhumators'.

referred to as 'parties of daring men'. The evil of their practice in the eyes of the Committee seemed to rest in (1) fights and feuds between gangs competing for the same source of bodies; (2) public disorder when 'vigilante' groups fought back against the bodysnatchers; (3) the cost of bodies, as scarcity and the risks to the bodysnatchers drove up the price of corpses to dissect. The Committee appeared to concede that as long as there was profit to be made bodysnatchers would continue their business, and if they remained the principal suppliers of dead bodies the anatomists would continue to do business with them.

> So long as there is no legalised mode of supplying the dissecting schools, so long the practice of disinterment will continue; but if other measures were devised, which would legalise and ensure a regular, plentiful and cheap supply, the practice of disinterring bodies, and of receiving them, would of necessity, be entirely abandoned.[73]

Given public disgust of dissection and the paucity of people prepared to donate their bodies, where was this supply of bodies to be found? The Committee looked to France. In Paris when a patient died in a public hospital, he was to be attended by a priest with the usual rites of the Roman Catholic Church. The body should be examined by a medical officer attached to the hospital and remain in the hospital for twenty-four hours unless claimed by a relative or friend. If unclaimed after twenty-four hours, the body would be sent to one of the dissecting schools in Paris. Witnesses endorsing the French precedent submitted that:

> the bodies of those who during life have been *maintained at the public charge,* and who die in workhouses, hospitals and other charitable institutions, should, if not claimed by next of kin within a certain time after death, be given up, under proper regulations to the Anatomist [my emphasis].[74]

The Committee endorsed the Parisian model authorising the supply of unclaimed corpses to the anatomists. They stated that evidence demonstrating that such a system would 'yield a supply of subjects that, in London at least, would be adequate to the wants of the Anatomist' was an essential factor in their recommendations. Moreover, the Committee added, creating a system that met the needs of the Anatomy Schools would 'eventually be the means of suppressing the practice of exhumation'.[75]

A delicate problem for the Committee derived from evidence that many people, not just the uneducated classes, still had visceral objections to the

73 Select Committee (n 63) 8.
74 Ibid 9.
75 Ibid 10.

dissection of their bodies or the bodies of relatives. Recognising strong feelings among the public that the bodies of the dead should lie 'undisturbed', the Committee crafted an ingenious argument, illustrating its Benthamite philosophy. If most of the dead were to lie peacefully in their graves, some corpses had to available for dissection because, without a legal supply of bodies, bodysnatching would continue. For the good of all, some must 'give' their remains. The current system of selection was random. Any corpse was at risk. Everyone might fear the 'exhumators'. The Committee proposed a 'just system for selection' rightly described by Richardson as 'appropriation of the corpses of the poor'.[76] Legislation should prescribe which bodies should be selected for dissection. The Committee acknowledged that their system of selecting bodies could be seen as discriminating against the poor as better off people were highly unlikely to die in workhouses or similar institutions. The Committee denied the charge, stating that only unclaimed bodies could be given up to the anatomists. In such cases there would either be no known relatives to be outraged or distressed by the fate of the corpse, or those relatives were indifferent to the prospect of dissection of the remains of the deceased. The meaning of unclaimed was unclear. For a relative to claim the body was it sufficient for them to come forward and state their relationship to the deceased and intention to attend the parish funeral? Or was the relative required to undertake responsibility for arranging and paying for the funeral? If the latter, the families of workhouse inmates were unlikely to be able meet such costs.

The Committee, somewhat ungraciously, recognised 'feelings' averse to their proposals. Insofar as such aversion was based on religious feelings, the Committee opined that such objections (presumably rooted in belief in the Resurrection) logically entailed opposition to dissection at all and the prohibition altogether of 'the study of practical Anatomy'. With some satisfaction, the Committee declared that several witnesses 'adduced facts to prove that those feeling of aversion are on the decline'. Those witnesses did not include people likely to be candidates for the dissection table. Later events proved predictions of decline to be wrong. The Committee's only concession to public aversion to dissection was its proposal that the 'Murder Act' 1752 be repealed. That Act was perceived as aggravating aversion to dissection by tainting the process with the mark of infamy.

The report ended with a sanctimonious flourish. The Committee lauded its proposals as important to the public interest and in particular the interests of the poor and middle classes. Anatomy was the key to advances in medicine and the education of the medical professions. The poorer classes

---

76 Richardson (n 2) 121.

could not afford the fees of those practitioners with a reputation for excellence. Medical practitioners of the 'lower orders' needed to learn Anatomy, for if such medical men did not practise dissection as students, they must learn the working of the human body 'by mangling the living'.

The Committee reported on 28 July 1828. In 1829, Henry Warburton introduced the first and unsuccessful Anatomy Bill, 'A Bill for preventing the Unlawful Disinterment of Human Bodies and for Regulating Schools of Anatomy'. A crucial omission from this Bill was the Committee's recommendation to repeal the detested 'Murder Act'.[77] Richardson has charted the failure of this first attempt at legislative reform and I can add little to her comprehensive treatment of the arguments deployed within and outside Parliament.

The 1829 Bill had four principal objectives, to make grave robbing a criminal offence by creating a new offence of unlawful disinterment of human bodies, to require dissecting schools to be licensed, to establish Commissioners responsible for licensing such schools and most importantly to set out the conditions on the basis of which bodies could lawfully be provided for dissection. At the core of the Bill were the proposed conditions for the lawful provision of bodies for dissection. The Bill made provision for voluntary bequests which was retained in the later successful Bill (discussed below). The controversy surrounding the first Bill arose from its proposals relating to 'unclaimed bodies'. It set out conditions for the lawful practice of dissection, providing:

> That it shall be lawful for any party to whom a license has been granted by the said Commissioners, or any party acting by authority of such party ... to receive from or by order of any of the persons herein after authorised to deliver up the same, any such human body as is hereinafter permitted to be delivered up, and to remove such body from the place of delivery to the place appointed for dissection in the license to such party granted, and there to dissect the same.

The next clause set out when, absent a voluntary bequest, bodies could lawfully be delivered to the dissecting schools for dissection:

> That when any person shall die during imprisonment in any prison, or shall die in any hospital or workhouse, and the body of such person shall not be claimed as hereinafter mentioned, or the disposition of such body shall not be otherwise provided for by law, it shall be lawful for the party having the custody of the body so dying in prison ... and for the party having the care of the person dying in any hospital or workhouse ... to deliver up the body of such person to any party duly licensed under this Act: Provided always, That

---

77 Ibid 107.

if within seventy-two hours after the death of any such person … any person shall attend to remove the body, and there shall be sufficient reason to believe that such body, if delivered to such person will by him be duly buried and not delivered up for dissection, the same shall be delivered up to the person attending …And provided also that if within the said period of seventy two hours, a person, representing himself to be a relative of the deceased, shall request that such body may not be delivered up for dissection and no nearer relative, and there is sufficient reason to believe that the person making such request is really a relative of the deceased, and no nearer relative has made any request to the contrary, such body shall not be delivered up for dissection.

The 1829 Bill was honest about its aim to ensure a sufficient supply of corpses for dissection. Prisoners and the destitute were to be the source of the supply. Such people were unlikely to have friends willing to claim the body with the funds to ensure the deceased was 'duly buried'. As to relatives objecting, if someone was poor enough to end up in the workhouse their family were likely either to be similarly situated and so unlikely to challenge the Workhouse Master, or to live so far away that they would not be aware of the deaths. There was no provision to notify families. The Bill excited passionate debate in Parliament and opposition from many different quarters, including senior medical men. It ultimately failed in the House of Lords in June 1829 and was withdrawn. Opponents of the Bill included the Archbishop of Canterbury and the Lord Chief Justice. The poor had a right to decent burial and many people had a fixed objection to dissection.[78] The then Prime Minister, the Duke of Wellington, accepted advice from the archbishop that the Bill be withdrawn, alert to the high level of opposition to the Bill.[79]

The 1829 Bill was withdrawn in the expectation that the government would introduce a further amended Bill. No such Bill was forthcoming and in 1831 Warburton introduced his second Bill 'An Act for regulating Schools of Anatomy'. This Bill was enacted in 1832. Richardson describes the public unrest provoked by the Act and continuing opposition to the Bill within Parliament. She locates the debates on the Anatomy Act within the broader historical context of other highly significant debates of the time, the 'Great Reform Bill' of 1832 and the 'new' Poor Law of 1834.

The Anatomy Act 1832

The Preamble makes it crystal clear that the legislature shared the Select Committee's Benthamite philosophy. The primary goal of the Act was to

---

78 Richardson (n 2) 157.
79 Ibid 157–158.

ensure a lawful, sufficient and affordable supply of dead bodies for dissection. The suppression of the bodysnatchers was a secondary objective driven by the aim of facilitating the practice of anatomy. Measures to regulate the schools may be seen as in part an attempt to calm public disquiet.

Substantive differences between the first unsuccessful Bill and the 1832 Act are small. 'Conscription of the poor' remained the central principle of legislation. Skilful drafting made the 1832 Act appear more palatable. One key difference in the 1832 Act was that the detested 'Murder Act' was repealed and express references to dissection of the bodies of prisoners were removed. The link between dissection and criminality was formally severed but remained part of public consciousness for long after 1832. The Act was much shorter than its predecessor. The creation of a new criminal offence of unlawful disinterment was dropped. Section 18 provided that any breach of the Act constituted a misdemeanour punishable by up to three months' imprisonment. One nod to public sentiment was the provision in Section 13 that after the corpse had been dissected, the remains must be decently interred.

The Anatomy Act 1832 is of interest as part of medico-legal history in three key respects. First, the Act addressed the conditions rendering the removal and use of bodies for dissection lawful. Second, the passage of the Act highlights conflict relating to bodies and body parts exposing a continuing gulf between 'Science' and popular feeling. And finally, the Act in introducing specific regulation of controversial biomedical activity provided glimmers of modern medical law.

Authorising anatomical examination

The Act did not mention dissection. That word was replaced by a more neutral term 'anatomical examination'; dissection by another name. Nor did the word consent feature in the Act. Sections 7 and 8 set out the conditions on the basis of which a dead body might be subjected to anatomical examination and identified how and who could permit such examination.

Section 8 provided, as had the earlier Bill, that an individual could authorise the anatomical examination of their body before death, expressly donating their corpse to the anatomists.

> [I]f any Person, either in writing at any Time during his Life, or verbally in the Presence of Two or more Witnesses during the Illness whereof he died, shall direct that his Body after Death be examined anatomically, *or shall nominate any Party by this Act authorised to examine Bodies anatomically to make such Examination*, and if, before the Burial of the Body of such Person, such Direction or Nomination shall be made known to the Party having lawful Possession of the dead Body, then such last mentioned Party shall direct such Examination to be made, and in the case of any such Nomination as aforesaid,

shall request and permit any Party so authorised and nominated as aforesaid to make such Examination, unless the deceased Person's surviving Husband, or Wife, or nearest known Relatives, or any One or more for such Person's nearest known Relatives, being Kin of the same Degree, shall require the Body to be interred without such Examination.

Read literally, Section 8 could be viewed as endorsing a system of voluntary donation delivering an ethical source of bodies regardless of social class. Better educated people might be more willing to follow Bentham's example and permit dissection of their bodies in the cause of medical science. Richardson shows that in practice voluntary donations were so rare that in the first ten years after the passing of the 1832 Act, only six donations are recorded,[80] and that where such voluntary bequests were attempted the Home Office and the Inspectorate of Anatomy were at a loss as to how to deal with them.[81] Not until the twentieth century did the numbers of voluntary donations rise to any significant extent.[82] Note too that even if the deceased had in their lifetime authorised donation of their corpse for anatomical examination, the deceased's spouse or nearest known relative could veto the donation. Family veto preventing doctors from implementing the wishes of the deceased being carried out remains a source of controversy today.[83]

For decades after 1832 the lawful supply of bodies for dissection relied almost entirely on Section 7 and unclaimed bodies of the poor:

That it shall be lawful for any Executor or other Party having lawful Possession of the Body of any deceased Person, and not being an Undertaker intrusted with the Body for the Purpose only of interment, to permit the Body of such deceased Person to undergo Anatomical Examination, unless to the Knowledge of such Executor or other Party, such Person shall have expressed his Desire, either in Writing at any Time during his Life, or verbally in the presence of Two or more Witnesses during the Illness whereof he died, that his Body after Death might not undergo such Examination, or unless the surviving Husband or Wife, or any known Relative of the deceased Person, shall require the Body to be interred without such Examination.

Section 7 avoids any reference to prisons, hospitals or workhouses. It looks misleadingly like a universal system of opt-out. A person's body could be given to the anatomy schools unless they had objected to donation before

---

80 Richardson (n 2) 237.
81 Ibid.
82 Ibid 256–260.
83 Human Tissue Authority Codes of Practice: Code A *Guiding principles and the fundamental principle of consent;* paras 37–38; Code F *Donation of solid organs and tissue for transplantation* Part 2 *Deceased Organ and tissue donation,* paras 13–14.

their death/or their family objected after death. On the face of the statute no distinction was made between paupers dying in the workhouse and the duke in his castle. The reality was very different. Paupers, indeed most of the population, were highly unlikely to have made a will and appointed an executor. They would have no estate to bequeath. Thus, there was no one appointed by the deceased to whom they might express in writing the desire not to be dissected, even if they could write. As to verbal objection in their final illness, how many people would be aware of this provision? Might the dying man or woman not have other matters on their mind? As to the right of the spouse or relatives to object there was no obligation to inform them of the death or expressly ask for their view.

The practical effect of Section 7 and its utility in implementing the objectives of the Select Committee to conscript the unclaimed bodies of the poor lay in the apparently innocuous words 'Executor or other Party having lawful Possession of the Body'. If there was no Executor, the crucial question became: who was the 'other party having lawful Possession of the body'? The answer, confirmed in *R v Feist*,[84] was in the case of paupers dying in the workhouse, the master of the workhouse. The person in actual physical possession of the body was the person in lawful possession. Should the deceased die in prison, the governor of the prison enjoyed such possession, and should they expire in a hospital, the hospital authority was the authority in possession. In all such cases the master, the gaoler or the hospital only enjoyed such possession unless or until a person with a better claim, i.e. the executors, claimed the body. No 'Body' could be removed for anatomical examination until forty-eight hours after the death in theory allowing time for an executor to come forward to claim the body.[85] Paupers in the workhouse, most prisoners and many people who died in hospital would have no executor. If a person of some means died in hospital, Sections 7 and 9 of the Act might work to ensure that the executor once appraised of the death could come forward and take custody of the body, allowing consideration of any wishes of the deceased and the family. Another twist to the tale was that the right to possession of a dead body carried with it a duty to dispose of the body. A relative who lacked the means to pay for interment of the corpse could not claim the body without risk of crippling debt. Richardson comments:

> The parliamentary passage of the second Anatomy Bill reveals that though everyone present was aware of the Bill's intention to single out the very poor for dissection, assertions of its social equity won the day. Invited by

84 (1858) 169 English Reports 1132.
85 Anatomy Act 1832, s 9.

the Benthamites to participate in a collective fiction, Parliament knowingly complied.[86]

The 'fiction' did not dupe the public.[87] The Act provoked fury, graphically illustrated in attacks on anatomy schools in Cambridge in 1833[88] and the burning of the Sheffield school in 1835.[89] The anger and terror inspired by the Anatomy Act has to be understood in the light of the nearly contemporaneous passage of the Poor Law (Amendment) Act 1834, the 'new' Poor Law.[90] The 'new' Poor Law, while implemented differently across the realm, sought to restrict the provision of 'outdoor relief' and offer the pauper the unpalatable choice between destitution and the dreaded workhouse where families would be separated and inmates subjected to a punitive regime.[91] Playwright William Cobbett expressed the sentiments of many of those who lived in terror of the workhouse, having a farm hand say to his master of his sweetheart:

> I'd rather die than see her begging a morsel of bread from the flint-hearted overseer ... hear of her dying perhaps and her body being cut to pieces like the carcass of a dead horse at the dog kennel.[92]

From 1832 to 1932, 99.5 per cent of nearly 57,000 bodies dissected in London were unclaimed bodies from public institutions.[93] Nor did the Act achieve its objective in assuring a sufficient supply of bodies for the anatomists.

Regulation: model for the future?

Putting aside for the moment the grisly images of half-starved inmates of the workhouse suffering further indignity in death, the Anatomy Act introduced a model for licensing and regulating a controversial field of medical activity which was to be 'copied' over a century and a half later in, for example, the regulation of assisted reproduction in the Human Fertilisation and Embryology Acts of 1990 and 2008, and the Human Tissue Act 2004 which

---

86 Richardson (n 2) 215.
87 Ibid Chapter 11 'The Unpardonable Offence'.
88 Richardson (n 2) 263.
89 Ibid.
90 Ibid 271.
91 K Price *Medical Negligence in Victorian Britain: The Crisis of Care under the English Poor Law c 1834–1900* (Bloomsbury, 2016) 8.
92 W Cobbett *Surplus Population and the Poor Law Bill: A Comedy in Three Acts* (Publisher unknown, 1834).
93 Richardson (n 2) 271.

replaced the earlier Anatomy Acts and sought to regulate the majority of uses of human bodies and their parts including anatomical examination.[94]

Section 1 of the 1832 Act empowered the Home Secretary in Great Britain or the Chief Secretary in Ireland to grant a personal licence to practise anatomy (i.e. dissection) to any fellow or member of any College of Physicians or Surgeons, or any person lawfully qualified to practise medicine or any professor or teacher of Anatomy, Medicine or Surgery, or to any student attending a School of Anatomy. Apothecaries who undertook the bulk of medical care to the less well-off sector of society were ineligible for a licence, exposing as fraudulent claims by the Select Committee that education of doctors treating the poor was a primary objective of law reform. Applicants seeking a licence were required to submit an application countersigned by two magistrates. Once a person was licensed it was lawful for the licensee to 'receive or possess for Anatomical Examination or to examine anatomically the Body of any Person deceased' whose body had been lawfully surrendered by the person in lawful possession of the body in conformity with Sections 7–9 of the Act.[95] Any person practising anatomy was additionally required to notify the relevant Secretary of State at least one week in advance of the first receipt of bodies for anatomical examination of the 'Place where it is intended to practise Anatomy'.[96] The Act further provided for the appointment of at least three Inspectors of Anatomy. The inspectors were required to provide the relevant Secretary of State with quarterly returns giving details of every dead body which had been removed for anatomical examination in 'every separate Place in his [the Inspector's] District where Anatomy is carried on distinguishing the Sex, and as far as is known at the Time the Name and Age of each person whose Body was so removed as aforesaid'.[97] Section 5 of the Act granted the inspectors powers to 'visit and inspect at any Time, any Place within his District, Notice of which Place has been given … that it is intended there to practise Anatomy'.

In some respects, the excoriated Anatomy Act 1832 created the template for modern regulation of biomedical activity which is deemed to need a higher level of external regulation than that provided by the general framework relating to medical practice. The State, not the medical corporations, or the General Medical Council, had the power to regulate the practice of anatomy. In theory, the Act ensured that the persons carrying

94 The similarity between the modern regulators and the nineteenth century Anatomy Act would have been even more marked had the proposal in the 1829 Bill for a Commission including lay representation had been retained.

95 S 2.

96 S 12.

97 S 4.

out anatomical examinations (including students) were suitably qualified, that the place where such examinations were conducted was appropriate, and that government received regular information relating to the numbers of bodies removed for dissection. The inspectors enforcing the Act were granted access to any site where dissection was practised, access to all schools of anatomy, public or private.

Theory did not translate into good practice. Richardson recounts how the early inspectors struggled to carry out their duties.[98] Old problems which the Act was supposed to eradicate endured, 'opposition, riots, shortage [of bodies], maldistribution, speculation, disinterment and non-interment of corpses, indecency, misconduct, collusion, corruption'.[99] A passion for secrecy, to cover up problems and failures of the Act proved, as it has done in later years, counter-productive. Accounts of the failures of these early regulators offer their later counterparts lessons in what not to do and much more importantly demonstrate that deeply flawed policy cannot be put right even by better processes than the efforts of the early inspectors.

The enduring spectre

Nearly 200 years have passed since the 1832 Act provoked riots in the streets.[100] Workhouses closed over half a century ago. Yet the Act's spectre endured, illustrated by dread of a pauper funeral, and haunting the retained organs 'scandals'. In 1961, debates in Parliament on the Human Tissue Bill had rather smugly compared 'bitter and superstitious opposition'[101] to the Anatomy Bill with the more sophisticated and scientific milieu of the twentieth century. Failure to recall and learn from the battles about dissection played a key role in the public outcry generated by revelations about organ retention in 2001. The 1832 Act is additionally significant for two other reasons; the precedent it set for regulation of medical science, and the evidence that in the nineteenth century the legislature had embraced medicine as the equal of law. The medical 'voice' which had played so large a part in framing abortion law, also succeeded in framing the law governing the treatment of the body post-mortem.

---

98 Richardson (n 2) Chapter 10 'The Bureaucrat's Bad Dream'.
99 Ibid 252.
100 The 1832 Act was amended in 1871 and repealed by the Anatomy Act 1984 which was itself repealed by the Human Tissue Act 2004.
101 Dr Horace King, MP, House of Commons Deb Vol 632 Column 1243, 20 December 1961.

Postscript

Some weeks after I submitted the final manuscript of this book to the publisher, medico-legal history became international news. In *Dobbs v Jackson Women's Health Organization*[1] the US Supreme Court overruled *Roe v Wade*[2] and abolished a woman's constitutional right to terminate her pregnancy. The history of abortion law in England played a small but significant role in that decision. I was able to add a very brief account of *Dobbs* into Chapter 9. Whatever my view on the outcome of *Dobbs*, given my passion for medico-legal history, I might have been expected to welcome the attention accorded to that history by the highest court in the USA. To the contrary, the deployment of history by the majority in *Dobbs* caused me unease, and prompted some final reflections on the use of history.

In *Dobbs*, the Supreme Court cited eminent common law authorities, the great jurists of the past,[3] in support of their finding that abortion was a common law crime. Popular outcry generated by *Dobbs* included amazement and fury that in 2022, addressing women's rights, the Court should consider the opinion of Henry de Bracton, a thirteenth-century monk, to be relevant – or take account of an admittedly less 'ancient' authority, the seventeenth-century judge, Matthew Hale, a jurist known for his misogyny. It was Hale who opined that a husband could not be guilty of marital rape,[4] and regarded a wife as an object of her husband's sexual property.[5] Historians complained that the Supreme Court in *Dobbs*, as in other recent high-profile cases, got the history wrong, either by 'cherry-picking the authorities or leaving

---

1 572 US (2022).
2 410 US 702 (1973).
3 Discussed more fully in Chapter 9.
4 An immunity only abolished in *R v R* [1991] 1 AC 599.
5 M Hale *The History of Pleas of the Crown* Vol 1 (London Professional, 1971 reprint of 1736 edition) 515 cited in M Davies and N Naffine *Are Persons Property? Legal Debates about Property and Personality* (Ashgate, 2001) 80.

out important nuances or both'.[6] Determined to overrule *Roe v Wade*, the majority in *Dobbs* distorted history to fit their desired ends.

Supporters of *Roe* should not feel smug. The Court in *Roe* was guilty of the same 'offence' in adopting Cyril Means' 'novel thesis' that before Lord Ellenborough's Act 1803, English women had a common law liberty to choose to end a pregnancy.[7] Justice Blackmun held that it was *undisputed* that, at common law, abortion performed before 'quickening' was not a criminal offence and *doubtful* if abortion was ever a common law crime at any stage in gestation.[8] But Means was wrong, and thus so was Blackmun. Despite Means' ingenious interpretations of the cases to suit his thesis, case law before 1803 establishes that abortion was a common law crime possibly at any stage in gestation and certainly after quickening. Addressing the eminent jurists, Means sought to neutralise Edward Coke's clear statement that abortion was a 'great misprision' by claiming that Coke's visceral hatred of abortion and his battle with the ecclesiastical courts led him to 'make up' a crime when no such crime existed.

Justice Alito, delivering the Opinion of the majority in *Dobbs*, mounted a stinging attack on Means, describing his two articles as discredited – the work of a pro-abortion advocate. He highlights Means', and therefore Blackmun's, errors. With the exception of Staunford, Alito considers the same common law jurists relied on by Means to reach a very different conclusion. Turning Blackmun's ruling on its head, *Dobbs* held that it is *undisputed* that at common law, abortion performed after 'quickening' was a criminal offence, and possible that abortion was a common law crime at any stage in gestation. Selectively citing De Bracton, Blackstone and Hale, Alito further indicated that, at common law, abortion at some point in gestation might constitute homicide. He quoted De Bracton:

[i]f one strikes a pregnant woman or gives her a potion in order to procure an abortion, if the foetus is already formed or animated, especially if it is animated, he commits homicide.[9]

---

6 A O Larsen 'The Supreme Court Decisions on Guns and Abortion Rely Heavily on History: But Whose History?' *Politico* 26 July 2022.

7 C C Means Jr 'The Law of New York Concerning Abortion and the Status of the Foetus 1664–1968: A Case of Cessation of Constitutionality' (1968) 14 *New York Law Forum* 411; C C Means Jr 'The Phoenix of Abortional Freedom: Is a Penumbral or Ninth-Amendment Right about to Arise from the Nineteenth-Century Legislative Ashes of a Fourteenth-Century Common-Law Liberty?' (1971) 17 *New York Law Forum* 335.

8 See above in Chapter 9.

9 Bracton *De Legibus et Consuetudinibus Anglise* (c. 1250) as cited in J Keown *Abortion, Doctors and the Law: Some Aspects of the Legal Regulation of Abortion in England from 1803 to 1982* (Cambridge University Press, 1988) 5.

Note that William Staunford, the jurist principally relied on by Means, is ignored altogether.[10] Nor are the implications of Coke's finding that abortion while a crime was not a felony addressed.

The manipulation of history in *Roe* and *Dobbs* questions the role and value of medico-legal history risking the charge that the historical evidence may be unreliable and self-serving, and undermining the view that an understanding of medico-legal history is valuable and important. In Chapter 1, I quoted Lord Atkin addressing the convoluted and sometimes incomprehensible rules of procedure developed by the common law:

> When these ghosts of the past stand in the path of justice clanking their medieval chains the proper course for the judge is to pass through them undeterred.[11]

I suggested that we might offer a warmer welcome to a ghost of medico-legal history. So I conclude that, encountering such a ghost, do not ignore them, pause and interrogate them. The spectre might cast light on the present, counselling us as much about what *not* to do, or as to how we might do better, and moreover, even if the ghost offers no positive prescriptions from their time, they may have a story to engage us.

There is no shortage of stories, dating back to the Middle Ages and before. Setting out to write this book, I feared that I might struggle to find material and in particular find little to say about law and healing before about 1500. How wrong I was. The snapshots at the start of Chapter 1 are not isolated or rare incidents but representative of the significant role played by the law relating to healing across time and class; from the ban on clerics performing surgery in 1215, to the effect on proposals for a national system of regulation of a king's untimely death in 1421, the persecution of doctors who defied the mighty medical corporations, the alliance against non-orthodox healers, to the pauper railing against the Anatomy Act 1832, and battles over regulating midwives. Medieval case law for medical negligence remains the foundation of clinical negligence claims, casting light on problems which still trouble the judges in the twenty-first century. And, within the accounts of litigation and legislation, hide vignettes depicting everyday life long ago. Stories entertain. They add to our knowledge of past lives and can inform us how difficult questions have been answered differently across the ages.

How far medico-legal history does and/or should be used to affect the making of law relating to medicine now is a tougher call. Does usefulness matter? I agreed with Margaret Pelling that history is valuable for its own sake but that there is no reason 'why history should not inform the present

---

10 *Les plees del Coron* (Pleas of the Crown) 1557 as cited in Keown ibid 4.
11 *United Australia Ltd v Barclays Bank* [1941] AC 1, 29.

especially since the subject we choose, and the ways in which we write about them, undoubtedly reflect current concerns'.[12]

I have not changed my mind. Unease prompted by *Dobbs* and *Roe* arises from how the Court misused history and more generally how scholars and practitioners use selective evidence to support their views about what the law should be. The reliability of the historical evidence becomes more crucial should we look to the past for positive direction about what *not* to do, or as to how we might do better.

Practical difficulties such as language, accessibility, erratic law reporting, and the complications of common law procedure make it impossible to be wholly certain of the accuracy of evidence advanced. Caution should be exercised. The further back in time the history addressed, the harder it is to establish the facts. Antiquity alone should not exclude the evidence from consideration. De Bracton should not be ignored *only* because he wrote eight centuries ago. 'Old' law is often less remote than it appears to be. Recall that not until 1982 were the last remnants of a husband's proprietary rights in his wife abolished by the Administration of Justice Act 1982.

Considering the use of history in US Supreme Court decisions, it has been said that it is imperative to ask where the judges are getting their historical sources, whether those resources are fact-checked, and most importantly who is narrating them.[13] In most instances in which medico-legal history is invoked in the law courts, the legislature or the academy, an immediate link between the 'lessons of history' and an impact on current law is weaker than in the constitutional jurisdiction of the US Supreme Court. Factual claims should still be made with caution and kept distinct from argument about *why* the law in issue evolved as it did. For example, claiming that a crime of maim punished self-harm requires documentary evidence from reliable sources, ideally court reports or legislation. Secondary sources such as the treatises of the jurists, contemporary literature and in more recent centuries textbooks such as Willcock[14] may be called on to supplement primary sources and develop an explanation of why sixteenth-century law criminalised injuring yourself. Authorities may well disagree vehemently with each other as graphically illustrated in the history of abortion law. A fair hearing should be afforded to all the combatants.

12 M Pelling *The Common Lot: Sickness, Medical Occupations and the Urban Poor in Early Modern England* (Routledge, 1998) 8.

13 Larsen (n 6).

14 J W Willcock *Laws Relating to the Medical Profession with an Account of the Rise and Progress of the Various Orders* (J & W T Clarke, 1830).

Index

EU authorised representative for GPSR:
Easy Access System Europe, Mustamäe tee 50,
10621 Tallinn, Estonia
gpsr.requests@easproject.com